The definitive
management ideas
of the year from
Harvard Business Review.

2020

HBR's 10 Must Reads series is the definitive collection of ideas and best practices for aspiring and experienced leaders alike. These books offer essential reading selected from the pages of *Harvard Business Review* on topics critical to the success of every manager.

Titles include:

HBR's 10 Must Reads 2015
HBR's 10 Must Reads 2016
HBR's 10 Must Reads 2017
HBR's 10 Must Reads 2018
HBR's 10 Must Reads 2019
HBR's 10 Must Reads 2020
HBR's 10 Must Reads for CEOs
HBR's 10 Must Reads for New Managers
HBR's 10 Must Reads on AI, Analytics, and the New Machine Age
HBR's 10 Must Reads on Business Model Innovation
HBR's 10 Must Reads on Change Management
HBR's 10 Must Reads on Collaboration
HBR's 10 Must Reads on Communication
HBR's 10 Must Reads on Diversity
HBR's 10 Must Reads on Emotional Intelligence
HBR's 10 Must Reads on Entrepreneurship and Startups
HBR's 10 Must Reads on Innovation
HBR's 10 Must Reads on Leadership
HBR's 10 Must Reads on Leadership for Healthcare
HBR's 10 Must Reads on Leadership Lessons from Sports
HBR's 10 Must Reads on Making Smart Decisions
HBR's 10 Must Reads on Managing Across Cultures
HBR's 10 Must Reads on Managing People
HBR's 10 Must Reads on Managing Yourself
HBR's 10 Must Reads on Mental Toughness
HBR's 10 Must Reads on Negotiation
HBR's 10 Must Reads on Nonprofits and the Social Sectors

HBR's 10 Must Reads on Reinventing HR
HBR's 10 Must Reads on Sales
HBR's 10 Must Reads on Strategic Marketing
HBR's 10 Must Reads on Strategy
HBR's 10 Must Reads on Strategy for Healthcare
HBR's 10 Must Reads on Teams
HBR's 10 Must Reads on Women and Leadership
HBR's 10 Must Reads: The Essentials

HBR'S 10 MUST READS

The definitive
management ideas
of the year from
Harvard Business Review.

2020

HARVARD BUSINESS REVIEW PRESS
Boston, Massachusetts

Copyright 2020 Harvard Business Publishing Corporation
Printed in the United States of America
10 9 8 7 6 5 4 3 2 1

The web addresses referenced in this book were live and correct at the time of the book's publication but may be subject to change.

Library of Congress Cataloging-in-Publication Data

Title: HBR's 10 must reads 2020: the definitive management ideas of the year from Harvard Business Review.
Other titles: HBR's 10 must reads (2020) | Harvard Business Review's ten must reads 2020 | Definitive management ideas of the year from Harvard Business Review | HBR's 10 must reads (Series)
Description: Hudson exclusive edition. | Boston, Massachusetts : Harvard Business Review Press, [2020] | Series: HBR's 10 must reads series | Edition statement from cover. | This edition includes two additional articles. | Includes index.
Identifiers: LCCN 2019012130 | ISBN 9781633698567 (pbk.)
Subjects: LCSH: Management.
Classification: LCC HD31.2 .H367 2020b | DDC 658—dc23
LC record available at https://lccn.loc.gov/2019012130

ISBN: 978-1-63369-856-7

The paper used in this publication meets the requirements of the American National Standard for Permanence of Paper for Publications and Documents in Libraries and Archives Z39.48-1992.

Contents

Editors' Note   ix

The Surprising Power of Questions   1
   by Alison Wood Brooks and Leslie K. John

Strategy Needs Creativity   15
   by Adam Brandenburger

What Most People Get Wrong about Men and Women   27
   by Catherine H. Tinsley and Robin J. Ely

Collaborative Intelligence: Humans and AI Are Joining Forces   43
   by H. James Wilson and Paul R. Daugherty

Stitch Fix's CEO on Selling Personal Style to the Mass Market   61
   by Katrina Lake

Strategy for Start-Ups   71
   by Joshua Gans, Erin L. Scott, and Scott Stern

Agile at Scale   87
   by Darrell K. Rigby, Jeff Sutherland, and Andy Noble

Operational Transparency   103
   by Ryan W. Buell

The Dual-Purpose Playbook   121
   by Julie Battilana, Anne-Claire Pache, Metin Sengul, and Marissa Kimsey

How CEOs Manage Time   137
   by Michael E. Porter and Nitin Nohria

When No One Retires   163
   by Paul Irving

HUDSON EXCLUSIVE EDITION ARTICLES
Why Design Thinking Works 179
    by Jeanne Liedtka

Time for Happiness 193
    by Ashley Whillans

About the Contributors 213
Index 217

Each year as we pare twelve months' worth of HBR articles down to a handful of the very best, certain trends and themes emerge. Sometimes the economy, politics, and technology loom largest. Other times new twists on the basics of leadership, strategy, and marketing dominate. This year's choices are united not by a trend or a theme but by a *feeling*: the surprise we experience when some long-held truth is gently challenged and is revealed to be different or more complex than we had thought. Educators and psychologists know that novelty reinforces understanding and learning. Indeed, the sense of surprise that distinguishes the pieces in this collection makes them stay with us, tugging at loose threads in our minds, helping us see connections as we seek to improve our organizations and ourselves. It spurs us out of complacency and encourages the mindset needed to learn, grow, and innovate. Embrace that feeling while you read and as you and your business prepare for coming challenges.

Some professionals are trained to ask questions: Think of litigators, journalists, and doctors. But few executives regard questioning as a skill to be honed. That's a missed opportunity, say Alison Wood Brooks and Leslie K. John. Thoughtful inquiry and the conversational exchange of ideas can yield a kind of magic, a whole that is greater than the sum of its parts. In **"The Surprising Power of Questions,"** the authors describe several carefully researched techniques that will help you boost your learning, persuade others, and negotiate more effectively.

The traditional analytical tools of strategy may be well suited to understanding an existing business context, but they're of little value when you need to reinvent your business. To generate a breakthrough strategy, Adam Brandenburger suggests building one with tools explicitly designed to foster creativity. **"Strategy Needs Creativity"** details approaches for kindling a spark of intuition, making a connection between disparate ways of thinking, or taking a leap into the unexpected that can lead you to a game-changing way of doing business.

"Women lack the desire and ability to negotiate"; "Women are more committed to family than men are." Statements like these are often proffered to explain why women have failed to gain parity with men in the workplace, but Catherine H. Tinsley and Robin J. Ely fell them with a few deft strokes. "Science, by and large, does not actually support these claims," they write. "The sexes are far more similar in their inclinations, attitudes, and skills than popular opinion would have us believe." The authors show that managers who are advancing gender equity in their firms take an inquisitive approach: They seek an evidence-based understanding of how women experience the workplace, and then create conditions that increase their prospects for success. **"What Most People Get Wrong About Men and Women"** is a clarion call for rejecting the script that encourages women to act more like men and instead fixing the things that undermine women and reinforce gender stereotypes.

Artificial intelligence is becoming good at many "human" jobs—diagnosing disease, translating languages, providing customer service. And it's improving fast, raising reasonable fears that AI will ultimately replace human workers throughout the economy. Accenture technology leaders H. James Wilson and Paul R. Daugherty argue that that's not the inevitable, or even the most likely, outcome. In **"Collaborative Intelligence: Humans and AI Are Joining Forces,"** they show that AI has the most significant impact—and companies see the biggest performance gains—when people and smart machines work together, enhancing one another's strengths. Organizations that use machines merely to displace workers, they say, will miss the full potential of AI.

Stitch Fix demonstrates human and machine collaboration in action. The company has a simple business model: It sends you clothing and accessories it thinks you'll like; you keep the items you want and send the others back. But behind the curtain is a relentlessly data-driven organization built on the belief that a good person plus a good algorithm is better than either the best person or the best algorithm alone. In **"Stitch Fix's CEO on Selling Personal Style to the Mass Market,"** company founder and chief executive Katrina Lake describes overcoming skeptics (one of her business school professors called her idea an "inventory nightmare") and surmounting the challenges of raising capital for a clothing start-up in the male-dominated VC field.

Is **"Strategy for Start-Ups"** the beginning of a new paradigm, or is it entrepreneurial heresy? HBR's most divisive article of the year details how entrepreneurs often run with the first plausible strategy they identify in their haste to get to market. As a result they lose out to second or even third movers with superior strategies. Having worked with and studied hundreds of start-ups over the past 20 years, Joshua Gans, Erin L. Scott, and Scott Stern have developed a framework that helps founders take a practical, clarifying approach to the critical choices they face. The authors delineate four go-to-market strategies for entrepreneurs to consider as they move from idea to launch. Each option offers a distinct way for the venture to create and capture value.

Agile innovation teams are small, entrepreneurial groups designed to stay close to customers and adapt quickly to changing conditions. When implemented correctly, they almost always result in greater productivity, better morale, faster time to market, higher quality, and lower risk than traditional approaches can achieve. In **"Agile at Scale,"** Darrell K. Rigby, Jeff Sutherland, and Andy Noble explore how your company can go from a handful of agile teams to hundreds. Making agile the dominant way you operate, they say, means committing all the way to the top: Leaders should adopt agile values, create a taxonomy of opportunities to set priorities, and break the journey of transformation into small steps.

Conventional wisdom holds that the more contact an operation has with its customers, the less efficiently it will run. But when customers are walled off, they are unlikely to fully understand and appreciate the work going on behind the scenes. **"Operational Transparency"** advocates for the deliberate design of windows into and out of an organization's processes so that customers can recognize the value being added. Take open kitchens: Research shows that when diners can see who's making their food, their satisfaction increases—and it's even greater if the chef can see the diners. Ryan W. Buell describes how managers can bring this sort of transparency to their companies, exploring what to reveal, when to reveal it, and how to avoid going too far.

What does it take for companies to both do well and do good? Many corporations are seeking to dial down their single-minded pursuit of financial gain and pay closer attention to their impact on the environment and society—but the business ecosystem is still motivated above all by shareholder wealth. In **"The Dual-Purpose Playbook,"** Julie Battilana, Anne-Claire Pache, Metin Sengul, and Marissa Kimsey look at how companies can find a balance. Examining dual-purpose companies around the globe, they find that successful ones build a commitment to both economic and social value into their core organizational activities. The authors outline four key management practices, which range from setting and monitoring dual goals to hiring and socializing employees to embrace them.

Strategy guru Michael E. Porter and Harvard Business School dean Nitin Nohria teamed up for 12 years to collect 60,000 hours' worth of data from 27 chief executives, all to better understand what their days consist of. Although CEOs have tremendous resources at their disposal, time remains an area of acute scarcity. **"How CEOs Manage Time,"** a fine-grained, first-of-a-kind study, reveals similarities in how CEOs structure their schedules (they all attend a lot of meetings) along with differences (some dedicate far more face time to investors and customers than others do). It sheds light on the crucial trade-offs executives must make and describes how any leader can manage his or her calendar more effectively.

It's often called the silver tsunami: In many countries the population is aging rapidly. In the United States alone about 10,000 people turn 65 each day—and one in five Americans will be 65 or older by 2030. This societal shift will affect every aspect of business, but Paul Irving finds that many corporate leaders have not yet considered its effects. And those who have, he says, typically foresee a looming crisis and miss the potential contributions that older adults—healthier and more active than their predecessors—can make as both workers and consumers. **"When No One Retires"** helps companies develop a "longevity strategy" for fostering a vibrant multigenerational workforce.

The last two articles are special additions for the **Hudson Exclusive Edition** of this book, which means you probably picked up a copy while traveling. If you're in an airport right now (or worse, crumpled in the middle seat while flying coach), odds are you'll agree that our world needs a *lot* more design thinking. But if you still see it as just a way to develop new products, now is the time to consider its greater potential. In **"Why Design Thinking Works,"** Jeanne Liedtka describes how the methodology helps innovators break free of counterproductive tendencies that thwart the imagination and hinder innovation. It does this not only by overcoming workplace politics but by blending practical tools with insights into human nature to shape the experiences of innovators and their key stakeholders and implementers at every step. Cases from the social services industry and health care provide inspiring examples of how you can use design thinking to spur engagement, dialogue, and learning.

Do you pay extra to fly direct, skip the main security line, or avoid a long layover? If so, Ashley Whillans would say you're probably making the right choice. People feel increasingly starved for time, and the fallout is profound: higher anxiety and depression and decreased health and productivity. Yet data shows that people have *more* discretionary time now than 50 years ago. We're stressed out, Whillans argues, because we've fallen into the trap of using our time to get more money. And we've got it backward: Study after study reveals that the happiest people consistently use their money to buy time. It's not easy to break ingrained habits, but the final piece in this volume, **"Time for Happiness,"** outlines concrete steps individuals and employers can take to promote time-savvier choices. If we learn to value time properly, we'll make trade-offs that significantly improve our well-being.

In the spirit of saving time, on to the articles! These standout pieces of the year explore some of the most compelling and important developments in business today. Did anything you just read in these descriptions surprise you? We hope so. Use that feeling to view yourself and your business through a new lens as you seek to improve and grow in the coming year.

—The Editors

HBR'S 10 MUST READS

The definitive
management ideas
of the year from
Harvard Business Review.

2020

The Surprising Power of Questions

by Alison Wood Brooks and Leslie K. John

MUCH OF AN EXECUTIVE'S WORKDAY is spent asking others for information—requesting status updates from a team leader, for example, or questioning a counterpart in a tense negotiation. Yet unlike professionals such as litigators, journalists, and doctors, who are taught how to ask questions as an essential part of their training, few executives think of questioning as a skill that can be honed—or consider how their own answers to questions could make conversations more productive.

That's a missed opportunity. Questioning is a uniquely powerful tool for unlocking value in organizations: It spurs learning and the exchange of ideas, it fuels innovation and performance improvement, it builds rapport and trust among team members. And it can mitigate business risk by uncovering unforeseen pitfalls and hazards.

For some people, questioning comes easily. Their natural inquisitiveness, emotional intelligence, and ability to read people put the ideal question on the tip of their tongue. But most of us don't ask enough questions, nor do we pose our inquiries in an optimal way.

The good news is that by asking questions, we naturally improve our emotional intelligence, which in turn makes us better questioners—a virtuous cycle. In this article, we draw on insights from behavioral science research to explore how the way we frame questions and choose to answer our counterparts can influence the outcome of conversations. We offer guidance for choosing the best type, tone, sequence, and framing of questions and for deciding what and how much information to share to reap the most benefit from our interactions, not just for ourselves but for our organizations.

Don't Ask, Don't Get

"Be a good listener," Dale Carnegie advised in his 1936 classic *How to Win Friends and Influence People.* "Ask questions the other person will enjoy answering." More than 80 years later, most people still fail to heed Carnegie's sage advice. When one of us (Alison) began studying conversations at Harvard Business School several years ago, she quickly arrived at a foundational insight: People don't ask enough questions. In fact, among the most common complaints people make after having a conversation, such as an interview, a first date, or a work meeting, is "I wish [s/he] had asked me more questions" and "I can't believe [s/he] didn't ask me any questions."

Why do so many of us hold back? There are many reasons. People may be egocentric—eager to impress others with their own thoughts, stories, and ideas (and not even think to ask questions). Perhaps they are apathetic—they don't care enough to ask, or they anticipate being bored by the answers they'd hear. They may be overconfident in their own knowledge and think they already know the answers (which sometimes they do, but usually not). Or perhaps they worry that they'll ask the wrong question and be viewed as rude or incompetent. But the biggest inhibitor, in our opinion, is that most people just don't understand how beneficial good questioning can be. If they did, they would end far fewer sentences with a period—and more with a question mark.

Dating back to the 1970s, research suggests that people have conversations to accomplish some combination of two major goals: information exchange (learning) and impression management (liking). Recent research shows that asking questions achieves both. Alison and Harvard colleagues Karen Huang, Michael Yeomans, Julia Minson, and Francesca Gino scrutinized thousands of natural conversations among participants who were getting to know each other, either in online chats or on in-person speed dates. The

Idea in Brief

The Problem

Some professionals such as litigators, journalists, and even doctors are taught to ask questions as part of their training. But few executives think about questioning as a skill that can be honed. That's a missed opportunity.

The Opportunity

Questioning is a powerful tool for unlocking value in companies: It spurs learning and the exchange of ideas, it fuels innovation and better performance, it builds trust among team members. And it can mitigate business risk by uncovering unforeseen pitfalls and hazards.

The Approach

Several techniques can enhance the power and efficacy of queries: Favor follow-up questions, know when to keep questions open-ended, get the sequence right, use the right tone, and pay attention to group dynamics.

researchers told some people to ask many questions (at least nine in fifteen minutes) and others to ask very few (no more than four in fifteen minutes). In the online chats, the people who were randomly assigned to ask many questions were better liked by their conversation partners and learned more about their partners' interests. For example, when quizzed about their partners' preferences for activities such as reading, cooking, and exercising, high question askers were more likely to be able to guess correctly. Among the speed daters, people were more willing to go on a second date with partners who asked more questions. In fact, asking just one more question on each date meant that participants persuaded one additional person (over the course of 20 dates) to go out with them again.

Questions are such powerful tools that they can be beneficial—perhaps particularly so—in circumstances when question asking goes against social norms. For instance, prevailing norms tell us that job candidates are expected to answer questions during interviews. But research by Dan Cable, at the London Business School, and Virginia Kay, at the University of North Carolina, suggests that most people excessively self-promote during job interviews. And when interviewees focus on selling themselves, they are likely to forget to ask questions—about the interviewer, the organization, the work—that

3

would make the interviewer feel more engaged and more apt to view the candidate favorably and could help the candidate predict whether the job would provide satisfying work. For job candidates, asking questions such as "What am I not asking you that I should?" can signal competence, build rapport, and unlock key pieces of information about the position.

Most people don't grasp that asking a lot of questions unlocks learning and improves interpersonal bonding. In Alison's studies, for example, though people could accurately recall how many questions had been asked in their conversations, they didn't intuit the link between questions and liking. Across four studies, in which participants were engaged in conversations themselves or read transcripts of others' conversations, people tended not to realize that question asking would influence—or had influenced—the level of amity between the conversationalists.

The New Socratic Method

The first step in becoming a better questioner is simply to ask more questions. Of course, the sheer number of questions is not the only factor that influences the quality of a conversation: The type, tone, sequence, and framing also matter.

In our teaching at Harvard Business School, we run an exercise in which we instruct pairs of students to have a conversation. Some students are told to ask as few questions as possible, and some are instructed to ask as many as possible. Among the low-low pairs (both students ask a minimum of questions), participants generally report that the experience is a bit like children engaging in parallel play: They exchange statements but struggle to initiate an interactive, enjoyable, or productive dialogue. The high-high pairs find that too many questions can also create a stilted dynamic. However, the high-low pairs' experiences are mixed. Sometimes the question asker learns a lot about her partner, the answerer feels heard, and both come away feeling profoundly closer. Other times, one of the participants may feel uncomfortable in his role or unsure about how much to share, and the conversation can feel like an interrogation.

Our research suggests several approaches that can enhance the power and efficacy of queries. The best approach for a given situation depends on the goals of the conversationalists—specifically, whether the discussion is cooperative (for example, the duo is trying to build a relationship or accomplish a task together) or competitive (the parties seek to uncover sensitive information from each other or serve their own interests), or some combination of both. (See the sidebar "Conversational Goals Matter.") Consider the following tactics.

Favor follow-up questions

Not all questions are created equal. Alison's research, using human coding and machine learning, revealed four types of questions: introductory questions ("How are you?"), mirror questions ("I'm fine. How are you?"), full-switch questions (ones that change the topic entirely), and follow-up questions (ones that solicit more information). Although each type is abundant in natural conversation, follow-up questions seem to have special power. They signal to your conversation partner that you are listening, care, and want to know more. People interacting with a partner who asks lots of follow-up questions tend to feel respected and heard.

An unexpected benefit of follow-up questions is that they don't require much thought or preparation—indeed, they seem to come naturally to interlocutors. In Alison's studies, the people who were told to ask more questions used more follow-up questions than any other type without being instructed to do so.

Know when to keep questions open-ended

No one likes to feel interrogated—and some types of questions can force answerers into a yes-or-no corner. Open-ended questions can counteract that effect and thus can be particularly useful in uncovering information or learning something new. Indeed, they are wellsprings of innovation—which is often the result of finding the hidden, unexpected answer that no one has thought of before.

A wealth of research in survey design has shown the dangers of narrowing respondents' options. For example, "closed" questions

Conversational goals matter

Conversations fall along a continuum from purely competitive to purely co-operative. For example, discussions about the allocation of scarce resources tend to be competitive; those between friends and colleagues are generally cooperative; and others, such as managers' check-ins with employees, are mixed—supportive but also providing feedback and communicating expectations. Here are some challenges that commonly arise when asking and answering questions and tactics for handling them.

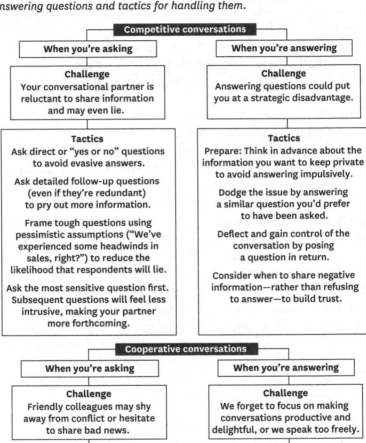

Competitive conversations

When you're asking

Challenge
Your conversational partner is reluctant to share information and may even lie.

Tactics
Ask direct or "yes or no" questions to avoid evasive answers.

Ask detailed follow-up questions (even if they're redundant) to pry out more information.

Frame tough questions using pessimistic assumptions ("We've experienced some headwinds in sales, right?") to reduce the likelihood that respondents will lie.

Ask the most sensitive question first. Subsequent questions will feel less intrusive, making your partner more forthcoming.

When you're answering

Challenge
Answering questions could put you at a strategic disadvantage.

Tactics
Prepare: Think in advance about the information you want to keep private to avoid answering impulsively.

Dodge the issue by answering a similar question you'd prefer to have been asked.

Deflect and gain control of the conversation by posing a question in return.

Consider when to share negative information—rather than refusing to answer—to build trust.

Cooperative conversations

When you're asking

Challenge
Friendly colleagues may shy away from conflict or hesitate to share bad news.

Tactics
Ask open-ended questions ("If you were to play devil's advocate, what would you say?") to draw out negative feedback.

Begin with the least-sensitive questions to build rapport, and escalate slowly.

As in competitive contexts, frame tough questions using negative assumptions.

When you're answering

Challenge
We forget to focus on making conversations productive and delightful, or we speak too freely.

Tactics
Avoid droning on and on. Use energy, humor, and storytelling to engage your partners.

Avoid talking too much about yourself, and remember to ask questions of others.

Deflect tough questions by answering with another question or a joke.

can introduce bias and manipulation. In one study, in which parents were asked what they deemed "the most important thing for children to prepare them in life," about 60% of them chose "to think for themselves" from a list of response options. However, when the same question was asked in an open-ended format, only about 5% of parents spontaneously came up with an answer along those lines.

Of course, open-ended questions aren't always optimal. For example, if you are in a tense negotiation or are dealing with people who tend to keep their cards close to their chest, open-ended questions can leave too much wiggle room, inviting them to dodge or lie by omission. In such situations, closed questions work better, especially if they are framed correctly. For example, research by Julia Minson, the University of Utah's Eric VanEpps, Georgetown's Jeremy Yip, and Wharton's Maurice Schweitzer indicates that people are less likely to lie if questioners make pessimistic assumptions ("This business will need some new equipment soon, correct?") rather than optimistic ones ("The equipment is in good working order, right?").

Sometimes the information you wish to ascertain is so sensitive that direct questions won't work, no matter how thoughtfully they are framed. In these situations, a survey tactic can aid discovery. In research Leslie conducted with Alessandro Acquisti and George Loewenstein of Carnegie Mellon University, she found that people were more forthcoming when requests for sensitive information were couched within another task—in the study's case, rating the ethicality of antisocial behaviors such as cheating on one's tax return or letting a drunk friend drive home. Participants were asked to rate the ethicality using one scale if they had engaged in a particular behavior and another scale if they hadn't—thus revealing which antisocial acts they themselves had engaged in. Although this tactic may sometimes prove useful at an organizational level—we can imagine that managers might administer a survey rather than ask workers directly about sensitive information such as salary expectations—we counsel restraint in using it. If people feel that you are trying to trick them into revealing something, they may lose trust in you, decreasing the likelihood that they'll share information in the future and potentially eroding workplace relationships.

Get the sequence right

The optimal order of your questions depends on the circumstances. During tense encounters, asking tough questions first, even if it feels socially awkward to do so, can make your conversational partner more willing to open up. Leslie and her coauthors found that people are more willing to reveal sensitive information when questions are asked in a decreasing order of intrusiveness. When a question asker begins with a highly sensitive question—such as "Have you ever had a fantasy of doing something terrible to someone?"—subsequent questions, such as "Have you ever called in sick to work when you were perfectly healthy?" feel, by comparison, less intrusive, and thus we tend to be more forthcoming. Of course, if the first question is *too* sensitive, you run the risk of offending your counterpart. So it's a delicate balance, to be sure.

If the goal is to build relationships, the opposite approach—opening with less sensitive questions and escalating slowly—seems to be most effective. In a classic set of studies (the results of which went viral following a write-up in the "Modern Love" column of the *New York Times*), psychologist Arthur Aron recruited strangers to come to the lab, paired them up, and gave them a list of questions. They were told to work their way through the list, starting with relatively shallow inquiries and progressing to more self-revelatory ones, such as "What is your biggest regret?" Pairs in the control group were asked simply to interact with each other. The pairs who followed the prescribed structure liked each other more than the control pairs. This effect is so strong that it has been formalized in a task called "the relationship closeness induction," a tool used by researchers to build a sense of connection among experiment participants.

Good interlocutors also understand that questions asked previously in a conversation can influence future queries. For example, Norbert Schwarz, of the University of Southern California, and his coauthors found that when the question "How satisfied are you with your life?" is followed by the question "How satisfied are you with your marriage?" the answers were highly correlated: Respondents who reported being satisfied with their life also said they were

The Power of Questions in Sales

THERE ARE FEW BUSINESS SETTINGS in which asking questions is more important than sales. A recent study of more than 500,000 business-to-business sales conversations—over the phone and via online platforms—by tech company Gong.io reveals that top-performing salespeople ask questions differently than their peers.

Consistent with past research, the data shows a strong connection between the number of questions a salesperson asks and his or her sales conversion rate (in terms of both securing the next meeting and eventually closing the deal). This is true even after controlling for the gender of the salesperson and the call type (demo, proposal, negotiation, and so on). However, there is a point of diminishing returns. Conversion rates start to drop off after about 14 questions, with 11 to 14 being the optimal range.

The data also shows that top-performing salespeople tend to scatter questions throughout the sales call, which makes it feel more like a conversation than an interrogation. Lower performers, in contrast, frontload questions in the first half of the sales call, as if they're making their way through a to-do list.

Just as important, top salespeople listen more and speak less than their counterparts overall. Taken together, the data from Gong.io affirms what great salespeople intuitively understand: When sellers ask questions rather than just make their pitch, they close more deals.

---

satisfied with their marriage. When asked the questions in this order, people implicitly interpreted that life satisfaction "ought to be" closely tied to marriage. However, when the same questions were asked in the opposite order, the answers were less closely correlated.

Use the right tone

People are more forthcoming when you ask questions in a casual way, rather than in a buttoned-up, official tone. In one of Leslie's studies, participants were posed a series of sensitive questions in an online survey. For one group of participants, the website's user interface looked fun and frivolous; for another group, the site looked official. (The control group was presented with a neutral-looking site.) Participants were about twice as likely to reveal sensitive information on the casual-looking site than on the others.

People also tend to be more forthcoming when given an escape hatch or "out" in a conversation. For example, if they are told that they can change their answers at any point, they tend to open up more—even though they rarely end up making changes. This might explain why teams and groups find brainstorming sessions so productive. In a whiteboard setting, where anything can be erased and judgment is suspended, people are more likely to answer questions honestly and say things they otherwise might not. Of course, there will be times when an off-the-cuff approach is inappropriate. But in general, an overly formal tone is likely to inhibit people's willingness to share information.

Pay attention to group dynamics

Conversational dynamics can change profoundly depending on whether you're chatting one-on-one with someone or talking in a group. Not only is the willingness to answer questions affected simply by the presence of others, but members of a group tend to follow one another's lead. In one set of studies, Leslie and her coauthors asked participants a series of sensitive questions, including ones about finances ("Have you ever bounced a check?") and sex ("While an adult, have you ever felt sexual desire for a minor?"). Participants were told either that most others in the study were willing to reveal stigmatizing answers or that they were unwilling to do so. Participants who were told that others had been forthcoming were 27% likelier to reveal sensitive answers than those who were told that others had been reticent. In a meeting or group setting, it takes only a few closed-off people for questions to lose their probing power. The opposite is true, too. As soon as one person starts to open up, the rest of the group is likely to follow suit.

Group dynamics can also affect how a question asker is perceived. Alison's research reveals that participants in a conversation enjoy being asked questions and tend to like the people asking questions more than those who answer them. But when third-party observers watch the same conversation unfold, they prefer the person who answers questions. This makes sense: People who mostly ask questions tend to disclose very little about themselves or their thoughts.

To those listening to a conversation, question askers may come across as defensive, evasive, or invisible, while those answering seem more fascinating, present, or memorable.

The Best Response

A conversation is a dance that requires partners to be in sync—it's a mutual push-and-pull that unfolds over time. Just as the way we ask questions can facilitate trust and the sharing of information—so, too, can the way we answer them.

Answering questions requires making a choice about where to fall on a continuum between privacy and transparency. Should we answer the question? If we answer, how forthcoming should we be? What should we do when asked a question that, if answered truthfully, might reveal a less-than-glamorous fact or put us in a disadvantaged strategic position? Each end of the spectrum—fully opaque and fully transparent—has benefits and pitfalls. Keeping information private can make us feel free to experiment and learn. In negotiations, withholding sensitive information (such as the fact that your alternatives are weak) can help you secure better outcomes. At the same time, transparency is an essential part of forging meaningful connections. Even in a negotiation context, transparency can lead to value-creating deals; by sharing information, participants can identify elements that are relatively unimportant to one party but important to the other—the foundation of a win-win outcome.

And keeping secrets has costs. Research by Julie Lane and Daniel Wegner, of the University of Virginia, suggests that concealing secrets during social interactions leads to the intrusive recurrence of secret thoughts, while research by Columbia's Michael Slepian, Jinseok Chun, and Malia Mason shows that keeping secrets—even outside of social interactions—depletes us cognitively, interferes with our ability to concentrate and remember things, and even harms long-term health and well-being.

In an organizational context, people too often err on the side of privacy—and underappreciate the benefits of transparency. How often do we realize that we could have truly bonded with a colleague only after he or she has moved on to a new company? Why are better deals often uncovered after the ink has dried, the tension has broken, and negotiators begin to chat freely?

To maximize the benefits of answering questions—and minimize the risks—it's important to decide before a conversation begins what information you want to share and what you want to keep private.

Deciding what to share

There is no rule of thumb for how much—or what type—of information you should disclose. Indeed, transparency is such a powerful bonding agent that sometimes it doesn't matter what is revealed—even information that reflects poorly on us can draw our conversational partners closer. In research Leslie conducted with HBS collaborators Kate Barasz and Michael Norton, she found that most people assume that it would be less damaging to refuse to answer a question that would reveal negative information—for example, "Have you ever been reprimanded at work?"—than to answer affirmatively. But this intuition is wrong. When they asked people to take the perspective of a recruiter and choose between two candidates (equivalent except for how they responded to this question), nearly 90% preferred the candidate who "came clean" and answered the question. Before a conversation takes place, think carefully about whether refusing to answer tough questions would do more harm than good.

Deciding what to keep private

Of course, at times you and your organization would be better served by keeping your cards close to your chest. In our negotiation classes, we teach strategies for handling hard questions without lying. Dodging, or answering a question you *wish* you had been asked, can be effective not only in helping you protect information you'd rather keep private but also in building a good rapport with your conversational partner, especially if you speak eloquently. In a study led by Todd Rogers, of Harvard's Kennedy School, participants were shown clips of political candidates responding to questions by either answering them or dodging them. Eloquent dodgers were liked more than ineloquent answerers, but only when their dodges went undetected. Another effective strategy is deflecting, or answering a probing question with another question or a joke. Answerers can use this approach to lead the conversation in a different direction.

"Question everything," Albert Einstein famously said. Personal creativity and organizational innovation rely on a willingness to seek out novel information. Questions and thoughtful answers foster smoother and more-effective interactions; they strengthen rapport and trust and lead groups toward discovery. All this we have documented in our research. But we believe questions and answers have a power that goes far beyond matters of performance. The wellspring of all questions is wonder and curiosity and a capacity for delight. We pose and respond to queries in the belief that the magic of a conversation will produce a whole that is greater than the sum of its parts. Sustained personal engagement and motivation—in our lives as well as our work—require that we are always mindful of the transformative joy of asking and answering questions.

Originally published in May–June 2018. Reprint R1803C

Strategy Needs Creativity

by Adam Brandenburger

I'VE NOTICED THAT BUSINESS SCHOOL STUDENTS often feel frustrated when they're taught strategy. There's a gap between what they learn and what they'd like to learn. Strategy professors (including me) typically teach students to think about strategy problems by introducing them to rigorous analytical tools—assessing the five forces, drawing a value net, plotting competitive positions. The students know that the tools are essential, and they dutifully learn how to use them. But they also realize that the tools are better suited to understanding an existing business context than to dreaming up ways to reshape it. Game-changing strategies, they know, are born of creative thinking: a spark of intuition, a connection between different ways of thinking, a leap into the unexpected.

They're right to feel this way—which is not to say that we should abandon the many powerful analytical tools we've developed over the years. We'll always need them to understand competitive landscapes and to assess how companies can best deploy their resources and competencies there. But we who devote our professional lives to thinking about strategy need to acknowledge that just giving people those tools will not help them break with conventional ways of thinking. If we want to teach students—and executives—how to generate groundbreaking strategies, we must give them tools explicitly designed to foster creativity.

A number of such tools already exist, often in practitioner-friendly forms. In "How Strategists Really Think: Tapping the Power of Analogy" (HBR, April 2005), Giovanni Gavetti and Jan W. Rivkin write compellingly about using analogies to come up with new business models. Charles Duhigg talks in his book *Smarter Faster Better* about introducing carefully chosen creative "disturbances" into work processes to spur new thinking. Youngme Moon, in "Break Free from the Product Life Cycle" (HBR, May 2005), suggests redefining products by boldly limiting—rather than augmenting—the features offered.

What these approaches have in common is the goal of moving strategy past the insights delivered by analytic tools (which are close at hand) and into territory that's further afield, or—to use a bit of academic jargon—*cognitively distant*. They take their inspiration more from how our thought processes work than from how industries or business models are structured. For that reason they can help strategists make the creative leap beyond what already exists to invent a genuinely new way of doing business. Simply waiting for inspiration to strike is not the answer.

In this article I explore four approaches to building a breakthrough strategy:

- **Contrast.** The strategist should identify—and challenge—the assumptions undergirding the company's or the industry's status quo. This is the most direct and often the most powerful way to reinvent a business.

- **Combination.** Steve Jobs famously said that creativity is "just connecting things"; many smart business moves come from linking products or services that seem independent from or even in tension with one another.

- **Constraint.** A good strategist looks at an organization's limitations and considers how they might actually become strengths.

- **Context.** If you reflect on how a problem similar to yours was solved in an entirely different context, surprising insights

Idea in Brief

The Problem

The field of strategy overfocuses on analytic rigor and underfocuses on creativity.

Why It Matters

Analytic tools are good at helping strategists develop business ideas that are close at hand—but less good at discovering transformative strategies.

In Practice

The wise strategist can work with four creativity-enhancing tools: contrast, combination, constraint, and context.

---

may emerge. (I wrote about these ideas more academically in "Where Do Great Strategies Really Come From?" *Strategy Science,* December 2017.)

These approaches aren't exhaustive—or even entirely distinct from one another—but I've found that they help people explore a wide range of possibilities.

Contrast: What Pieces of Conventional Wisdom Are Ripe for Contradiction?

To create a strategy built on contrast, first identify the assumptions implicit in existing strategies. Elon Musk seems to have a knack for this approach. He and the other creators of PayPal took a widely held but untested assumption about banking—that transferring money online was feasible and safe between institutions but not between individuals—and disproved it. With SpaceX he is attempting to overturn major assumptions about space travel: that it must occur on a fixed schedule, be paid for by the public, and use onetime rockets. He may be on track toward a privately funded, on-demand business that reuses rockets.

It's best to be precise—even literal—when naming such assumptions. Consider the video rental industry in 2000. Blockbuster ruled the industry, and the assumptions beneath its model seemed self-evident: People pick up videos at a retail location close to home. Inventory must be limited because new videos are expensive. Since the demand for them is high, customers must be charged for late returns. (It was basically a public-library model.) But Netflix put those assumptions under a microscope. Why is a physical location necessary? Mailing out videos would be cheaper and more convenient. Is there a way around the high fees for new releases? If the studios were open to a revenue-sharing agreement, both parties could benefit. Those two changes allowed Netflix to carry lots more movies, offer long rental periods, do away with late fees—and remake an industry.

Most of the time, strategy from contrast may look less revolutionary than Netflix (which remade itself again by streaming videos and becoming a content creator) or SpaceX (should it succeed). Any organization can ask whether it might usefully flip the order in which it performs activities, for example. The traditional model in retail is to start with a flagship store (usually in a city center) and add satellites (in suburban locations). Now consider pop-up stores: In some cases they conform to the old model—they are like mini-satellites; but in others the pop-up comes first, and if that's successful, a larger footprint is added. The Soho area of New York City has become a testing ground for this strategy.

Another approach is to consider shaking up the value chain, which in any industry is conventionally oriented in a particular way, with some players acting as suppliers and others as customers. Inverting the value chain may yield new business models. In the charitable sector, for example, donors have been seen as suppliers of financial resources. DonorsChoose.org is a model that treats them more like customers. The organization puts up a "storefront" of requests posted by schoolteachers around the United States who are looking for materials for their (often underresourced) classrooms. Donors can choose which requests to respond to and receive photos of the schoolwork that their money has supported. In effect, they are buying the satisfaction of seeing a particular classroom before and after.

In some industries the status quo has dictated highly bundled, expensive products or services. Unbundling them is another way to build a contrast strategy. Various segments of the market may prefer to get differing subsets of the bundle at better prices. Challengers' unbundling of the status quo has been facilitated by the internet in one industry after another: Music, TV, and education are leading examples. Incumbents have to make major internal changes to compete with unbundlers, rendering this approach especially effective.

How to begin

1. Precisely identify the assumptions that underlie conventional thinking in your company or industry.

2. Think about what might be gained by proving one or more of them false.

3. Deliberately disturb an aspect of your normal work pattern to break up ingrained assumptions.

What to watch out for

Because the assumptions underlying your business model are embedded in all your processes—and because stable businesses need predictability—it won't be easy to change course. Organizations are very good at resisting change.

Combination: How Can You Connect Products or Services That Have Traditionally Been Separate?

Combination is a canonical creative approach in both the arts and the sciences. As Anthony Brandt and David Eagleman note in *The Runaway Species,* it was by combining two very different ideas—a ride in an elevator and a journey into space—that Albert Einstein found his way to the theory of general relativity. In business, too, creative and successful moves can result from combining things that have been separate. Often these opportunities arise with complementary products and services. Products and payment systems, for example, have traditionally been separate nodes in value chains. But the Chinese social media platform WeChat (owned by Tencent) now includes an integrated mobile payment platform called WeChat Pay that enables users to buy and sell products within their social networks. Expanding beyond the Chinese ecosystem, Tencent and Alibaba are coordinating with overseas payment firms to enable retailers in other countries to accept their mobile payment services.

Sometimes competitors can benefit from joining forces to grow the pie. (Barry Nalebuff and I explored this idea in our 1996 book *Co-opetition.*) For example, BMW and Daimler have announced plans to combine their mobility services—car sharing, ride hailing, car parking, electric vehicle charging, and tickets for public transport. Presumably, the two automakers hope that this move will be an effective counterattack against Uber and other players that are encroaching on the traditional car industry.

In other instances, companies from wholly separate industries have created new value for customers by combining offerings. Apple and Nike have done so since the 2006 introduction of the Nike+ iPod Sport Kit, which enabled Nike shoes to communicate with an iPod for tracking steps. More recently, versions of the Apple Watch have come with the Nike+ Run Club app fully integrated. Nest Labs and Amazon also complement each other: Nest's intelligent home thermostat becomes even more valuable when it can deploy voice control via Amazon's virtual assistant, Alexa.

New technologies are a rich source of combinatorial possibilities. AI and blockchain come together naturally to protect the privacy of the large amounts of personal data needed to train algorithms in health care and other sensitive areas. Blockchain and the internet of things come together in the form of sensors and secure data in decentralized applications such as food supply chains, transportation systems, and smart homes, with automated insurance included in smart contracts.

Perhaps the biggest combination today is the one emerging between humans and machines. Some commentators see the future of that relationship as more competitive than cooperative, with humans losing out in many areas of economic life. Others predict a more positive picture, in which machines take on lower-level cognition, freeing humans to be more creative. Martin Reeves and Daichi Ueda have written about algorithms that allow companies to make frequent, calibrated adjustments to their business models, enabling humans to work on high-level objectives and think beyond the present. (See "Designing the Machines That Will Design Strategy," HBR.org, April 2016.)

Strategy from combination involves looking for connections across traditional boundaries, whether by linking a product and a service, two technologies, the upstream and the downstream, or other ingredients. Here, too, the creative strategist must challenge the status quo—this time by thinking not just outside the box but across two or more boxes.

How to begin
1. Form groups with diverse expertise and experience; brainstorm new combinations of products and services.

2. Look for ways to coordinate with providers of complementary products (who may even be competitors).

What to watch out for
Businesses often manage for and measure profits at the individual product or activity level. But combinations require system-level thinking and measurements.

Constraint: How Can You Turn Limitations or Liabilities into Opportunities?

The world's first science fiction story, *Frankenstein,* was written when its author, Mary Wollstonecraft Shelley, was staying near Lake Geneva during an unusually cold and stormy summer and found herself trapped indoors with nothing to do but exercise her imagination. Artists know a lot about constraints—from profound ones, such as serious setbacks in their lives, to structural ones, such as writing a 14-line poem with a specified rhyming structure. In business, too, creative thinking turns limitations into opportunities.

That constraints can spark creative strategies may seem paradoxical. Lift a constraint, and any action that was previously possible is surely still possible; most likely, more is now possible.

But that misses the point that one can think multiple ways in a given situation—and a constraint may prompt a whole new line of thinking. Of course, the Goldilocks principle applies: Too many constraints will choke off all possibilities, and a complete absence of constraints is a problem too.

Tesla hasn't lacked financial resources in entering the car industry, but it doesn't have a traditional dealership network (considered a key part of automakers' business models) through which to sell. Rather than get into the business of building one, Tesla has chosen to sell cars online and to build Apple-like stores staffed with salespeople on salary. This actually positions the company well relative to competitors, whose dealers may be conflicted about promoting electric vehicles over internal-combustion ones. In addition, Tesla controls its pricing directly, whereas consumers who buy electric vehicles from traditional dealers may encounter significant variations in price.

I should note that this attitude toward constraints is very different from that suggested by the classic SWOT analysis. Strategists are supposed to identify the strengths, weaknesses, opportunities, and threats impinging on an organization and then figure out ways to exploit strengths and opportunities and mitigate weaknesses and threats.

In stark contrast, a constraint-based search would look at how those weaknesses could be turned to the company's advantage. Constraint plus imagination may yield an opportunity.

This approach to strategy turns the SWOT tool upside down in another way as well. Just as an apparent weakness can be turned into a strength, an apparent strength can prove to be a weakness. The likelihood of this often increases over time, as the assets that originally enabled a business to succeed become liabilities when the environment changes. For example, big retailers have historically considered "success" to be moving product out the door; to that end, they needed large physical footprints with on-site inventory. Among the many changes they face today is the rise of "guideshops"—a term used by the menswear retailer Bonobos—where shoppers try on items, which they can have shipped to them or later order online. In the new environment, traditional retail footprints become more of a liability than an asset.

Another way to approach strategy from constraint is to ask whether you might benefit from self-imposed constraints. (Artists do something similar when they choose to work only within a particular medium.) The famous Copenhagen restaurant Noma adheres to the New Nordic Food manifesto (emphasizing purity, simplicity, beauty, seasonality, local tradition, and innovation). A similar strategy of working only with local suppliers has been adopted by thousands of restaurants around the world. A commitment to high environmental standards, fair labor practices, and ethical supply-chain management can be powerful for organizations looking to lead change in their industries or sectors.

Self-imposed constraints can also spur innovation. Adam Morgan and Mark Barden, in their book *A Beautiful Constraint*, describe the efforts of the Audi racing team in the early 2000s to win Le Mans under the assumption that its cars couldn't go faster than the competition's. Audi developed diesel-powered racers, which required fewer fuel stops than gasoline-powered cars, and won Le Mans three years in succession (2004–2006). In 2017 Audi set itself a new constraint—and a new ambition: to build winning all-electric racers for the new Formula E championship.

How to begin
1. List the "incompetencies" (rather than the competencies) of your organization—and test whether they can in fact be turned into strengths.

2. Consider deliberately imposing some constraints to encourage people to find new ways of thinking and acting.

What to watch out for
Successful businesses face few obvious constraints; people may feel no need to explore how new ones might create new opportunities.

Context: How Can Far-Flung Industries, Ideas, or Disciplines Shed Light on Your Most Pressing Problems?

An entire field, biomimetics, is devoted to finding solutions in nature to problems that arise in engineering, materials science, medicine, and elsewhere. For example, the burrs from the burdock plant, which propagate by attaching to the fur of animals via tiny hooks, inspired George de Mestral in the 1940s to create a clothing fastener that does not jam (as zippers are prone to do). Thus the invention of Velcro. This is a classic problem-solving technique. Start with a problem in one context, find another context in which an analogous problem has already been solved, and import the solution.

Intel did that when it came up with its famous Intel Inside logo, in the early 1990s. The goal was to turn Intel microprocessors into a branded product to speed up consumers' adoption of next-generation chips and, more broadly, to improve the company's ability to drive the PC industry forward. Branded ingredients were well established in certain consumer product sectors—examples include Teflon and NutraSweet—but hadn't been tried in the world of technology. Intel imported the approach to high tech with a novel advertising campaign, successfully branding what had previously been an invisible computer component.

Context switching can be done across industries, as in Intel's case, or even across time. The development of the graphical user interface (GUI) for computers was in a sense the result of a step backward: The developers moved from immersion in the text-based context in which programming had grown up to thinking about the highly visual hand-eye environment in which young children operate. Similarly, some AI researchers are currently looking at how children learn in order to inform processes for machine learning.

Companies are always eager to see into the future, of course, and techniques for trying to do so are well established. That is the purpose of lead-user and extreme-user innovation strategies, which ask companies to shift their attention from mainstream customers to people who are designing their own versions or using products in unexpected ways in especially demanding environments. Information about where the edges of the market are today can signal where the mainstream will be tomorrow. Extreme sports, such as mountain biking, skateboarding, snowboarding, and windsurfing, are good examples. In an MIT Sloan School working paper, Sonali Shah relates that aficionados led many of the innovations in those areas, starting in the 1950s, and big manufacturers added cost efficiencies and marketing to take them mainstream.

When companies locate R&D functions far from headquarters, they're acknowledging the importance of jumping into someone else's context. This is not just a strategy for large companies that move people to Silicon Valley for tech or the Boston area for biotech. Start-ups, too, should put themselves in the best context for learning and growth. The hardware accelerator HAX, located in Shenzhen, hosts hardware start-up teams from numerous countries and enables them to tap into the high-speed ecosystem of the "hardware capital of the world," quadrupling the rate at which they cycle through iterations of their prototypes.

Strategy focused on context may involve transferring a solution from one setting to another more or less as is. It may mean uncovering entirely new thinking about problems (or opportunities) by finding pioneers who are ahead of the game. At bottom, it's about not being trapped in a single narrative.

How to begin
1. Explain your business to an outsider in another industry. Fresh eyes from a different context can help uncover new answers and opportunities.

2. Engage with lead users, extreme users, and innovation hotspots.

What to watch out for
Businesses need to focus on internal processes to deliver on their current value propositions—but the pressure to focus internally can get in the way of learning from the different contexts in which other players operate.

In the world of management consulting, aspects of "strategy" and "innovation" have started to converge. IDEO, the design and innovation powerhouse, has moved into strategy consulting, for example—while McKinsey has added design-thinking methods to its strategy consulting. This convergence raises an obvious question: If the distinction between strategy and innovation is less clear than it once was, do we really need to think carefully about the role of creativity in the strategy-making process?

I believe strongly that the answer is yes. At its core, strategy is still about finding ways to create and claim value through differentiation. That's a complicated, difficult job. To be sure, it requires tools that can help identify surprising, creative breaks from conventional thinking. But it also requires tools for analyzing the competitive landscape, the dynamics threatening that landscape, and a company's resources and competencies. We need to teach business school students—and executives—how to be creative and rigorous at the same time.

Originally published in March–April 2019. Reprint R1902C

What Most People Get Wrong about Men and Women

by Catherine H. Tinsley and Robin J. Ely

THE CONVERSATION ABOUT the treatment of women in the workplace has reached a crescendo of late, and senior leaders—men as well as women—are increasingly vocal about a commitment to gender parity. That's all well and good, but there's an important catch. The discussions, and many of the initiatives companies have undertaken, too often reflect a faulty belief: that men and women are fundamentally *different*, by virtue of their genes or their upbringing or both. Of course, there are biological differences. But those are not the differences people are usually talking about. Instead, the rhetoric focuses on the idea that women are inherently unlike men in terms of disposition, attitudes, and behaviors. (Think headlines that tout "Why women do X at the office" or "Working women don't Y.")

One set of assumed differences is marshaled to explain women's failure to achieve parity with men: Women negotiate poorly, lack confidence, are too risk-averse, or don't put in the requisite hours at work because they value family more than their careers. Simultaneously, other assumed differences—that women are more caring, cooperative, or mission-driven—are used as a rationale for companies to invest in women's success. But whether framed as a barrier or a benefit, these beliefs hold women back. We will not level the playing field so long as the bedrock on which it rests is our conviction about how the sexes are different.

The reason is simple: Science, by and large, does not actually support these claims. There is wide variation among women and among men, and meta-analyses show that, on average, the sexes are far more similar in their inclinations, attitudes, and skills than popular opinion would have us believe. We do see sex differences in various settings, including the workplace—but those differences are not rooted in fixed gender traits. Rather, they stem from organizational structures, company practices, and patterns of interaction that position men and women differently, creating systematically different experiences for them. When facing dissimilar circumstances, people respond differently—not because of their sex but because of their situations.

Emphasizing sex differences runs the risk of making them seem natural and inevitable. As anecdotes that align with stereotypes are told and retold, without addressing why and when stereotypical behaviors appear, sex differences are exaggerated and take on a determinative quality. Well-meaning but largely ineffectual interventions then focus on "fixing" women or accommodating them rather than on changing the circumstances that gave rise to different behaviors in the first place.

Take, for example, the common belief that women are more committed to family than men are. Research simply does not support that notion. In a study of Harvard Business School graduates that one of us conducted, nearly everyone, regardless of gender, placed a higher value on their families than on their work (see "Rethink What You 'Know' About High-Achieving Women," HBR, December 2014). Moreover, having made career decisions to accommodate family responsibilities didn't explain the gender achievement gap. Other research, too, makes it clear that men and women do not have fundamentally different priorities.

Numerous studies show that what does differ is the treatment mothers and fathers receive when they start a family. Women (but not men) are seen as needing support, whereas men are more likely

Idea in Brief

The Belief

There's a popular notion that men and women are fundamentally different in important (nonbiological) ways—and those differences are cited to explain women's lagged achievement.

The Truth

According to numerous meta-analyses of published research, men and women are actually very similar with respect to key attri-

butes such as confidence, appetite for risk, and negotiating skill.

Why It Matters

Too many managers try to "fix" women or accommodate their supposed differences—and that doesn't work. Companies must instead address the organizational conditions that lead to lower rates of retention and promotion for women.

to get the message—either explicit or subtle—that they need to "man up" and not voice stress and fatigue. If men do ask, say, for a lighter travel schedule, their supervisors may cut them some slack—but often grudgingly and with the clear expectation that the reprieve is temporary. Accordingly, some men attempt an under-the-radar approach, quietly reducing hours or travel and hoping it goes unnoticed, while others simply concede, limiting the time they spend on family responsibilities and doubling down at work. Either way, they maintain a reputation that keeps them on an upward trajectory. Meanwhile, mothers are often expected, indeed encouraged, to ratchet back at work. They are rerouted into less taxing roles and given less "demanding" (read: lower-status, less career-enhancing) clients.

To sum up, men's and women's desires and challenges about work/family balance are remarkably similar. It is what they experience at work once they become parents that puts them in very different places.

Things don't have to be this way. When companies observe differences in the overall success rates of women and men, or in behaviors that are critical to effectiveness, they can actively seek to understand the organizational conditions that might be responsible, and then they can experiment with changing those conditions.

Consider the example of a savvy managing director concerned about the leaky pipeline at her professional services firm. Skeptical that women were simply "opting out" following the birth of a child, she investigated and found that one reason women were leaving the firm stemmed from the performance appraisal system: Supervisors had to adhere to a forced distribution when rating their direct reports, and women who had taken parental leave were unlikely to receive the highest rating because their performance was ranked against that of peers who had worked a full year. Getting less than top marks not only hurt their chances of promotion but also sent a demoralizing message that being a mother was incompatible with being on a partner track. However, the fix was relatively easy: The company decided to reserve the forced distribution for employees who worked the full year, while those with long leaves could roll over their rating from the prior year. That applied to both men and women, but the policy was most heavily used by new mothers. The change gave women more incentive to return from maternity leave and helped keep them on track for advancement. Having more mothers stay on track, in turn, helped chip away at assumptions within the firm about women's work/family preferences.

As this example reveals, companies need to dive deeper into their beliefs, norms, practices, and policies to understand how they position women relative to men and how the different positions fuel inequality. Seriously investigating the context that gives rise to differential patterns in the way men and women experience the workplace—and intervening accordingly—can help companies chart a path to gender parity.

Below, we address three popular myths about how the sexes differ and explain how each manifests itself in organizational discourse about women's lagged advancement. Drawing on years of social science research, we debunk the myths and offer alternative explanations for observed sex differences—explanations that point to ways that managers can level the playing field. We then offer a four-pronged strategy for undertaking such actions.

Popular Myths

We've all heard statements in the media and in companies that women lack *the desire or ability to negotiate,* that they lack *confidence,* and that they lack *an appetite for risk.* And, the thinking goes, those shortcomings explain why women have so far failed to reach parity with men.

For decades, studies have examined sex differences on these three dimensions, enabling social scientists to conduct meta-analyses—investigations that reveal whether or not, on average across studies, sex differences hold, and if so, how large the differences are. (See the sidebar "The Power of Meta-Analysis.") Just as importantly, meta-analyses also reveal the circumstances under which differences between men and women are more or less likely to arise. The aggregated findings are clear: Context explains any sex differences that exist in the workplace.

Take negotiation. Over and over, we hear that women are poor negotiators—they "settle too easily," are "too nice," or are "too cooperative." But not so, according to research. Jens Mazei and colleagues recently analyzed more than 100 studies examining whether men and women negotiate different outcomes; they determined that gender differences were small to negligible. Men have a slight advantage in negotiations when they are advocating exclusively for themselves and when ambiguity about the stakes or opportunities is high. Larger disparities in outcomes occur when negotiators either have no prior experience or are forced to negotiate, as in a mandated training exercise. But such situations are atypical, and even when they do arise, statisticians would deem the resulting sex differences to be small. As for the notion that women are more cooperative than men, research by Daniel Balliet and colleagues refutes that.

The belief that women lack confidence is another fallacy. That assertion is commonly invoked to explain why women speak up less in meetings and do not put themselves forward for promotions unless they are 100% certain they meet all the job requirements. But research does not corroborate the idea that women are less confident than men. Analyzing more than 200 studies, Kristen Kling and colleagues concluded that the only noticeable differences occurred during adolescence; starting at age 23, differences become negligible.

What about risk taking—are women really more conservative than men? Many people believe that's true—though they are split on whether being risk-averse is a strength or a weakness. On the positive side, the thinking goes, women are less likely to get caught up in macho displays of bluff and bravado and thus are less likely to take unnecessary risks. Consider the oft-heard sentiment following the demise of Lehman Brothers: "If Lehman Brothers had been Lehman Sisters, the financial crisis might have been averted." On the negative side, women are judged as too cautious to make high-risk, potentially high-payoff investments.

But once again, research fails to support either of these stereotypes. As with negotiation, sex differences in the propensity to take risks are small and depend on the context. In a meta-analysis performed by James Byrnes and colleagues, the largest differences arise in contexts unlikely to exist in most organizations (such as among people asked to participate in a game of pure chance). Similarly, in a study Peggy Dwyer and colleagues ran examining the largest, last, and riskiest investments made by nearly 2,000 mutual fund investors, sex differences were very small. More importantly, when investors' specific knowledge about the investments was added to the equation, the sex difference diminished to near extinction, suggesting that access to information, not propensity for risk taking, explains the small sex differences that have been documented.

In short, a wealth of evidence contradicts each of these popular myths. Yet they live on through oft-repeated narratives routinely invoked to explain women's lagged advancement.

More-Plausible Explanations

The extent to which employees are able to thrive and succeed at work depends partly on the kinds of opportunities and treatment they receive. People are more likely to behave in ways that undermine their chances for success when they are disconnected from information networks, when they are judged or penalized dispropor-

Why the Sex-Difference Narrative Persists

BELIEFS IN SEX DIFFERENCES have staying power partly because they uphold conventional gender norms, preserve the gender status quo, and require no upheaval of existing organizational practices or work arrangements. But they are also the path of least resistance for our brains. Three well-documented cognitive errors help explain the endurance of the sex-difference narrative.

First, when seeking to explain others' behavior, we gravitate to explanations based on intrinsic *personality traits*—including stereotypically "male" traits and stereotypically "female" traits"—rather than *contextual factors*. (Social psychologists call this "the fundamental attribution error.") For example, if a man speaks often and forcefully in a meeting, we are more likely to conclude that he is assertive and confident than to search for a situational explanation, such as that he's been repeatedly praised for his contributions. Likewise, if a woman is quiet in a meeting, the easier explanation is that she's meek or underconfident; it takes more cognitive energy to construct an alternative account, such as that she is used to being cut off or ignored when she speaks. In short, when we see men and women behaving in gender-stereotypical ways, we tend to make the most cognitively simple assumption—that the behavior reflects who they are rather than the situation they are in.

Second, mere exposure to a continuing refrain, such as "Women are X, and men are Y," makes people judge the statement as true. Many beliefs—that bats are blind, that fresh produce is always more nutritious than frozen, that you shouldn't wake a sleepwalker—are repeated so often that their mere familiarity makes them easier for our minds to accept as truth. (This is called the "mere exposure effect.")

Third, once people believe something is true, they tend to seek, notice, and remember evidence that confirms the position and to ignore or forget evidence that would challenge it. (Psychologists call this "confirmation bias.") If we believe that gender stereotypes are accurate, we are more likely to expect, notice, and remember times when men and women behave in gender-stereotypical ways and to overlook times when they don't.

tionately harshly for mistakes or failures, and when they lack feedback. Unfortunately, women are more likely than men to encounter each of these situations. And the way they respond—whether that's by failing to drive a hard bargain, to speak up, or to take risks—gets unfairly attributed to "the way women are," when in fact the culprit is very likely the differential conditions they face.

Multiple studies show, for example, that women are less embedded in networks that offer opportunities to gather vital information and garner support. When people lack access to useful contacts and information, they face a disadvantage in negotiations. They may not know what is on the table, what is within the realm of possibility, or even that a chance to strike a deal exists. When operating under such conditions, women are more likely to conform to the gender stereotype that "women don't ask."

We saw this dynamic vividly play out when comparing the experiences of two professionals we'll call Mary and Rick. (In this example and others that follow, we have changed the names and some details to maintain confidentiality.) Mary and Rick were both midlevel advisers in the wealth management division of a financial services firm. Rick was able to bring in more assets to manage because he sat on the board of a nonprofit, giving him access to a pool of potential clients with high net worth. What Mary did not know for many years is how Rick had gained that advantage. Through casual conversations with one of the firm's senior partners, with whom he regularly played tennis, Rick had learned that discretionary funds existed to help advisers cultivate relationships with clients. So he arranged for the firm to make a donation to the nonprofit. He then began attending the nonprofit's fund-raising events and hobnobbing with key players, eventually parlaying his connections into a seat on the board. Mary, by contrast, had no informal relationships with senior partners at the firm and no knowledge of the level of resources that could have helped her land clients.

When people are less embedded, they are also less aware of opportunities for stretch assignments and promotions, and their supervisors may be in the dark about their ambitions. But when women fail to "lean in" and seek growth opportunities, it is easy to assume that they lack the confidence to do so—not that they lack pertinent information. Julie's experience is illustrative. Currently the CEO of a major investment fund, Julie had left her previous employer of 15 years after learning that a more junior male colleague had leapfrogged over her to fill an opening she didn't even know existed. When she announced that she was leaving and why, her boss was surprised. He told her that if he had realized she wanted to move up, he would have gladly helped position her for the promotion. But because she hadn't put her hat in the ring, he had assumed she lacked confidence in her ability to handle the job.

How people react to someone's mistake or failure can also affect that person's ability to thrive and succeed. Several studies have found that because women operate under a higher-resolution microscope than their male counterparts do, their mistakes and failures are scrutinized more carefully and punished more severely. People who are scrutinized more carefully will, in turn, be less likely to speak up in meetings, particularly if they feel no one has their back. However, when women fail to speak up, it is commonly assumed that they lack confidence in their ideas.

We saw a classic example of this dynamic at a biotech company in which team leaders noticed that their female colleagues, all highly qualified research scientists, participated far less in team meetings than their male counterparts did, yet later, in one-on-one conversations, often offered insightful ideas germane to the discussion. What these leaders had failed to see was that when women did speak in meetings, their ideas tended to be either ignored until a man restated them or shot down quickly if they contained even the slightest flaw. In contrast, when men's ideas were flawed, the meritorious elements were salvaged. Women therefore felt they needed to be 110% sure of their ideas before they would venture to share them. In a context in which being smart was the coin of the realm, it seemed better to remain silent than to have one's ideas repeatedly dismissed.

It stands to reason that people whose missteps are more likely to be held against them will also be less likely to take risks. That was the case at a Big Four accounting firm that asked us to investigate why so few women partners were in formal leadership roles. The reason, many believed, was that women did not want such roles because of their family responsibilities, but our survey revealed a more complex story. First, women and men were equally likely to say they would accept a leadership role if offered one, but men were nearly 50% more likely to have been offered one. Second, women were more likely than men to say that worries about jeopardizing their careers deterred them from pursuing leadership positions—they feared they would not recover from failure and thus could not afford to take the risks an effective leader would need to take. Research confirms that such concerns are valid. For example, studies by Victoria Brescoll and colleagues found that if women in male-dominated occupations make mistakes, they are accorded less status and seen as less competent than men making the same mistakes; a study by Ashleigh Rosette and Robert Livingston demonstrated that black women leaders are especially vulnerable to this bias.

Research also shows that women get less frequent and lower-quality feedback than men. When people don't receive feedback, they are less likely to know their worth in negotiations. Moreover, people who receive little feedback are ill-equipped to assess their strengths, shore up their weaknesses, and judge their prospects for success and are therefore less able to build the confidence they need to proactively seek promotions or make risky decisions.

An example of this dynamic comes from a consulting firm in which HR staff members delivered partners' annual feedback to associates. The HR folks noticed that when women were told they were "doing fine," they "freaked out," feeling damned by faint praise; when men received the same feedback, they left the meeting "feeling great." HR concluded that women lack self-confidence and are therefore more sensitive to feedback, so the team advised partners to be especially encouraging to the women associates and to soften any criticism. Many of the partners were none too pleased to have to treat a subset of their associates with kid gloves, grousing that "if women can't stand the heat, they should get out of the kitchen." What these partners failed to realize, however, is that the kitchen was a lot hotter for women in the firm than for men. Why? Because the partners felt more comfortable with the men and so were systematically giving them more informal, day-to-day feedback. When women heard in their annual review that they were doing "fine," it was often the first feedback they'd received all year; they had nothing else to go on and assumed it meant their performance was merely adequate. In contrast, when men heard they were doing "fine," it was but one piece of information amidst a steady stream. The upshot was disproportionate turnover among women associates, many of whom left the firm because they believed their prospects for promotion were slim.

An Alternative Approach

The problem with the sex-difference narrative is that it leads companies to put resources into "fixing" women, which means that women miss out on what they need—and what every employee deserves: a context that enables them to reach their potential and maximizes their chances to succeed.

Managers who are advancing gender equity in their firms are taking a more inquisitive approach—rejecting old scripts, seeking an evidence-based understanding of how women experience the workplace, and then creating the conditions that increase women's prospects for success. Their approach entails four steps:

1. Question the narrative
A consulting firm we worked with had recruited significant numbers of talented women into its entry ranks—and then struggled to promote them. Their supervisors' explanations? Women are insufficiently competitive, lack "fire in the belly," or don't have the requisite confidence to excel in the job. But those narratives did not ring true to Sarah, a regional head, because a handful of women—those within her region—were performing and advancing at par. So rather than accept her colleagues' explanations, she got curious.

2. Generate a plausible alternative explanation
Sarah investigated the factors that might have helped women in her region succeed and found that they received more hands-on training and more attention from supervisors than did women in other regions. This finding suggested that the problem lay not with women's deficiencies but with their differential access to the conditions that enhance self-confidence and success.

To test that hypothesis, Sarah designed an experiment, with our help. First, we randomly split 60 supervisors into two groups of 30 for a training session on coaching junior consultants. Trainers gave both groups the same lecture on how to be a good coach. With one group, however, trainers shared research showing that differences in men's and women's self-confidence are minuscule, thus subtly giving the members of this "treatment" group reason to question gender stereotypes. The "control" group didn't get that information. Next, trainers gave all participants a series of hypotheticals in which an employee—sometimes a man and sometimes a woman—was underperforming. In both groups, participants were asked to write down the feedback they would give the underperforming employee.

Clear differences emerged between the two groups. Supervisors in the control group took different tacks with the underperforming man and woman: They were far less critical of the woman and focused largely on making her feel good, whereas they gave the man feedback that was more direct, specific, and critical, often with concrete suggestions for how he could improve. In contrast, the supervisors who had been shown research that refuted sex differences in self-confidence gave both employees the same kind of feedback; they also asked for more-granular information about the employee's performance so that they could deliver constructive comments. We were struck by how the participants who had been given a reason to question gender stereotypes focused on learning more about individuals' specific performance problems.

The experiment confirmed Sarah's sense that women's lagged advancement might be due at least partly to supervisors' assumptions about the training and development needs of their female direct reports. Moreover, her findings gave supervisors a plausible alternative explanation for women's lagged advancement—a necessary precondition for taking the next step. Although different firms find different types of evidence more or less compelling—not all require as rigorous a test as this firm did—Sarah's evidence-based approach illustrates a key part of the strategy we are advocating.

3. Change the context and assess the results

Once a plausible alternative explanation has been developed, companies can make appropriate changes and see if performance improves. Two stories help illustrate this step. Both come from a midmarket private equity firm that was trying to address a problem that had persisted for 10 years: The company's promotion and retention rates for white women and people of color were far lower than its hiring rates.

The first story involves Elaine, an Asian-American senior associate who wanted to sharpen her financing skills and asked Dave, a partner, if she could assist with that aspect of his next deal. He invited her to lunch, but when they met, he was underwhelmed. Elaine struck him as insufficiently assertive and overly cautious. He decided against putting her on his team—but then he had second thoughts. The partners had been questioning their ability to spot and develop talent, especially in the case of associates who didn't look like them. Dave thus decided to try an experiment: He invited Elaine to join the team and then made a conscious effort to treat her exactly as he would have treated someone he deemed a superstar. He introduced her to the relevant players in the industry, told the banks she would be leading the financing, and gave her lots of rope but also enough feedback and coaching so that she wouldn't hang herself. Elaine did not disappoint; indeed, her performance was stellar. While quiet in demeanor, Dave's new protégée showed an uncanny ability to read the client and come up with creative approaches to the deal's financing.

A second example involves Ned, a partner who was frustrated that Joan, a recent-MBA hire on his team, didn't assert herself on management team calls. At first Ned simply assumed that Joan lacked confidence. But then it occurred to him that he might be falling back on gender stereotypes, and he took a closer look at his own behavior. He realized that he wasn't doing anything to make participation easier for her and was actually doing things that made it harder, like taking up all the airtime on calls. So they talked about it, and Joan admitted that she was afraid of making a mistake and was hyperaware that if she spoke, she needed to say something very smart. Ned realized that he, too, was afraid she would make a mistake or wouldn't add value to the discussion, which is partly why he took over. But on reflection, he saw that it wouldn't be the end of the world if she did stumble—he did the same himself now and again.

The Power of Meta-Analysis

A META-ANALYSIS is a statistical technique used to combine the results of many studies, providing a more reliable basis for drawing conclusions from research. This approach has three advantages over a single study.

First, it is more *accurate*, because it is based on a very large sample—the total of the samples across all the studies—and because it contains data collected in many different contexts. Any single set of findings may reflect idiosyncrasies of the study's sample or context and thus may not yield conclusions that are truly generalizable. A meta-analysis, in essence, averages across these idiosyncrasies to give us a truer answer to the research question (in this case, "Are men and women different with regard to a particular trait or behavior?").

Second, a meta-analysis is more *comprehensive*. Because it contains studies conducted in many different contexts, it can tell us in which kinds of contexts we are more or less likely to see sex differences.

Third, a meta-analysis is more *precise:* It can tell us just how different men and women are. For any given trait or behavior, there is variability *among* men and *among* women; typically, those within-group differences are distributed around some "true" average for each group. Using the averages and the variability within each group, we can calculate an "effect size" that can be thought of as the impact that sex has on a particular trait. When testing for a sex difference, we are in essence asking the question "How much overlap is there between women and men, or, stated another way, how far apart are their respective averages, relative to the variability within each sex?"

Take the left-hand graph, which shows the distribution of men's and women's heights in the UK. We can see from the curves that men, on average, are quite a bit taller than women. In fact, men average five feet, nine inches, and

---

For their next few calls, they went over the agenda beforehand and worked out which parts she would take the lead on; he then gave her feedback after the call. Ned now has a junior colleague to whom he can delegate more; Joan, meanwhile, feels more confident and has learned that she can take risks and recover from mistakes.

4. Promote continual learning

Both Dave and Ned recognized that their tendency to jump to conclusions based on stereotypes was robbing them—and the firm—of

women five feet, three inches—a six-inch difference. We can also see that a number of women are taller than the average man, just as a number of men are shorter than the average woman. The size of the sex effect on height is 1.72, which is considered "large."

Using that sex difference as a reference point, we can see from the right-hand graph that the difference between men and women in self-esteem, or confidence, is much smaller, with an effect size of 0.10. Although the difference in each graph is statistically significant, the difference in confidence is considered, from a statistical point of view, "trivial"—and from a managerial point of view, essentially meaningless. This same analysis for men's and women's negotiation outcomes and for their propensity to take risks yielded effect sizes of 0.20 ("small") and 0.13 ("trivial"), respectively. In short, contrary to popular belief, all three sex differences we consider in this article are, for all intents and purposes, meaningless.

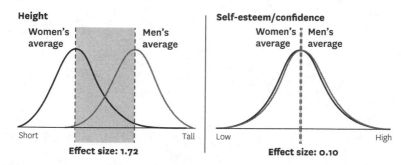

Height

Women's average | Men's average

Short | Tall

Effect size: 1.72

Self-esteem/confidence

Women's average | Men's average

Low | High

Effect size: 0.10

Note: Statisticians consider an effect size of less than 0.20 to be "trivial," 0.20–0.49 to be "small," 0.50–0.79 to be "medium," and 0.80 or more to be "large."

vital talent. Moreover, they have seen firsthand how questioning assumptions and proactively changing conditions gives women the opportunity to develop and shine. The lessons from these small-scale experiments are ongoing: Partners at the firm now meet regularly to discuss what they're learning. They also hold one another accountable for questioning and testing gender-stereotypical assessments as they arise. As a result, old narratives about women's limitations are beginning to give way to new narratives about how the firm can better support all employees.

The four steps we've outlined are consistent with research suggesting that on difficult issues such as gender and race, managers respond more positively when they see themselves as part of the solution rather than simply part of the problem. The solution to women's lagged advancement is not to fix women or their managers but to fix the conditions that undermine women and reinforce gender stereotypes. Furthermore, by taking an inquisitive, evidence-based approach to understanding behavior, companies can not only address gender disparities but also cultivate a learning orientation and a culture that gives all employees the opportunity to reach their full potential.

Originally published in May–June 2018. Reprint R1803J

Collaborative Intelligence

Humans and AI Are Joining Forces.
by H. James Wilson and Paul R. Daugherty

ARTIFICIAL INTELLIGENCE IS BECOMING good at many "human" jobs—diagnosing disease, translating languages, providing customer service—and it's improving fast. This is raising reasonable fears that AI will ultimately replace human workers throughout the economy. But that's not the inevitable, or even most likely, outcome. Never before have digital tools been so responsive to us, nor we to our tools. While AI will radically alter how work gets done and who does it, the technology's larger impact will be in complementing and augmenting human capabilities, not replacing them.

Certainly, many companies have used AI to automate processes, but those that deploy it mainly to displace employees will see only short-term productivity gains. In our research involving 1,500 companies, we found that firms achieve the most significant performance improvements when humans and machines work together (see the exhibit "The value of collaboration"). Through such collaborative intelligence, humans and AI actively enhance each other's complementary strengths: the leadership, teamwork, creativity, and social skills of the former, and the speed, scalability, and quantitative capabilities of the latter. What comes naturally to people (making a joke, for example) can be tricky for machines, and

The value of collaboration

Companies benefit from optimizing collaboration between humans and artificial intelligence. Five principles can help them do so: Reimagine business processes; embrace experimentation/employee involvement; actively direct AI strategy; responsibly collect data; and redesign work to incorporate AI and cultivate related employee skills. A survey of 1,075 companies in 12 industries found that the more of these principles companies adopted, the better their AI initiatives performed in terms of speed, cost savings, revenues, or other operational measures.

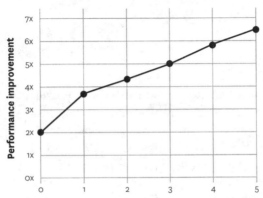

Number of human-machine collaboration principles adopted
(0 indicates the adoption of only basic, noncollaborative AI)

what's straightforward for machines (analyzing gigabytes of data) remains virtually impossible for humans. Business requires both kinds of capabilities.

To take full advantage of this collaboration, companies must understand how humans can most effectively augment machines, how machines can enhance what humans do best, and how to redesign business processes to support the partnership. Through our research and work in the field, we have developed guidelines to help companies achieve this and put the power of collaborative intelligence to work.

Idea in Brief

The Outlook

Artificial intelligence is transforming business—and having the most significant impact when it augments human workers instead of replacing them.

The Details

Companies see the biggest performance gains when humans and smart machines collaborate. People are needed to train machines, explain their outputs, and ensure their responsible use. AI, in turn, can enhance humans' cognitive skills and creativity, free workers from low-level tasks, and extend their physical capabilities.

The Prescription

Companies should reimagine their business processes, focusing on using AI to achieve more operational flexibility or speed, greater scale, better decision making, or increased personalization of products and services.

Humans Assisting Machines

Humans need to perform three crucial roles. They must *train* machines to perform certain tasks; *explain* the outcomes of those tasks, especially when the results are counterintuitive or controversial; and *sustain* the responsible use of machines (by, for example, preventing robots from harming humans).

Training

Machine-learning algorithms must be taught how to perform the work they're designed to do. In that effort, huge training data sets are amassed to teach machine-translation apps to handle idiomatic expressions, medical apps to detect disease, and recommendation engines to support financial decision making. In addition, AI systems must be trained how best to interact with humans. While organizations across sectors are now in the early stages of filling trainer roles, leading tech companies and research groups already have mature training staffs and expertise.

Consider Microsoft's AI assistant, Cortana. The bot required extensive training to develop just the right personality: confident, caring, and helpful but not bossy. Instilling those qualities took countless hours of attention by a team that included a poet, a novelist, and a playwright. Similarly, human trainers were needed to develop the personalities of Apple's Siri and Amazon's Alexa to ensure that they accurately reflected their companies' brands. Siri, for example, has just a touch of sassiness, as consumers might expect from Apple.

AI assistants are now being trained to display even more complex and subtle human traits, such as sympathy. The start-up Koko, an offshoot of the MIT Media Lab, has developed technology that can help AI assistants seem to commiserate. For instance, if a user is having a bad day, the Koko system doesn't reply with a canned response such as "I'm sorry to hear that." Instead it may ask for more information and then offer advice to help the person see his issues in a different light. If he were feeling stressed, for instance, Koko might recommend thinking of that tension as a positive emotion that could be channeled into action.

Explaining

As AIs increasingly reach conclusions through processes that are opaque (the so-called black-box problem), they require human experts in the field to explain their behavior to nonexpert users. These "explainers" are particularly important in evidence-based industries, such as law and medicine, where a practitioner needs to understand how an AI weighed inputs into, say, a sentencing or medical recommendation. Explainers are similarly important in helping insurers and law enforcement understand why an autonomous car took actions that led to an accident—or failed to avoid one. And explainers are becoming integral in regulated industries— indeed, in any consumer-facing industry where a machine's output could be challenged as unfair, illegal, or just plain wrong. For instance, the European Union's new General Data Protection Regulation (GDPR) gives consumers the right to receive an explanation for any algorithm-based decision, such as the rate offer on a credit card or mortgage. This is one area where AI will contribute to *increased* employment: Experts estimate that companies will have to create about 75,000 new jobs to administer the GDPR requirements.

Sustaining

In addition to having people who can explain AI outcomes, companies need "sustainers"—employees who continually work to ensure that AI systems are functioning properly, safely, and responsibly.

For example, an array of experts sometimes referred to as safety engineers focus on anticipating and trying to prevent harm by AIs. The developers of industrial robots that work alongside people have paid careful attention to ensuring that they recognize humans nearby and don't endanger them. These experts may also review analysis from explainers when AIs do cause harm, as when a self-driving car is involved in a fatal accident.

Other groups of sustainers make sure that AI systems uphold ethical norms. If an AI system for credit approval, for example, is found to be discriminating against people in certain groups (as has happened), these ethics managers are responsible for investigating and addressing the problem. Playing a similar role, data compliance officers try to ensure that the data that is feeding AI systems complies with the GDPR and other consumer-protection regulations. A related data-use role involves ensuring that AIs manage information responsibly. Like many tech companies, Apple uses AI to collect personal details about users as they engage with the company's devices and software. The aim is to improve the user experience, but unconstrained data gathering can compromise privacy, anger customers, and run afoul of the law. The company's "differential privacy team" works to make sure that while the AI seeks to learn as much as possible about a group of users in a statistical sense, it is protecting the privacy of individual users.

Machines Assisting Humans

Smart machines are helping humans expand their abilities in three ways. They can *amplify* our cognitive strengths; *interact* with customers and employees to free us for higher-level tasks; and *embody* human skills to extend our physical capabilities.

Enhancing performance

At organizations in all kinds of industries, humans and AI are collaborating to improve five elements of business processes.

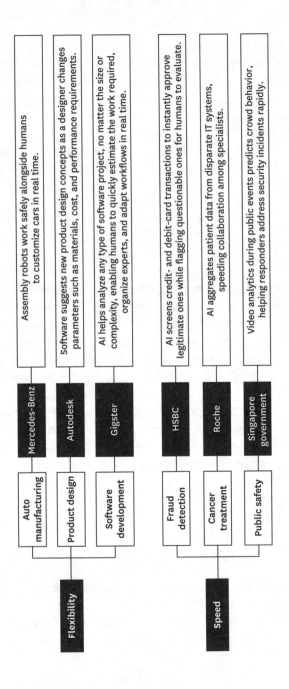

Flexibility

- **Auto manufacturing** — Mercedes-Benz — Assembly robots work safely alongside humans to customize cars in real time.
- **Product design** — Autodesk — Software suggests new product design concepts as a designer changes parameters such as materials, cost, and performance requirements.
- **Software development** — Gigster — AI helps analyze any type of software project, no matter the size or complexity, enabling humans to quickly estimate the work required, organize experts, and adapt workflows in real time.

Speed

- **Fraud detection** — HSBC — AI screens credit- and debit-card transactions to instantly approve legitimate ones while flagging questionable ones for humans to evaluate.
- **Cancer treatment** — Roche — AI aggregates patient data from disparate IT systems, speeding collaboration among specialists.
- **Public safety** — Singapore government — Video analytics during public events predicts crowd behavior, helping responders address security incidents rapidly.

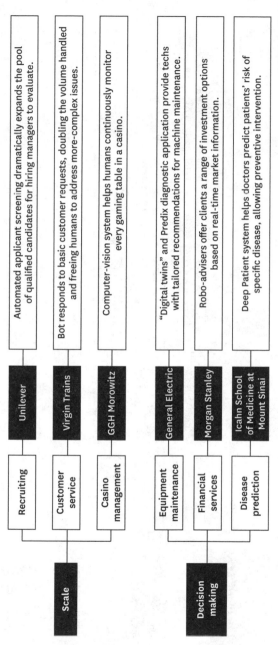

Scale			
Recruiting	Unilever		Automated applicant screening dramatically expands the pool of qualified candidates for hiring managers to evaluate.
Customer service	Virgin Trains		Bot responds to basic customer requests, doubling the volume handled and freeing humans to address more-complex issues.
Casino management	GGH Morowitz		Computer-vision system helps humans continuously monitor every gaming table in a casino.

Decision making			
Equipment maintenance	General Electric		"Digital twins" and Predix diagnostic application provide techs with tailored recommendations for machine maintenance.
Financial services	Morgan Stanley		Robo-advisers offer clients a range of investment options based on real-time market information.
Disease prediction	Icahn School of Medicine at Mount Sinai		Deep Patient system helps doctors predict patients' risk of specific disease, allowing preventive intervention.

(continued)

Enhancing performance (*continued*)

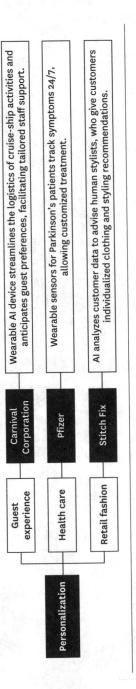

Personalization

Guest experience	Carnival Corporation	Wearable AI device streamlines the logistics of cruise-ship activities and anticipates guest preferences, facilitating tailored staff support.
Health care	Pfizer	Wearable sensors for Parkinson's patients track symptoms 24/7, allowing customized treatment.
Retail fashion	Stitch Fix	AI analyzes customer data to advise human stylists, who give customers individualized clothing and styling recommendations.

Amplifying

Artificial intelligence can boost our analytic and decision-making abilities by providing the right information at the right time. But it can also heighten creativity. Consider how Autodesk's Dreamcatcher AI enhances the imagination of even exceptional designers. A designer provides Dreamcatcher with criteria about the desired product—for example, a chair able to support up to 300 pounds, with a seat 18 inches off the ground, made of materials costing less than $75, and so on. She can also supply information about other chairs that she finds attractive. Dreamcatcher then churns out thousands of designs that match those criteria, often sparking ideas that the designer might not have initially considered. She can then guide the software, telling it which chairs she likes or doesn't, leading to a new round of designs.

Throughout the iterative process, Dreamcatcher performs the myriad calculations needed to ensure that each proposed design meets the specified criteria. This frees the designer to concentrate on deploying uniquely human strengths: professional judgment and aesthetic sensibilities.

Interacting

Human-machine collaboration enables companies to interact with employees and customers in novel, more effective ways. AI agents like Cortana, for example, can facilitate communications between people or on behalf of people, such as by transcribing a meeting and distributing a voice-searchable version to those who couldn't attend. Such applications are inherently scalable—a single chatbot, for instance, can provide routine customer service to large numbers of people simultaneously, wherever they may be.

SEB, a major Swedish bank, now uses a virtual assistant called Aida to interact with millions of customers. Able to handle natural-language conversations, Aida has access to vast stores of data and can answer many frequently asked questions, such as how to open an account or make cross-border payments. She can also ask callers follow-up questions to solve their problems, and she's able to analyze a caller's tone of voice (frustrated versus appreciative, for instance) and use that information to provide better service later. Whenever the system can't resolve an issue—which happens in about 30% of cases—it turns the caller over to a human customer-service representative and then monitors that interaction to learn how to resolve similar problems in the future. With Aida handling basic requests, human reps can concentrate on addressing more-complex issues, especially those from unhappy callers who might require extra hand-holding.

Embodying

Many AIs, like Aida and Cortana, exist principally as digital entities, but in other applications the intelligence is embodied in a robot that augments a human worker. With their sophisticated sensors, motors, and actuators, AI-enabled machines can now recognize people and objects and work safely alongside humans in factories, warehouses, and laboratories.

In manufacturing, for example, robots are evolving from potentially dangerous and "dumb" industrial machines into smart, context-aware "cobots." A cobot arm might, for example, handle repetitive actions that require heavy lifting, while a person performs complementary tasks that require dexterity and human judgment, such as assembling a gear motor.

Hyundai is extending the cobot concept with exoskeletons. These wearable robotic devices, which adapt to the user and location in real time, will enable industrial workers to perform their jobs with superhuman endurance and strength.

Reimagining Your Business

In order to get the most value from AI, operations need to be redesigned. To do this, companies must first discover and describe an operational area that can be improved. It might be a balky internal process (such as HR's slowness to fill staff positions), or it could be a previously intractable problem that can now be addressed using AI (such as quickly identifying adverse drug reactions across patient

Revealing Invisible Problems

FORMER U.S. DEFENSE SECRETARY Donald Rumsfeld once famously distinguished among "known knowns," "known unknowns," and "unknown unknowns"—things you're not even aware you don't know. Some companies are now using AI to uncover unknown unknowns in their businesses. Case in point: GNS Healthcare applies machine-learning software to find overlooked relationships among data in patients' health records and elsewhere. After identifying a relationship, the software churns out numerous hypotheses to explain it and then suggests which of those are the most likely. This approach enabled GNS to uncover a new drug interaction hidden in unstructured patient notes. CEO Colin Hill points out that this is not garden-variety data mining to find associations. "Our machine-learning platform is not just about seeing patterns and correlations in data," he says. "It's about actually discovering causal links."

populations). Moreover, a number of new AI and advanced analytic techniques can help surface previously invisible problems that are amenable to AI solutions (see the sidebar "Revealing Invisible Problems").

Next, companies must develop a solution through co-creation—having stakeholders envision how they might collaborate with AI systems to improve a process. Consider the case of a large agricultural company that wanted to deploy AI technology to help farmers. An enormous amount of data was available about soil properties, weather patterns, historical harvests, and so forth, and the initial plan was to build an AI application that would more accurately predict future crop yields. But in discussions with farmers, the company learned of a more pressing need. What farmers really wanted was a system that could provide real-time recommendations on how to increase productivity—which crops to plant, where to grow them, how much nitrogen to use in the soil, and so on. The company developed an AI system to provide such advice, and the initial outcomes were promising; farmers were happy about the crop yields obtained with the AI's guidance. Results from that initial test were then fed back into the system to refine the algorithms used. As with the discovery step, new AI and analytic techniques can assist in co-creation by suggesting novel approaches to improving processes.

The third step for companies is to scale and then sustain the proposed solution. SEB, for example, originally deployed a version of Aida internally to assist 15,000 bank employees but thereafter rolled out the chatbot to its one million customers.

Through our work with hundreds of companies, we have identified five characteristics of business processes that companies typically want to improve: flexibility, speed, scale, decision making, and personalization. When reimagining a business process, determine which of these characteristics is central to the desired transformation, how intelligent collaboration could be harnessed to address it, and what alignments and trade-offs with other process characteristics will be necessary.

Flexibility

For Mercedes-Benz executives, inflexible processes presented a growing challenge. Increasingly, the company's most profitable customers had been demanding individualized S-class sedans, but the automaker's assembly systems couldn't deliver the customization people wanted.

Traditionally, car manufacturing has been a rigid process with automated steps executed by "dumb" robots. To improve flexibility, Mercedes replaced some of those robots with AI-enabled cobots and redesigned its processes around human-machine collaborations. At the company's plant near Stuttgart, Germany, cobot arms guided by human workers pick up and place heavy parts, becoming an extension of the worker's body. This system puts the worker in control of the build of each car, doing less manual labor and more of a "piloting" job with the robot.

The company's human-machine teams can adapt on the fly. In the plant, the cobots can be reprogrammed easily with a tablet, allowing them to handle different tasks depending on changes in the workflow. Such agility has enabled the manufacturer to achieve unprecedented levels of customization. Mercedes can individualize vehicle production according to the real-time choices consumers make at dealerships, changing everything from a vehicle's dashboard components to the seat leather to the tire valve caps. As a result, no two cars rolling off the assembly line at the Stuttgart plant are the same.

Speed

For some business activities, the premium is on speed. One such operation is the detection of credit-card fraud. Companies have just seconds to determine whether they should approve a given transaction. If it's fraudulent, they will most likely have to eat that loss. But if they deny a legitimate transaction, they lose the fee from that purchase and anger the customer.

Like most major banks, HSBC has developed an AI-based solution that improves the speed and accuracy of fraud detection. The AI monitors and scores millions of transactions daily, using data on purchase location and customer behavior, IP addresses, and other information to identify subtle patterns that signal possible fraud. HSBC first implemented the system in the United States, significantly reducing the rate of undetected fraud and false positives, and then rolled it out in the UK and Asia. A different AI system used by Danske Bank improved its fraud-detection rate by 50% and decreased false positives by 60%. The reduction in the number of false positives frees investigators to concentrate their efforts on equivocal transactions the AI has flagged, where human judgment is needed.

The fight against financial fraud is like an arms race: Better detection leads to more-devious criminals, which leads to better detection, which continues the cycle. Thus the algorithms and scoring models for combating fraud have a very short shelf life and require continual updating. In addition, different countries and regions use different models. For these reasons, legions of data analysts, IT professionals, and experts in financial fraud are needed at the interface between humans and machines to keep the software a step ahead of the criminals.

Scale

For many business processes, poor scalability is the primary obstacle to improvement. That's particularly true of processes that depend on intensive human labor with minimal machine assistance.

Consider, for instance, the employee recruitment process at Unilever. The consumer goods giant was looking for a way to diversify its 170,000-person workforce. HR determined that it needed to focus on entry-level hires and then fast-track the best into management. But the company's existing processes weren't able to evaluate potential recruits in sufficient numbers—while giving each applicant individual attention—to ensure a diverse population of exceptional talent.

Here's how Unilever combined human and AI capabilities to scale individualized hiring: In the first round of the application process, candidates are asked to play online games that help assess traits such as risk aversion. These games have no right or wrong answers, but they help Unilever's AI figure out which individuals might be best suited for a particular position. In the next round, applicants are asked to submit a video in which they answer questions designed for the specific position they're interested in. Their responses are analyzed by an AI system that considers not just what they say but also their body language and tone. The best candidates from that round, as judged by the AI, are then invited to Unilever for in-person interviews, after which humans make the final hiring decisions.

It's too early to tell whether the new recruiting process has resulted in better employees. The company has been closely tracking the success of those hires, but more data is still needed. It is clear, however, that the new system has greatly broadened the scale of Unilever's recruiting. In part because job seekers can easily access the system by smartphone, the number of applicants doubled to 30,000 within a year, the number of universities represented surged from 840 to 2,600, and the socioeconomic diversity of new hires increased. Furthermore, the average time from application to hiring decision has dropped from four months to just four weeks, while the time that recruiters spend reviewing applications has fallen by 75%.

Decision making

By providing employees with tailored information and guidance, AI can help them reach better decisions. This can be especially valuable for workers in the trenches, where making the right call can have a huge impact on the bottom line.

Consider the way in which equipment maintenance is being improved with the use of "digital twins"—virtual models of physical equipment. General Electric builds such software models of its turbines and other industrial products and continually updates them with operating data streaming from the equipment. By collecting readings from large numbers of machines in the field, GE has amassed a wealth of information on normal and aberrant performance. Its Predix application, which uses machine-learning algorithms, can now predict when a specific part in an individual machine might fail.

This technology has fundamentally changed the decision-intensive process of maintaining industrial equipment. Predix might, for example, identify some unexpected rotor wear and tear in a turbine, check the turbine's operational history, report that the damage has increased fourfold over the past few months, and warn that if nothing is done, the rotor will lose an estimated 70% of its useful life. The system can then suggest appropriate actions, taking into account the machine's current condition, the operating environment, and aggregated data about similar damage and repairs to other machines. Along with its recommendations, Predix can generate information about their costs and financial benefits and provide a confidence level (say, 95%) for the assumptions used in its analysis.

Without Predix, workers would be lucky to catch the rotor damage on a routine maintenance check. It's possible that it would go undetected until the rotor failed, resulting in a costly shutdown. With Predix, maintenance workers are alerted to potential problems before they become serious, and they have the needed information at their fingertips to make good decisions—ones that can sometimes save GE millions of dollars.

Personalization

Providing customers with individually tailored brand experiences is the holy grail of marketing. With AI, such personalization can now be achieved with previously unimaginable precision and at vast scale. Think of the way the music streaming service Pandora uses AI algorithms to generate personalized playlists for each of its millions of users according to their preferences in songs, artists, and genres. Or consider Starbucks, which, with customers' permission, uses AI to recognize their mobile devices and call up their ordering history to help baristas make serving recommendations. The AI technology does what it does best, sifting through and processing copious amounts of data to recommend certain offerings or actions, and humans do what they do best, exercising their intuition and judgment to make a recommendation or select the best fit from a set of choices.

The Carnival Corporation is applying AI to personalize the cruise experience for millions of vacationers through a wearable device called the Ocean Medallion and a network that allows smart devices to connect. Machine learning dynamically processes the data flowing from the medallion and from sensors and systems throughout the ship to help guests get the most out of their vacations. The medallion streamlines the boarding and debarking processes, tracks the guests' activities, simplifies purchasing by connecting their credit cards to the device, and acts as a room key. It also connects to a system that anticipates guests' preferences, helping crew members deliver personalized service to each guest by suggesting tailored itineraries of activities and dining experiences.

The Need for New Roles and Talent

Reimagining a business process involves more than the implementation of AI technology; it also requires a significant commitment to developing employees with what we call "fusion skills"—those that enable them to work effectively at the human-machine interface. To start, people must learn to delegate tasks to the new technology, as when physicians trust computers to help read X-rays and MRIs. Employees should also know how to combine their distinctive human skills with those of a smart machine to get a better outcome than either could achieve alone, as in robot-assisted surgery. Workers must be able to teach intelligent agents new skills and undergo training to work well within AI-enhanced processes. For example, they must know how best to put questions to an AI agent to get the information they need. And there must be employees, like those on Apple's differential privacy team, who ensure that their companies' AI systems are used responsibly and not for illegal or unethical purposes.

We expect that in the future, company roles will be redesigned around the desired outcomes of reimagined processes, and corporations will increasingly be organized around different types of skills rather than around rigid job titles. AT&T has already begun that transition as it shifts from landline telephone services to mobile networks and starts to retrain 100,000 employees for new positions. As part of that effort, the company has completely overhauled its organizational chart: Approximately 2,000 job titles have been streamlined into a much smaller number of broad categories encompassing similar skills. Some of those skills are what one might expect (for example, proficiency in data science and data wrangling), while others are less obvious (for instance, the ability to use simple machine-learning tools to cross-sell services).

––––––––––––––

Most activities at the human-machine interface require people to *do new and different things* (such as train a chatbot) and to *do things differently* (use that chatbot to provide better customer service). So far, however, only a small number of the companies we've surveyed have begun to reimagine their business processes to optimize collaborative intelligence. But the lesson is clear: Organizations that use machines merely to displace workers through automation will miss the full potential of AI. Such a strategy is misguided from the get-go. Tomorrow's leaders will instead be those that embrace collaborative intelligence, transforming their operations, their markets, their industries, and—no less important—their workforces.

Originally published in July–August 2018. Reprint R1804J

Stitch Fix's CEO on Selling Personal Style to the Mass Market

by Katrina Lake

AT STITCH FIX OUR BUSINESS MODEL IS SIMPLE: We send you clothing and accessories we think you'll like; you keep the items you want and send the others back. We leverage data science to deliver personalization at scale, transcending traditional brick-and-mortar and e-commerce retail experiences. Customers enjoy having an expert stylist do the shopping for them and appreciate the convenience and simplicity of the service.

Of course, making something seem simple and convenient to consumers while working profitably and at scale is complex. It's even more complex in the fashion retail industry, which is crowded, fickle, and rapidly changing. Other apparel retailers attempt to differentiate themselves through the lowest price or the fastest shipping; we differentiate ourselves through personalization. Each Fix shipment, as we call it, is a box containing five clothing and accessory items we've chosen just for you. Those choices are based on information you and millions of others have given us—first in an extensive questionnaire you fill out when you sign up, and then in feedback you provide after each shipment.

Stitch Fix sold $730 million worth of clothing in 2016 and $977 million worth in 2017. One hundred percent of our revenue results directly from our recommendations, which are the core of our business. We have more than 2 million active clients in the United States, and we carry more than 700 brands. We're not upselling you belts that match that blouse you just added to your cart, or touting a certain brand because you've bought it before, or using browsing patterns to intuit that you might be shopping for a little black dress—all activities that have low conversion rates. Instead we make unique and personal selections by combining data and machine learning with expert human judgment.

Data science isn't woven into our culture; it *is* our culture. We started with it at the heart of the business, rather than adding it to a traditional organizational structure, and built the company's algorithms around our clients and their needs. We employ more than 80 data scientists, the majority of whom have PhDs in quantitative fields such as math, neuroscience, statistics, and astrophysics. Data science reports directly to me, and Stitch Fix wouldn't exist without data science. It's that simple.

Not a Valley Story

We're far from the prototypical Silicon Valley start-up. I don't consider myself a serial entrepreneur: Stitch Fix is the first company I've launched. But I'm fascinated by retail experiences and how untouched they were by modern technology in the 21st century. During my undergraduate years at Stanford, in the early 2000s, and in my first job, as a consultant at the Parthenon Group, I did a lot of work with retailers and restaurants. While I loved both industries and how meaningful they were to people, I was intrigued that they still provided fundamentally the same experience they had in the 1970s—or even the 1950s—despite how much the world had changed. I wondered how they might adapt, and I wanted to be part of that future.

I moved on from Parthenon to become an associate at Leader Ventures, a VC firm, just as the iPhone appeared, in 2007. Still, I was

Idea in Brief

Lake's experience as a consultant to retailers and restaurants led to a fascination with how untouched those industries were by 21st-century technology. As a lover of both clothes and data, she felt certain that data could create a better experience with apparel—as long as the human element was preserved.

From the beginning Lake planned to build a data science operation to make Stitch Fix scalable. The company's revenue is dependent on great recommendations from its algorithm, so its data scientists have a direct line to the CEO. Data science is deeply ingrained in the company culture: In addition to client recommendations of clothing, algorithms keep capital costs low, inventory moving, and deliveries efficient. Product development has adapted algorithms from genetics to find successful "traits" in clothing. Stitch Fix has even used machine learning to design apparel.

But, Lake says, shopping is inherently a personal and human activity, which is why human stylists can alter or override the product assortment a styling algorithm delivers before the client receives a shipment.

thinking about retail. I studied the economics of Blockbuster during the rise of Netflix. On one side was a company that dominated physical store sales; on the other was a company that dominated sales without stores. It was the perfect case study. And I could see exactly when the scale tipped. Whenever Netflix hit about 30% market share, the local Blockbuster closed. The remaining 70% of customers then faced a decision: try Netflix or travel farther to get movies. More of them tried Netflix, putting more pressure on Blockbuster. Another store would close, and more customers would face that try-or-travel decision, in a downward spiral.

I recognized that other retailers might suffer Blockbuster's fate if they didn't rethink their strategy. For example, how would someone buy jeans 10 years down the road? I knew it wouldn't be the traditional model: go to six stores, pull pairs of jeans off the racks, try them all on. And I didn't think it would resemble today's e-commerce model either: You have 15 tabs open on your browser while you check product measurements and look for what other shoppers are saying. Then you buy multiple pairs and return the ones that don't fit.

The part of me that loves data knew it could be used to create a better experience with apparel. After all, fit and taste are just a bunch of attributes: waist, inseam, material, color, weight, durability, and pattern. It's all just data. If you collect enough, you'll get a pretty good picture of what clothes people want.

But the part of me that loves clothes recognized the human element in shopping—the feeling of finding something you weren't expecting to and delighting in the fact that it fits you and your budget. I saw an opportunity to combine those two elements—data and human experience—to create a new model for buying clothes.

A Bad Idea?

At first I didn't plan to start a company; I was going to join a startup that wanted to pursue this idea. At Leader, I met with hundreds of entrepreneurs, hoping the right one would come through. That didn't happen. So I enrolled at Harvard Business School to pursue my risk-averse path to entrepreneurship. I used those two years to plan and launch my company. I received a term sheet to fund Stitch Fix in February 2011; I shipped the first Fix boxes from my apartment in April; and I graduated in May.

Not many people thought it was a good idea. One of my professors called it an inventory nightmare. I wanted to own all the inventory so that I could deeply understand each item and turn it into a lot of structured data. In retail, owning all the inventory is scary, and the professor thought it would make my strategy capital-intensive and risky. But the strategy was ultimately right. Using data to better understand what people want enables us to turn over inventory faster than many conventional retailers do, because we can buy the right things and get them to the right people. Selling inventory fast enough to pay vendors with cash from clients turns out to be a very capital-efficient model.

Then there were skeptical venture capitalists. I would come to pitch meetings with a box of clothes and a personalized card from the stylist. I remember that at one meeting, a VC said within the first five minutes, "I just don't understand why anyone would ever want to receive anything like this." I appreciated his honesty. Many of them were unexcited about warehouses full of clothes. Others were baffled that we employed human stylists who were paid hourly—a very un-VC idea at a time when everything was about automation and apps. Despite our early success, Series B funding conversations got a tepid response. "I think you're great, your team is amazing, and your business is working," one VC told me. "But I get to pick one or two boards a year, and I want to pick ones I feel connected to. I can't get passionate about retail or women's dresses."

That's fair—and frustrating. As it happens, 87% of the employees, 35% of the data scientists, and 32% of the engineers at Stitch Fix are women. More than 90% of venture capitalists are men, and I felt the industry's gender dynamic was working against us. In the end, what didn't kill us made us stronger, because it forced us to focus on profitability and capital efficiency. We've since used cash from our operations to launch new businesses, including men's apparel and plus sizes for women.

Finally, there was the industry itself. By making revenue dependent on fashion recommendations, I had picked one of the more difficult tasks for machine learning. Even people who think they're undiscerning about the clothes they wear do in fact care. Fit, style, material—these matter to all of us. It's a nuanced business. That makes it especially interesting but also more difficult. Early on, focus groups asserted that they just didn't believe we could pick out clothes they'd like. They'd say, "How will it work? Nothing will fit."

The idea of paying us a $20 styling fee up front, credited to your purchase if you keep something, also gave pause. Focus group participants would ask, "Why would I pay $20 when I don't get to pick anything out?" We needed customers to trust that they'd want to keep items. And that has turned out to be true—because of the data science.

Enter the Algorithms

When I started, my "data science" was rudimentary. I used Survey-Monkey and Google Docs along with some statistical methods to track preferences and try to make good recommendations. In the

Mix and Match

STITCH FIX USES DATA that clients supply—beginning with a "style profile"—and a suite of algorithms to capture their reactions to merchandise. Human stylists (algorithmically matched with clients) review and revise every box of five items before it is mailed. Clients respond with written answers to five survey questions about each item, along with comments. That feedback, together with purchase history, allows Stitch Fix to improve its picks over time.

The following illustrates how the algorithm and the stylist together might choose one client's very first Fix and two successive ones.

X Returned   **✔** Bought

Fix 1

 The client's style profile guided both the algorithm's choice of this shirt and the stylist's choice of pale pink. **✔**

 The stylist approved the algorithm's choice of this all-season top, even though it's out of the stated price range, because the client likes florals. **✔**

 These slip-on sneakers have a high match rate among clients looking for a casual shoe. The stylist thought the floral pattern would add originality. **✔**

 The client asked for skinny jeans. The stylist selected green from among the algorithm's denim recommendations. **X**

 Because the client's style profile said she loves textures, the stylist chose this studded blouse. **X**

beginning, I was essentially acting as a personal stylist. Sometimes I even delivered a Fix box in person. But my plan was always to build a data science operation that would make the business scalable. Our recommendations work because our algorithms are good, but our algorithms are good because data science underpins the company.

Three things make machine learning integral:

Data science reports to the CEO

At most companies, data science reports to the CTO, as part of the engineering team, or sometimes even to finance. Here it's separate, and we have a chief algorithms officer, Eric Colson, who has a seat

Fix 2

The client was looking for a versatile top. The algorithm identified this cashmere sweater because it has been extremely successful with women of her age and physical dimensions. ✔

The client did not like the fit of the green jeans, so the algorithm found a pair that fit better, and the stylist chose blue denim. **X**

The client loved the lightweight floral top in the previous box, so the stylist found this more vibrant variation, which the algorithm suggested would fit well. ✔

The client also loved the pink shirt in the previous box, so the stylist found a different take within the same color palette. ✔

The client wanted a new bag, and the algorithm found this one trending among women of her age. The stylist picked light green to pop against the red palette of the tops in the box. **X**

Fix 3

Because the client kept the cashmere sweater from the previous Fix, the stylist thought this piece, a little bolder, was worth taking a risk on. ✔

The algorithm chose this popular coat for its versatility and affordability. ✔

Stitch Fix now knows the client's preferred color and fit for jeans, so the stylist felt confident in exceeding her price range with this pair. ✔

The algorithm recommended this blouse because the client responded warmly to the color palette in the previous Fix. ✔

The stylist knows that the client is single and dating, so she chose these playful heels to dress up the skinny jeans. ✔

at the strategy table. Eric came from Netflix in August 2012. Before that he was an adviser to us. He became interested in our company because it presented a challenge. At Netflix, he recalls, someone said, "What if we just started playing a movie we think someone will like when they open the app?" That seemed like a bold but risky idea—to go all in on just one recommendation. He realized that's what Stitch Fix does. As an adviser, he found himself spending a vacation playing with some of our data. He decided to join us full-time—a huge coup for a little start-up.

Because our revenue is dependent on great recommendations from our algorithms, it's even more crucial that our data scientists have a direct line to the CEO. We also believe it sends a message to the organization as a whole about our values and our approach to strategy: Data science is extremely important, and other teams, such as marketing and engineering, will increase their capabilities by partnering closely with our data science team.

Innovation is done by data science

We've developed dozens of algorithms that no one ever asked for, because we allow our data science team to create new solutions and determine whether they have potential. No one explicitly asked the team to develop algorithms to do rebuy recommendations, for example. (Rebuys happen when a certain inventory item is selling well and we need to acquire more of it.) Our algorithms help us see these trends earlier and more accurately, so we can stock inventory more efficiently and be ready for spikes in demand. Recently the team came up with a way to track the movements of employees in our warehouses and created an algorithm that could help optimize routes without expensive remapping of the spaces as they change.

It's sometimes hard for people to imagine how deeply ingrained data science is in our culture. We use many kinds of algorithms now, and we're building many more. Personalized recommendations of clothing, of course, are driven by machine learning. Fulfillment and inventory management use algorithms to keep capital costs low, inventory moving, and deliveries efficient. Product development has adapted some algorithms from genetics to find successful "traits" in clothes. We've even started using machine learning to design apparel.

Hybrid Designs, our in-house clothing brand, came to life one rainy afternoon when a couple of data scientists were thinking about how to fill product gaps in the marketplace. For example, many female clients in their mid-40s were asking for capped-sleeve blouses, but that style was missing from our current inventory set. Fast-forward a year, and we have 29 apparel items for women and plus sizes that were designed by computer and meet some specific, previously unfilled needs our clients have.

Another way we apply a quantitative approach to fashion is with measurement data. We track anywhere from 30 to 100 measurements on a garment, depending on what type it is, and we now know—from the experiences of more than 2 million active clients—what kind of fit would make a customer spend outside her or his comfort zone. We know the optimal ratio of chest size to shirt width on a men's shirt. Using data analysis, we adjusted the distance from the collar to the first button on shirts for men with large chests. We know what proportion of the population fits a 27-inch inseam, and we can stock according to that proportion.

But in some ways, that's the easy part. The real challenge is having the right dress in the right color and the right size at the right time. The math around that is complex. We must account for all the measurements plus the taste of the customer, the season, the location, past trends—lots of variables.

Given a dollar to invest in the company and the choice to use it for marketing, product, or data science, we'd almost always choose data science. We're glad we started with data science at our core rather than trying to transform a traditional retailer, which I believe wouldn't have worked. For a traditional retailer to say, "Let's do what Stitch Fix does" would be like my saying, "I'd like to be taller now."

Don't forget the people

The analytical part of me loves our algorithmic approach. But shopping is inherently a personal and human activity. That's why we insist on combining data with a human stylist who can alter or override the product assortment our styling algorithm has delivered. Our stylists come from a range of design and retail backgrounds, but they all have an appreciation for the data and feel love and empathy for our clients. Humans are much better than machines at some things—and they are likely to stay that way for a long time.

For example, when a client writes in with a very specific request, such as "I need a dress for an outdoor wedding in July," our stylists immediately know what dress options might work for that event. In addition, our clients often share intimate details of a pregnancy, a major weight loss, or a new job opportunity—all occasions whose importance a machine can't fully understand. But our stylists know exactly how special such life moments are and can go above and beyond to curate the right look, connect with the clients, and improvise when needed. That creates incredible brand loyalty.

It's simple: A good person plus a good algorithm is far superior to the best person or the best algorithm alone. We aren't pitting people and data against each other. We need them to work together. We're not training machines to behave like humans, and we're certainly not training humans to behave like machines. And we all need to acknowledge that we're fallible—the stylist, the data scientist, me. We're all wrong sometimes—even the algorithm. The important thing is that we keep learning from that.

Originally published in May–June 2018. Reprint R1803A

Strategy for Start-Ups

by Joshua Gans, Erin L. Scott, and Scott Stern

AS A START-UP, RapidSOS was an easy sell: It would bring 911 calls into the smartphone age. Emergency-response systems had evolved in a premobile era, which meant that few of them could accurately identify the location of callers who were using mobile phones, compromising response times and medical outcomes. The founders of RapidSOS—Michael Martin, an HBS graduate, and Nick Horelik, an MIT engineer—had developed a way to transmit mobile phone locations to existing 911 systems that would require only minimal adaptation on the part of other players in the emergency-services sector. After attracting early-stage financing at business plan competitions, Martin and Horelik reached a crossroads: How should they take their technology to market?

The answer wasn't straightforward—in fact, they identified four possible paths. (See the exhibit "The Entrepreneurial Strategy Compass.") They could be wildly ambitious and attempt to replace the emergency-response system altogether—creating an "Uber for ambulances." They could try a classic disruption strategy—initially targeting poorly served populations, such as people with epilepsy, with the intention of eventually expanding to a wider swath of customers. They could avoid direct competition altogether, either by helping incumbents modernize their operations—perhaps working with 911 equipment suppliers such as Motorola—or by partnering with insurance companies, which ultimately cover the cost of ambulance service.

Many entrepreneurs, operating in the fog of uncertainty, worry that exploration will delay commercialization. They go, therefore, with the first practical strategy that comes to mind, deriding the deliberation and planning that accompany careful strategizing. As Richard Branson has famously claimed, "In the end you [have] to say, 'Screw it, just do it' and get on and try it."

There are times when that approach works, of course. But usually such ad hoc experimentation should be avoided, even when it requires few resources. Entrepreneurs who commit to the first promising route they see leave their start-ups vulnerable to competitors that take a less obvious but ultimately more powerful route to commercialization and customers. Shai Agassi, for example, spent almost $1 billion building an ecosystem to support Better Place, his "swappable battery" approach to the electric car business. Elon Musk's more deliberative, stepwise approach to developing an integrated, highly reliable Tesla turned out to be a smarter strategy.

And that's not the only problem with an action-first philosophy. Founders are both more confident and more persuasive to investors, employees, and partners when they can demonstrate an idea's potential across multiple strategies, validating the underlying assumptions and strength of the idea itself.

Is there a way to think through your strategic options without slowing down the process too much? After working with and studying hundreds of start-ups over the past 20 years, we have developed a framework, which we call the entrepreneurial strategy compass, that allows company founders to approach the critical choices they face in a practical and clarifying way. It delineates four generic go-to-market strategies they should consider as they move from an idea to the launch stage, each of which offers a distinct way for the venture to create and capture value.

The Entrepreneurial Strategy Compass

At the heart of our approach is the recognition that a go-to-market strategy for any innovation involves making choices about which customers to target, what technologies to apply, what organizational

Idea in Brief

The Problem

In their haste to get to market, entrepreneurs often run with the first plausible strategy they identify. As a result, they end up losing out to second or even third movers with superior strategies.

Why It Happens

In the innovation space it's easy to get overwhelmed by the apparent range of opportunities. Entrepreneurs fear that spending too much time weighing the alternatives will delay commercialization. The strategic commitments they make in moving forward limit their ability to pivot.

The Solution

Start-ups can improve their chances of picking the right path by investigating four generic go-to-market strategies, articulating multiple plausible versions of those strategies, and choosing the one that aligns most closely with their founders' values and motivations.

identity to assume, and how to position the company against which competitors. (See the sidebar "The Four Decisions.") To complicate matters, the decisions are interdependent—the choice of customers influences the company's organizational identity and its technology options.

For corporations with resources, the four decisions involve analyzing data they probably already have. They can also quite often afford to engage in market research and experimentation along multiple fronts. And they can draw on prior experience. A start-up on a shoestring, in contrast, lacks a history and the knowledge it brings. However, that can actually be an advantage, because prior experience, historical data, and commitments that drive existing practices may create blind spots for established corporations, possibly even causing them to overlook innovations that pose an existential threat. Nevertheless, start-ups may ultimately face competition when incumbents wake up to new innovations, and they will definitely face pressure from other start-ups trying to beat them to market.

Entrepreneurs may feel overwhelmed by the vast number of choices they face, even though some paths can be dismissed as impractical, and some won't coherently mesh. Our research

The Four Decisions

AT LEAST FOUR DOMAINS of decision making are crucial for every venture. Although any company will face additional choices that are particular to its context, a start-up that has not wrestled with at least these four decisions is unlikely to create and capture value on a sustainable basis. Amazon's story is illustrative.

Customers

Identifying customers and understanding their needs is usually the first step in any go-to-market strategy. But the target customer is not necessarily the first customer—and it is important that you understand the relationship between the two. You validate your product by getting the right early adopters. Amazon's decision to initially target book readers was a strategic choice. Its leadership recognized that books were a beachhead from which the company could expand into other retail categories.

Technology

Technology and customer choices are interrelated. Amazon could have built a simple online ordering system to service existing stores. Instead its goal was to let consumers buy the long tail of books that could not be stocked physically at the local mall. Thus the company had to invest beyond transaction services to build a database and a search engine capable of guiding readers through millions rather than thousands of books.

Identity, Culture, and Capabilities

Choices in this category should both create a narrative about what the company will stand for and communicate to all stakeholders what behavior to expect and what capabilities it will develop. Readers loved Amazon's offer, and Wall Street quickly saw how much money the company could make. But Amazon's founder, Jeff Bezos, wasn't building a bookstore. He wanted to create the "everything store." That would require that ordinary consumers trust they were getting a good deal, which meant that Amazon would focus relentlessly on lowering prices, despite pressure from investors for early returns.

Competitors

Amazon defined its competition as other retailers and chose to compete aggressively by offering consumers more choice, greater reliability, and lower prices. In its early days it could easily have chosen to work with existing retailers—perhaps even defining them as customers. Competitors would have been other search and logistics service providers, and the company could have established itself as a premium service provider by adding more value for booksellers.

The entrepreneurial strategy compass

Strategic opportunities for new ventures can be categorized along two dimensions: attitude toward incumbents (collaborate or compete?) and attitude toward the innovation (build a moat or storm a hill?). This compass produces four distinct strategies that will guide a venture's decisions regarding customers, technologies, identity, and competitive space. The emergency-services provider RapidSOS used the compass to explore its strategic options.

Maintain control of the innovation and find a way to create value within the existing marketplace. Focus on being an idea factory.

For example, Dolby is the global standard setter for sound technology; it licenses proprietary technology to Sony, Bose, Apple, and others.

Create and control a new value chain, often using a platform business. Protect intellectual property.

For example, OpenTable developed a proprietary platform that allowed diners to make reservations efficiently and in so doing established influence over customer flow to restaurants.

RapidSOS could keep the technology proprietary and work with existing 911 equipment suppliers such as Motorola to modernize operations.

RapidSOS could replace the existing emergency response system altogether.

RapidSOS could partner with insurance companies (which ultimately pay for ambulance services); the product might take the form of a smartphone app.

RapidSOS could first target poorly served populations (such as epilepsy patients) and later serve a larger swath of customers.

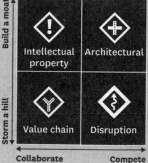

Build a moat / Storm a hill / Intellectual property / Architectural / Value chain / Disruption / Collaborate / Compete

Focus on creating value for partners in the existing value chain. Execute quickly.

For example, Peapod became the leading U.S. internet grocer by fitting into—and improving—the grocery industry.

Compete directly with incumbents. Take them by surprise with fast execution.

For example, Rent the Runway challenged high-end retailers by offering aspiring fashion-oriented women the ability to rent rather than buy designer clothes.

suggests, however, that the four categories of the compass make the process manageable, getting young companies to workable go-to-market strategies quickly and laying bare the assumptions that inform choices.

To sort through potential strategies, every new venture must consider two specific competitive trade-offs:

Collaborate or compete?

Working with established players provides access to resources and supply chains that may enable the start-up to enter a larger and better-established market more quickly. Then again, the venture may encounter significant delays owing to the bureaucratic nature of large organizations and may also capture a smaller fraction of that potentially larger pie. (The incumbent is likely to hold greater bargaining power in the relationship—particularly if it can appropriate key elements of the start-up's idea.)

The alternative, too, has pluses and minuses. Competing against established players in an industry means the start-up has more freedom to build the value chain it envisions, to work with customers that the incumbents may have overlooked, and to bring innovations to market that enhance value for customers while displacing otherwise successful products. However, it means taking on competitors that have greater financial resources and an established business infrastructure.

Build a moat or storm a hill?

Some companies believe that they have more to gain from maintaining tight control over a product or a technology and that imitation will leave them vulnerable. Thus they invest in protecting intellectual property. Formal IP protection, though expensive, can allow a technology-driven start-up to exclude others from direct competition or to wield significant bargaining power in negotiations with a supply chain partner. But prioritizing control raises the transaction costs and challenges of bringing an innovation to market and working with customers and partners.

In contrast, concentrating on quickly getting to market speeds up commercialization and development, which typically occurs in close collaboration with partners and customers. Start-ups that choose to pursue this route prioritize the ability to experiment and iterate on their ideas directly in the marketplace. Whereas a strategy built on control can delay entry, start-ups focused on getting to market expect competition and use their agility to respond when competitive threats arise. They move fast and break things.

Zeroing in on these two questions greatly simplifies the process of strategic reflection. Rather than seek to identify an á la carte combination of choices that are "right" for a given idea, a founding team can consider the potential for value creation and value capture from the various options that might be crafted within each of the four strategies.

Let's now consider the four.

The Intellectual Property Strategy

In this quadrant of the compass, the company collaborates with incumbents and retains control of its product or technology. The start-up focuses on idea generation and development and avoids the costs of downstream, customer-facing activities. The core idea must be of value to the customers of incumbents; therefore, development choices concerning it will dictate which incumbents are the most suitable partners for the venture.

In addition, because cooperation requires alignment with the incumbents' activities, the start-up will probably choose generalizable technology investments compatible with existing systems. Finally, the start-up's identity—as a kind of idea factory—will be reflected in its development of innovations that can be brought to market through chosen incumbents. But it will see itself as developing a small number of modular technologies that can make a decisive difference for the industry and it won't engage in unstructured experimentation with every potential new technology.

The sound company Dolby provides a quintessential example. Anyone in the market for a stereo system or watching a movie in a theater is guaranteed to come across the Dolby name. Dolby Laboratories' patented noise-reduction technologies, invented by Ray Dolby in 1965, became a global standard, retaining market leadership for 50 years. Dolby technologies have been credited with elevating the emotional intensity of iconic films such as Stanley Kubrick's *A Clockwork Orange* and George Lucas's *Star Wars*. Yet Dolby's multibillion-dollar valuation was achieved with only limited interaction with film directors, music producers, and audiophiles. The company has licensed its proprietary technology to many product developers and manufacturers, including Sony, Bose, Apple, and Yamaha.

Entrepreneurs that pursue a strategy like Dolby's take maintaining and protecting their intellectual property very seriously. Carefully conceived patents and trademarks, managed in combination with solid R&D, can create powerful defenses that allow a start-up to preserve bargaining power over long periods of time. This strategy dictates culture and capability choices: The start-up needs to invest not only in relevant R&D skills but also in smart and committed legal minds. The IP strategy has proved powerful not only in narrow cases like Dolby's but across whole industries, such as biotechnology; with leading technology platform players, including Qualcomm; and for market intermediaries, such as Getty Images.

The Disruption Strategy

This strategy is the polar opposite of an IP strategy. It involves a decision to compete directly with incumbents, emphasizing commercialization of the idea and the rapid growth of market share rather than control of the idea's development. Disruption entrepreneurs aim to redefine established value chains and the companies that dominate those chains. But the very nature of disruption permits others to follow. Thus the heart of this strategy is the ability to get ahead and stay ahead.

Although the word "disruption" connotes chaos, the entrepreneur's initial goal is in fact to avoid poking the beast and provoking a strong (and potentially fatal) response. The start-up strives to quickly build capabilities, resources, and customer loyalty so that when the incumbents finally wake up, the start-up is too far ahead for imitators to catch up.

For this reason, the initial choice of customers is usually a niche segment—typically one poorly served by incumbents and off their radar screen. This allows the start-up to establish credibility and explore (before anyone notices) new technologies that may have initial flaws but solid prospects for dramatic improvement. If they prove viable, these technologies are usually difficult for incumbents—whose capabilities and commitments are built around established technologies—to adopt.

The disruptive entrepreneur's identity projects hustle and verve. The start-up is staffed by the young and the hungry (and not just for ramen noodles). It doesn't fear the competitive war to come; rather, it's eager to engage. It must be lean and quick to respond. And it is intensely focused on growth.

Netflix is a poster child for this quadrant. Frustrated by movie-rental overdue fines, its founders, Marc Randolph and Reed Hastings, envisioned a solution that would leverage the then-emergent technology of DVDs. After testing their concept by sending a disc through the U.S. mail, they created a service in the late 1990s that allowed cinephiles—rather than mainstream consumers who simply wanted to watch the latest blockbuster—to receive and return DVDs that way. Netflix's strategy was to take advantage of the "long tail" of (low-cost) content and build a recommendation engine that would reinforce customer relationships, enabling the development of a new method of movie rental that would render the brick-and-mortar Blockbuster model obsolete. (Blockbuster initially dismissed Netflix as not serving mainstream customers in a timely manner but then saw the profitability of its stores drop and ultimately disappear.)

Rent the Runway is using the disruption playbook in its drive to reshape the women's high-end clothing market. Two Harvard MBAs, Jennifer Hyman and Jennifer Fleiss, founded the company in 2009 after identifying the challenge that fashion-oriented women faced in having to buy dresses that they might wear only once. Rent the Runway developed an online site offering aspirational women the option of renting rather than buying designer clothing and focused on solving the operational and logistical challenges of shipping dresses back and forth. Although the company has yet to displace Neiman Marcus and other more traditional players, whose focus is on wealthy haute couture customers seeking a personalized in-store experience, it has created a dedicated customer base that evangelizes the brand across social networks. Its extraordinary growth is testament to the power of execution in the face of less nimble incumbents.

The Value Chain Strategy

Disruption is exciting; by comparison, a value chain strategy seems somewhat pedestrian. The start-up invests in commercialization and day-to-day competitive strength, rather than in controlling the new product and erecting entry barriers, but its focus is on fitting into the existing value chain rather than upending it.

A pedestrian approach can nevertheless create very lucrative businesses. Consider Foxconn, the Chinese electronics manufacturer, which is one of the few global companies that can bring new products from Apple and others to market at scale and on time. The identity of such corporations arises from competence rather than aggressive competition. And although value chain entrepreneurs are driven by the customers and technology of other companies, they focus on developing scarce talent and unique capabilities to become preferred partners.

The value chain strategy is available to most start-ups. While the online grocery business Webvan, founded in 1996, was trying to disrupt the supermarket industry, Peapod became the leading U.S. internet grocer by serving as a value-added complement to traditional retailers. (Webvan went bankrupt in 2001.)

An early partnership with a Chicago-area food supplier, Jewel-Osco, allowed Peapod to clarify who its ideal customers were (professional women) and what they valued (the ability to repeat an order on a regular basis and to schedule deliveries for certain times, among other things). Whereas Webvan's disruption strategy required reconceptualizing the entire grocery-shopping experience, Peapod's more-focused approach allowed it to develop a meaningful value proposition for customers who were willing to pay a premium for automated ordering and delivery, resulting in a profitable partnership with the supermarket chain Stop & Shop. Peapod gained the knowledge and developed the specialized capabilities with which it has led the online grocery business for nearly 20 years.

Entrepreneurs who adopt Peapod's approach create and capture value by focusing on a single "horizontal" layer of the value chain in which their expertise and capabilities are unrivaled. In probably no other entrepreneurial strategy does the founder's team play a more important role. In addition to hiring salespeople who are focused on final customers, or engineers who can improve the technical functioning of the product, it must be able to integrate innovators, business development leaders, and supply chain partners.

The start-up's capabilities must translate into enhanced differentiation or cost advantage for the established companies. And even if the innovation does enhance the competitive position of the overall value chain, the new venture can prevail only if other players in the chain are unable to replicate the value it has created.

The Architectural Strategy

Whereas the value chain strategy is the domain of quiet achievers, entrepreneurs who choose and succeed with an architectural strategy tend to have very high public profiles. This strategy allows start-ups to both compete and achieve control, but it is out of reach for many if not most ideas and incredibly risky when it is feasible. This is the domain of Facebook and Google.

Entrepreneurs who follow an architectural strategy design an entirely new value chain and then control the key bottlenecks in it. They may not be the originators of an underlying innovation—search engines existed prior to Google, and social networks prior to Facebook—but they bring it to a mass market through careful alignment of customer, technology, and identity choices. Facebook committed early to not charging users, even though the dynamics of social media would lock them into the platform. Google adopted the motto "Don't Be Evil" so that it could achieve dominance without the pushback that had plagued other digital firms such as IBM and Microsoft. But in each case pivots were taken off the table. In other words, the risks for architectural entrepreneurs come from the fact that they may have only one shot at glory. (Remember the much-lamented Segway.)

It is perhaps not surprising that architectural entrepreneurs often end up trying to build platforms rather than products. Although platforms can be commercialized through the other strategies, if the core of a platform is closed, the entrepreneur may be able to control a new value chain.

Consider OpenTable, an online restaurant-reservation service founded in 1998 by Chuck Templeton. Motivated by the challenge of making a simple dinner reservation over the phone, Templeton hypothesized that in addition to offering a reservation platform, a successful online intermediary would have to solve the problem of restaurant-seating management. He decided to build systems that combined restaurant reservations with seating and management software, putting him in direct competition with established point-of-sale vendors such as IBM and NCR.

As Templeton recalls, OpenTable in its earliest days was "the one running wire through the rafters to get power and connectivity." To tip the market toward his start-up, he targeted the most influential restaurants first. "We were able to get the top 20 restaurants [in San Francisco]," he says, "and the next 50 would all want to be where those top 20 were. There began to be a critical mass on the website." Templeton reorganized the value chain of the dining industry so that the internal operations of restaurants were integrated into custom-ers' first engagement with them: the reservation phase. OpenTable achieved control over valuable proprietary data on customer prefer-ences and demand and established a hard-to-dislodge platform that is "table stakes" for a new restaurateur. This dominance underlay its $2.6 billion acquisition by Priceline in 2014.

Let's look now at how entrepreneurs can use the strategy com-pass to decide among the four basic approaches.

Making the Choice

The first step is to fill as many of the quadrants of the compass as possible with strategic options. This is no simple task. It involves gathering additional information and experimenting to some degree (but commitments should be modest until a choice is made).

Particularly effective approaches for start-ups can be found in Eric Ries's *The Lean Startup,* Alexander Osterwalder and Yves Pigneur's *Business Model Generation,* and Bill Aulet's *Disciplined Entrepreneurship.* Whatever framework is chosen, however, it should involve an explicit process of hypothesis building and testing—an observation that was nicely made in "Bringing Science to the Art of Strategy," by A.G. Lafley, Roger L. Martin, Jan W. Rivkin, and Nicolaj Siggelkow (HBR, September 2012).

This process at a minimum yields crucial insight into stumbling blocks associated with particular paths within the compass. Some alternatives can be dismissed owing to lack of feasibility or lack of alignment with the capabilities of the founding team. In other cases, the requirements—in terms of capital, commitment, and momentum—will be clear, allowing the start-up to focus on them to make the chosen strategy work.

Once the alternatives have been identified, how should the entrepreneur actually make a choice? Let's go back to RapidSOS. As the founders debated the next steps for their idea—mobile-centric emergency-response systems—they used the compass to identify four strategies. As noted earlier, they could use an architectural strategy to replace the existing 911 system with an "Uber for ambulances." They could use an IP strategy to collaborate with existing players in the emergency-response sector. They could use a value chain strategy to work with insurance companies and other consumer-facing partners, becoming a feature for a corporate smartphone app. Or they could use a disruption strategy to focus on a narrow customer segment for whom emergency response is a priority—such as epileptics—and partner with patient advocacy groups to meet its needs.

For each compass quadrant the company identified which customers to target, which technologies to focus on, what identity to assume, and whom to compete with and how. All four paths looked plausible, which was a striking validation of the founders' idea. If only one viable vision of the future exists, the entrepreneur probably doesn't have much of a business to begin with.

Having several good options need not be paralyzing. Quite simply, entrepreneurs should choose the strategy that aligns best with the purpose they originally brought to the venture. The RapidSOS mission to improve services for specific patient groups led the team to focus with a high level of conviction on a disruption strategy. This commitment—which Martin and Horelik could communicate with passion and purpose—allowed them to win over patient groups and stakeholders throughout the emergency-response sector, enabling RapidSOS to roll out its technology to the broader market over two years.

The founding team does not just make the choice; it has to live the choice. Alignment between strategy and purpose is crucial for motivating founders and persuading early stakeholders to travel the chosen path. To be clear, making a choice requires commitment but does not foreclose all other paths forward. RapidSOS's decision to engage with both patient advocates and the emergency-response community meant that the start-up was unlikely to bypass traditional 911 systems—at least in the medium term. But the focus on patient advocacy groups encouraged end-user engagement, which over time generated meaningful collaboration opportunities and attracted investment from more-established players, including Motorola.

Still, every strategy affects possible future pivots, removing some and opening up others. A venture must be mindful of this so that it doesn't raise future costs but does enable opportunities to move from the start-up to the scale-up phase.

———

The entrepreneurial strategy compass does not eliminate or minimize the uncertainty inherent in launching a start-up. What it does is provide a coherent framework for escaping the perceived realities of the existing environment and defining possible new environments to choose from. The word "choose" is critical here: When a start-up is competing with new products in the absence of a significant innovation, its success is largely determined by how its strategic choices are informed by the environment. Among established businesses, the winner is usually the company that understands the environment better. But entrepreneurs offering something significantly new have an opportunity to reshape the environment—perhaps, as with Dolby, to create a part of it that they will own or, as with Amazon, to create an altogether different reality. Which they choose is largely up to them. Our framework is designed to help them make that choice successfully and channel imagination and commitment toward the realization of their ideas.

Originally printed in May–June 2018. Reprint R1803B

Erin L. Scott and Scott Stern gratefully acknowledge financial support from the Jean Hammond (1986) and Michael Krasner (1974) Entrepreneurship Fund, the Edward B. Roberts (1957) Entrepreneurship Fund, and the MIT Sloan School of Management.

Agile at Scale

by Darrell K. Rigby, Jeff Sutherland, and Andy Noble

BY NOW MOST BUSINESS LEADERS are familiar with agile innovation teams. These small, entrepreneurial groups are designed to stay close to customers and adapt quickly to changing conditions. When implemented correctly, they almost always result in higher team productivity and morale, faster time to market, better quality, and lower risk than traditional approaches can achieve.

Naturally, leaders who have experienced or heard about agile teams are asking some compelling questions. What if a company were to launch dozens, hundreds, or even thousands of agile teams throughout the organization? Could whole segments of the business learn to operate in this manner? Would scaling up agile improve corporate performance as much as agile methods improve individual team performance?

In today's tumultuous markets, where established companies are furiously battling assaults from startups and other insurgent competitors, the prospect of a fast-moving, adaptive organization is highly appealing. But as enticing as such a vision is, turning it into a reality can be challenging. Companies often struggle to know which functions should be reorganized into multidisciplinary agile teams and which should not. And it's not unusual to launch hundreds of new agile teams only to see them bottlenecked by slow-moving bureaucracies.

We have studied the scaling up of agile at hundreds of companies, including small firms that run the entire enterprise with agile methods; larger companies that, like Spotify and Netflix, were born agile and have become more so as they've grown; and companies that, like Amazon and USAA (the financial services company for the military community), are making the transition from traditional hierarchies to more-agile enterprises. Along with the many success stories are some disappointments. For example, one prominent industrial company's attempts over the past five years to innovate like a lean start-up have not yet generated the financial results sought by activist investors and the board of directors, and several senior executives recently resigned.

Our studies show that companies can scale up agile effectively and that doing so creates substantial benefits. But leaders must be realistic. Not every function needs to be organized into agile teams; indeed, agile methods aren't well suited to some activities. Once you begin launching dozens or hundreds of agile teams, however, you can't just leave the other parts of the business alone. If your newly agile units are constantly frustrated by bureaucratic procedures or a lack of collaboration between operations and innovation teams, sparks will fly from the organizational friction, leading to meltdowns and poor results. Changes are necessary to ensure that the functions that don't operate as agile teams support the ones that do.

Leading Agile by Being Agile

For anyone who isn't familiar with agile, here's a short review. Agile teams are best suited to innovation—that is, the profitable application of creativity to improve products and services, processes, or business models. They are small and multidisciplinary. Confronted with a large, complex problem, they break it into modules, develop solutions to each component through rapid prototyping and tight feedback loops, and integrate the solutions into a coherent whole. They place more value on adapting to change than on sticking to a plan, and they hold themselves accountable for outcomes (such as growth, profitability, and customer loyalty), not outputs (such as lines of code or number of new products).

Conditions are ripe for agile teams in any situation where problems are complex, solutions are at first unclear, project requirements are likely to change, close collaboration with end users is feasible,

Idea in Brief

The Ambition

To go from a handful of agile innovation teams in a function like software development to scores, even hundreds, throughout your company—to make agile the dominant way you operate.

The Challenges

Figuring out where to start and how fast and far to go, deciding which functions can and should be converted to agile teams and which should not, and preventing slow-moving bureaucracies from impeding those that do convert.

The Solution

Leaders should use agile methods themselves and create a *taxonomy of opportunities* to set priorities and break the journey into small steps. Workstreams should be modularized and then seamlessly integrated. Functions not reorganized into agile teams should learn to operate with agile values. The annual budgeting process should be complemented with a VC-like approach to funding.

and creative teams will outperform command-and-control groups. Routine operations such as plant maintenance, purchasing, and accounting are less fertile ground. Agile methods caught on first in IT departments and are now widely used in software development. Over time they have spread into functions such as product development, marketing, and even HR. (See "Embracing Agile," HBR, May 2016, and "HR Goes Agile," HBR, March–April 2018.)

Agile teams work differently from chain-of-command bureaucracies. They are largely self-governing: Senior leaders tell team members where to innovate but not how. And the teams work closely with customers, both external and internal. Ideally, this puts responsibility for innovation in the hands of those who are closest to customers. It reduces layers of control and approval, thereby speeding up work and increasing the teams' motivation. It also frees up senior leaders to do what only they can do: create and communicate long-term visions, set and sequence strategic priorities, and build the organizational capabilities to achieve those goals.

When leaders haven't themselves understood and adopted agile approaches, they may try to scale up agile the way they have attacked other change initiatives: through top-down plans and directives. The track record is better when they behave like an agile team. That means viewing various parts of the organization as their customers—people and groups whose needs differ, are probably misunderstood, and will evolve as agile takes hold. The executive team sets priorities and sequences opportunities to improve those customers' experiences and increase their success. Leaders plunge in to solve problems and remove constraints rather than delegate that work to subordinates. The agile leadership team, like any other agile team, has an "initiative owner" who is responsible for overall results and a facilitator who coaches team members and helps keep everyone actively engaged.

Bosch, a leading global supplier of technology and services with more than 400,000 associates and operations in 60-plus countries, took this approach. As leaders began to see that traditional top-down management was no longer effective in a fast-moving, globalized world, the company became an early adopter of agile methods. But different business areas required different approaches, and Bosch's first attempt to implement what it called a "dual organization"— one in which hot new businesses were run with agile teams while traditional functions were left out of the action—compromised the goal of a holistic transformation. In 2015 members of the board of management, led by CEO Volkmar Denner, decided to build a more unified approach to agile teams. The board acted as a steering committee and named Felix Hieronymi, a software engineer turned agile expert, to guide the effort.

At first Hieronymi expected to manage the assignment the same way Bosch managed most projects: with a goal, a target completion date, and regular status reports to the board. But that approach felt inconsistent with agile principles, and the company's divisions were just too skeptical of yet another centrally organized program. So the team shifted gears. "The steering committee turned into a working committee," Hieronymi told us. "The discussions got far more interactive." The team compiled and rank-ordered a backlog of corporate priorities that was regularly updated, and it focused on steadily removing companywide barriers to greater agility. Members fanned out to engage division leaders in dialogue. "Strategy evolved from an annual project to a continuous process," Hieronymi says. "The members of the management board divided themselves into small agile teams and tested various approaches—some with a 'product owner' and an 'agile master'—to tackle tough problems or work on fundamental topics. One group, for instance, drafted the 10 new leadership principles released in 2016. They personally experienced the satisfaction of increasing speed and effectiveness. You can't gain this experience by reading a book." Today Bosch operates with a mix of agile teams and traditionally structured units. But it reports that nearly all areas have adopted agile values, are collaborating more effectively, and are adapting more quickly to increasingly dynamic marketplaces.

Getting Agile Rolling

At Bosch and other advanced agile enterprises, the visions are ambitious. In keeping with agile principles, however, the leadership team doesn't plan every detail in advance. Leaders recognize that they do not yet know how many agile teams they will require, how quickly they should add them, and how they can address bureaucratic constraints without throwing the organization into chaos. So they typically launch an initial wave of agile teams, gather data on the value those teams create and the constraints they face, and then decide whether, when, and how to take the next step. This lets them weigh the value of increasing agility (in terms of financial results, customer outcomes, and employee performance) against its costs (in terms of both financial investments and organizational challenges). If the benefits outweigh the costs, leaders continue to scale up agile—deploying another wave of teams, unblocking constraints in less agile parts of the organization, and repeating the cycle. If not, they can pause, monitor the market environment, and explore ways to increase the value of the agile teams already in place (for instance, by improving the prioritization of work or upgrading prototyping capabilities) and decrease the costs of change (by publicizing agile successes or hiring experienced agile enthusiasts).

To get started on this test-and-learn cycle, leadership teams typically employ two essential tools: a taxonomy of potential teams and a sequencing plan reflecting the company's key priorities. Let's first look at how each can be employed and then explore what more is needed to tackle large-scale, long-term agile initiatives.

Create a taxonomy of teams

Just as agile teams compile a backlog of work to be accomplished in the future, companies that successfully scale up agile usually begin by creating a full taxonomy of opportunities. Following agile's modular approach, they may break the taxonomy into three components—customer experience teams, business process teams, and technology systems teams—and then integrate them. The first component identifies all the experiences that could significantly affect external and internal customer decisions, behaviors, and satisfaction. These can usually be divided into a dozen or so major experiences (for example, one of a retail customer's major experiences is to buy and pay for a product), which in turn can be divided into dozens of more-specific experiences (the customer may need to choose a payment method, use a coupon, redeem loyalty points, complete the checkout process, and get a receipt). The second component examines the relationships among these experiences and key business processes (improved checkout to reduce time in lines, for instance), aiming to reduce overlapping responsibilities and increase collaboration between process teams and customer experience teams. The third focuses on developing technology systems (such as better mobile-checkout apps) to improve the processes that will support customer experience teams.

The taxonomy of a $10 billion business might identify anywhere from 350 to 1,000 or more potential teams. Those numbers sound daunting, and senior executives are often loath even to consider so much change ("How about if we try two or three of these things and see how it goes?"). But the value of a taxonomy is that it encourages exploration of a transformational vision while breaking the journey into small steps that can be paused, turned, or halted at any time. It also helps leaders spot constraints. Once you've identified the teams you could launch and the sorts of people you would need to staff them, for instance, you need to ask: Do we have those people? If so, where are they? A taxonomy reveals your talent gaps and the kinds of people you must hire or retrain to fill them. Leaders can also see how each potential team fits into the goal of delivering better customer experiences.

USAA has more than 500 agile teams up and running and plans to add 100 more in 2018. The taxonomy is fully visible to everyone across the enterprise. "If you don't have a really good taxonomy, you get redundancy and duplication," COO Carl Liebert told us. "I want to walk into an auditorium and ask, 'Who owns the member's change-of-address experience?' And I want a clear and confident response from a team that owns that experience, whether a member is calling us, logging into our website on a laptop, or using our mobile app. No finger-pointing. No answers that begin with 'It's complicated.'"

USAA's taxonomy ties the activities of agile teams to the people responsible for business units and product lines. The goal is to ensure that managers responsible for specific parts of the P&L understand how cross-functional teams will influence their results. The company has senior leaders who act as general managers in each line of business and are fully accountable for business results. But those leaders rely on customer-focused, cross-organizational teams to get much of the work done. The company also depends on technology and digital resources assigned to the experience owners; the goal here is to ensure that business leaders have the end-to-end resources to deliver the outcomes they have committed to. The intent of the taxonomy is to clarify how to engage the right people in the right work without creating confusion. This kind of link is especially important when hierarchical organizational structures do not align with customer behaviors. For example, many companies have separate structures and P&Ls for online and offline operations—but customers want seamlessly integrated omnichannel experiences. A clear taxonomy that launches the right cross-organizational teams makes such alignment possible.

Sequence the transition
Taxonomy in hand, the leadership team sets priorities and sequences initiatives. Leaders must consider multiple criteria, including strategic importance, budget limitations, availability of people, return on

investment, cost of delays, risk levels, and interdependencies among teams. The most important—and the most frequently overlooked— are the pain points felt by customers and employees on the one hand and the organization's capabilities and constraints on the other. These determine the right balance between how fast the rollout should proceed and how many teams the organization can handle simultaneously.

A few companies, facing urgent strategic threats and in need of radical change, have pursued big-bang, everything-at-once deployments in some units. For example, in 2015 ING Netherlands anticipated rising customer demand for digital solutions and increasing incursions by new digital competitors ("fintechs"). The management team decided to move aggressively. It dissolved the organizational structures of its most innovative functions, including IT development, product management, channel management, and marketing—essentially abolishing everyone's job. Then it created small agile "squads" and required nearly 3,500 employees to reapply for 2,500 redesigned positions on those squads. About 40% of the people filling the positions had to learn new jobs, and all had to profoundly change their mindset. (See "One Bank's Agile Team Experiment," HBR, March–April 2018.)

But big-bang transitions are hard. They require total leadership commitment, a receptive culture, enough talented and experienced agile practitioners to staff hundreds of teams without depleting other capabilities, and highly prescriptive instruction manuals to align everyone's approach. They also require a high tolerance of risk, along with contingency plans to deal with unexpected breakdowns. ING continues to iron out wrinkles as it expands agile throughout the organization.

Companies short on those assets are better off rolling out agile in sequenced steps, with each unit matching the implementation of opportunities to its capabilities. At the beginning of its agile initiative, the advanced technology group at 3M Health Information Systems launched eight to 10 teams every month or two; now, two years in, more than 90 teams are up and running. 3M's Corporate Research Systems Lab got started later but launched 20 teams in three months.

Whatever the pace or endpoint, results should begin showing up quickly. Financial results may take a while—Jeff Bezos believes that most initiatives take five to seven years to pay dividends for Amazon—but positive changes in customer behavior and team problem solving provide early signs that initiatives are on the right track. "Agile adoption has already enabled accelerated product deliveries and the release of a beta application six months earlier than originally planned," says Tammy Sparrow, a senior program manager at 3M Health Information Systems.

Division leaders can determine the sequencing just as any agile team would. Start with the initiatives that offer potentially the greatest value and the most learning. SAP, the enterprise software company, was an early scaler of agile, launching the process a decade ago. Its leaders expanded agile first in its software development units—a highly customer-centric segment where they could test and refine the approach. They established a small consulting group to train, coach, and embed the new way of working, and they created a results tracker so that everyone could see the teams' gains. "Showing concrete examples of impressive productivity gains from agile created more and more pull from the organization," says Sebastian Wagner, who was then a consulting manager in that group. Over the next two years the company rolled out agile to more than 80% of its development organizations, creating more than 2,000 teams. People in sales and marketing saw the need to adapt in order to keep up, so those areas went next. Once the front end of the business was moving at speed, it was time for the back end to make the leap, so SAP shifted its group working on internal IT systems to agile.

Too many companies make the mistake of going for easy wins. They put teams into offsite incubators. They intervene to create easy workarounds to systemic obstacles. Such coddling increases the odds of a team's success, but it doesn't produce the learning environment or organizational changes necessary to scale dozens or hundreds of teams. A company's early agile teams carry the burden of destiny. Testing them, just like testing any prototype, should reflect diverse, realistic conditions. Like SAP, the most successful companies focus on vital customer experiences that cause the greatest frustrations among functional silos.

Still, no agile team should launch unless and until it is ready to begin. *Ready* doesn't mean planned in detail and guaranteed to succeed. It means that the team is:

- focused on a major business opportunity with a lot at stake
- responsible for specific outcomes
- trusted to work autonomously—guided by clear decision rights, properly resourced, and staffed with a small group of multidisciplinary experts who are passionate about the opportunity
- committed to applying agile values, principles, and practices
- empowered to collaborate closely with customers
- able to create rapid prototypes and fast feedback loops
- supported by senior executives who will address impediments and drive adoption of the team's work

Following this checklist will help you plot your sequence for the greatest impact on both customers and the organization.

Master large-scale agile initiatives

Many executives have trouble imagining that small agile teams can attack large-scale, long-term projects. But in principle there is no limit to the number of agile teams you can create or how large the initiative can be. You can establish "teams of teams" that work on related initiatives—an approach that is highly scalable. Saab's aeronautics business, for instance, has more than 100 agile teams operating across software, hardware, and fuselage for its Gripen fighter jet—a $43 million item that is certainly one of the most complex products in the world. It coordinates through daily team-of-teams stand-ups. At 7:30 AM each frontline agile team holds a 15-minute meeting to flag impediments, some of which cannot be resolved within that team. At 7:45 the impediments requiring coordination are escalated to a team of teams, where leaders work to either settle or further escalate issues. This approach continues, and by 8:45 the executive action team has a list of the critical issues it must resolve to keep progress on track. Aeronautics also coordinates its teams through a common rhythm of three-week sprints, a project master plan that is treated as a living document, and the colocation of traditionally disparate parts of the organization—for instance, putting test pilots and simulators with development teams. The results are dramatic: IHS Jane's has deemed the Gripen the world's most cost-effective military aircraft.

Building Agility Across the Business

Expanding the number of agile teams is an important step toward increasing the agility of a business. But equally important is how those teams interact with the rest of the organization. Even the most advanced agile enterprises—Amazon, Spotify, Google, Netflix, Bosch, Saab, SAP, Salesforce, Riot Games, Tesla, and SpaceX, to name a few—operate with a mix of agile teams and traditional structures. To ensure that bureaucratic functions don't hamper the work of agile teams or fail to adopt and commercialize the innovations developed by those teams, such companies constantly push for greater change in at least four areas.

Values and principles

A traditional hierarchical company can usually accommodate a small number of agile teams sprinkled around the organization. Conflicts between the teams and conventional procedures can be resolved through personal interventions and workarounds. When a company launches several hundred agile teams, however, that kind of ad hoc accommodation is no longer possible. Agile teams will be pressing ahead on every front. Traditionally structured parts of the organization will fiercely defend the status quo. As with any change, skeptics can and will produce all kinds of antibodies that attack agile, ranging from refusals to operate on an agile timetable ("Sorry, we can't get to that software module you need for six months") to the withholding of funds from big opportunities that require unfamiliar solutions.

So a leadership team hoping to scale up agile needs to instill agile values and principles throughout the enterprise, including the parts that do not organize into agile teams. This is why Bosch's leaders developed new leadership principles and fanned out throughout the company: They wanted to ensure that everyone understood that things would be different and that agile would be at the center of the company's culture.

Operating architectures

Implementing agile at scale requires modularizing and then seamlessly integrating workstreams. For example, Amazon can deploy software thousands of times a day because its IT architecture was designed to help developers make fast, frequent releases without jeopardizing the firm's complex systems. But many large companies, no matter how fast they can code programs, can deploy software only a few times a day or a week; that's how their architecture works.

Building on the modular approach to product development pioneered by Toyota, Tesla meticulously designs interfaces among the components of its cars to allow each module to innovate independently. Thus the bumper team can change anything as long as it maintains stable interfaces with the parts it affects. Tesla is also abandoning traditional annual release cycles in favor of real-time responses to customer feedback. CEO Elon Musk says that the company makes about 20 engineering changes a week to improve the production and performance of the Model S. Examples include new battery packs, updated safety and autopilot hardware, and software that automatically adjusts the steering wheel and seat for easier entry and exit.

In the most advanced agile enterprises, innovative product and process architectures are attacking some of the thorniest organizational constraints to further scaling. Riot Games, the developer of the wildly successful multiplayer online battle arena League of Legends, is redesigning the interfaces between agile teams and support-and-control functions that operate conventionally, such as facilities, finance, and HR. Brandon Hsiung, the product lead for this ongoing initiative, says it involves at least two key steps. One is shifting the functions' definition of their customers. "Their customers are not their functional bosses, or the CEO, or even the board of directors," he explains. "Their customers are the development teams they serve, who ultimately serve our players." The company instituted Net Promoter surveys to collect feedback on whether those customers would recommend the functions to others and made it plain that dissatisfied customers could sometimes hire outside providers. "It's the last thing we want to happen, but we want to make sure our functions develop world-class capabilities that could compete in a free market," Hsiung says.

Riot Games also revamped how its corporate functions interact with its agile teams. Some members of corporate functions may be embedded in agile teams, or a portion of a function's capacity may be dedicated to requests from agile teams. Alternatively, functions might have little formal engagement with the teams after collaborating with them to establish certain boundaries. Says Hsiung: "Silos such as real estate and learning and development might publish philosophies, guidelines, and rules and then say, 'Here are our guidelines. As long as you operate within them, you can go crazy; do whatever you believe is best for our players.'"

In companies that have scaled up agile, the organization charts of support functions and routine operations generally look much as they did before, though often with fewer management layers and broader spans of control as supervisors learn to trust and empower people. The bigger changes are in the ways functional departments work. Functional priorities are necessarily more fully aligned with corporate strategies. If one of the company's key priorities is improving customers' mobile experience, that can't be number 15 on finance's funding list or HR's hiring list. And departments such as legal may need buffer capacity to deal with urgent requests from high-priority agile teams.

Over time even routine operations with hierarchical structures are likely to develop more-agile mindsets. Of course, finance departments will always manage budgets, but they don't need to keep questioning the decisions of the owners of agile initiatives. "Our CFO constantly shifts accountability to empowered agile teams," says Ahmed Sidky, the head of development management at Riot Games. "He'll say, 'I am not here to run the finances of the company. You are, as team leaders. I'm here in an advisory capacity.' In the day-to-day organization, finance partners are embedded in every team. They don't control what the teams do or don't do. They are more like finance coaches who ask hard questions and provide deep expertise. But ultimately it's the team leader who makes decisions, according to what is best for Riot players."

Some companies, and some individuals, may find these trade-offs hard to accept and challenging to implement. Reducing control is always scary—until you do so and find that people are happier and success rates triple. In a recent Bain survey of nearly 1,300 global executives, more respondents agreed with this statement about management than with any other: "Today's business leaders must trust and empower people, not command and control them." (Only 5% disagreed.)

Talent acquisition and motivation

Companies that are scaling up agile need systems for acquiring star players and motivating them to make teams better. (Treat your stars unfairly, and they will bolt to a sexy start-up.) They also need to unleash the wasted potential of more-typical team members and build commitment, trust, and joint accountability for outcomes. There's no practical way to do this without changing HR procedures. A company can no longer hire purely for expertise, for instance; it now needs expertise combined with enthusiasm for work on a collaborative team. It can't evaluate people according to whether they hit individual objectives; it now needs to look at their performance on agile teams and at team members' evaluations of one another. Performance assessments typically shift from an annual basis to a system that provides relevant feedback and coaching every few weeks or months. Training and coaching programs encourage the development of cross-functional skills customized to the needs of individual employees. Job titles matter less and change less frequently with self-governing teams and fewer hierarchical levels. Career paths show how product owners—the individuals who set the vision and own the results of an agile team—can continue their personal development, expand their influence, and increase their compensation.

Companies may also need to revamp their compensation systems to reward group rather than individual accomplishments. They need recognition programs that celebrate contributions immediately. Public recognition is better than confidential cash bonuses at bolstering agile values—it inspires recipients to improve even further, and it motivates others to emulate the recipients' behaviors. Leaders can also reward "A" players by engaging them in the most vital opportunities, providing them with the most advanced tools and the greatest possible freedom, and connecting them with the most talented mentors in their field.

Annual planning and budgeting cycles

In bureaucratic companies, annual strategy sessions and budget negotiations are powerful tools for aligning the organization and securing commitments to stretch goals. Agile practitioners begin with different assumptions. They see that customer needs change frequently and that breakthrough insights can occur at any time. In their view, annual cycles constrain innovation and adaptation: Unproductive projects burn resources until their budgets run out, while critical innovations wait in line for the next budget cycle to compete for funding.

In companies with many agile teams, funding procedures are different. Funders recognize that for two-thirds of successful innovations, the original concept will change significantly during the development process. They expect that teams will drop some features and launch others without waiting for the next annual cycle. As a result, funding procedures evolve to resemble those of a venture capitalist. VCs typically view funding decisions as opportunities to purchase options for further discovery. The objective is not to instantly create a large-scale business but, rather, to find a critical component of the ultimate solution. This leads to a lot of apparent failures but accelerates and reduces the cost of learning. Such an approach works well in an agile enterprise, vastly improving the speed and efficiency of innovation.

Companies that successfully scale up agile see major changes in their business. Scaling up shifts the mix of work so that the business is doing more innovation relative to routine operations. The business is better able to read changing conditions and priorities, develop adaptive solutions, and avoid the constant crises that so frequently hit traditional hierarchies. Disruptive innovations will come to feel less disruptive and more like adaptive business as usual. The scaling up also brings agile values and principles to business operations and support functions, even if many routine activities remain. It leads to greater efficiency and productivity in some of the business's big cost centers. It improves operating architectures and organizational models to enhance coordination between agile teams and routine operations. Changes come on line faster and are more responsive to customer needs. Finally, the business delivers measurable improvements in outcomes—not only better financial results but also greater customer loyalty and employee engagement.

Agile's test-and-learn approach is often described as incremental and iterative, but no one should mistake incremental development processes for incremental thinking. SpaceX, for example, aims to use agile innovation to begin transporting people to Mars by 2024, with the goal of establishing a self-sustaining colony on the planet. How will that happen? Well, people at the company don't really know . . . yet. But they have a vision that it's possible, and they have some steps in mind. They intend to dramatically improve reliability and reduce expenses, partly by reusing rockets much like airplanes. They intend to improve propulsion systems to launch rockets that can carry at least 100 people. They plan to figure out how to refuel in space. Some of the steps include pushing current technologies as far as possible and then waiting for new partners and new technologies to emerge.

That's agile in practice: big ambitions and step-by-step progress. It shows the way to proceed even when, as is so often the case, the future is murky.

Originally published in May–June 2018. Reprint R1803F

Operational Transparency

by Ryan W. Buell

BARCLAYS BANK INSTALLED the world's first successful automated teller machine to much fanfare in June 1967. Having a machine distribute cash was less expensive and more efficient than having a human teller do it. What's more, customers could access the ATM at any hour—even when the bank was closed. It seemed like a win-win, and ATMs quickly spread around the world. Today people are three times more likely to withdraw money from an ATM than from a human teller.

However, there's a wrinkle to the ATM success story. When customers use ATMs more and tellers less, their overall level of satisfaction with their bank goes down. It turns out that when consumers can't see the work that's being done to serve them, their perception is that less effort went into delivering the service, so they don't appreciate or value it as much. ATMs carry out complex work: They reliably identify customers, find their account information, and then accurately complete the transaction—all while protecting the confidentiality of their private information. But separated from this work by a hard, metallic surface and a vague "processing transaction" message, customers take the "wizardry" for granted in a way that they don't when they're face-to-face with tellers who are working in their behalf.

Automation has enabled enormous efficiencies in recent years, but it has also detached customers from operations. Thanks to fleets of order-picking robots and miles of automated conveyors, it takes less than one minute of human labor to pick, pack, and ship the typical Amazon package—a miraculous ballet among people and machines that customers never glimpse. Google has more than a million servers working to deliver answers to more than a trillion queries a year—information distributed in fractions of a second without a hint of the massive operation behind it.

And even where technology hasn't erected barriers between customers and the work being performed for them, leaders have put them up. At hospitals, as many as 70% of clinical diagnoses come from the pathology lab—but the people who run those tests are often hidden away in the basement or off-site. Hundreds of people have a hand in the successful takeoff and landing of a commercial flight—but for the most part, passengers see only the cabin crew. Consider all the people who work in offices, kitchens, warehouses, and factories whose efforts create immeasurable value but who never enter customers' minds.

Therein lies a crucial managerial dilemma that I've been studying over the past decade. It has long been believed that the more contact an operation has with its customers, the less efficiently it runs. Customers are, as a researcher in the 1960s boldly called them, "environmental disturbances." As the argument goes, separating customers from internal processes through physical distance, time, or the introduction of technology enables companies to perform more efficiently and, in turn, create more value for consumers. But my research shows that the pendulum can swing too far. When customers are cordoned off from a company's operation, they are less likely to fully understand and appreciate the value being created. As a result, they are less satisfied, less willing to pay, less trusting, and less loyal to the company over time. Employees also suffer when they are cut off from the business's front lines, as they lose the motivation and enjoyment that comes from making a difference in people's lives and are denied the opportunities to learn and improve that arise from interaction with customers.

One solution that my colleagues and I have investigated is the introduction of operational transparency—the deliberate design of

Idea in Brief

The Dilemma

Conventional wisdom holds that the more contact an operation has with its customers, the less efficiently it will run. But when customers are partitioned away from the operation, they are less likely to fully understand and appreciate the work going on behind the scenes, thereby placing a lower value on the product or service being offered.

The Solution

Managers should experiment with operational transparency—the deliberate design of windows into and out of the organization's operations to help customers understand and appreciate the value being added.

The Benefits

Witnessing the hidden work performed on their behalf makes customers more satisfied, more willing to pay, and more loyal. It can also make employees more satisfied by demonstrating to them that they are serving their customers well. However, managers should be aware of certain conditions in which transparency can backfire.

windows into and out of the organization's operations to help customers and employees alike understand and appreciate the value being created. To determine when and how to design such windows, managers must understand when and how customers and employees want to open up operations to scrutiny—and when both parties would prefer that work be undertaken behind the scenes.

Behind the Curtain

I first started documenting the beneficial effects of operational transparency in 2008, when I set up a mock website called Travel Finder, with my Harvard Business School colleague Michael Norton, as part of a study. We had noticed that travel agents, like bank tellers, were being made increasingly obsolete by technology—in this case, by online travel agencies. We also noticed that most online ticket sites hid the work they performed for customers behind progress bars and activity spinners, or behind marketing messages such as "Did you know you can book your hotel with us, too?" Online travel agency Kayak was an exception. The company showed customers how many different airlines it was searching while they waited, and it slotted itineraries into the results screen as they were found instead of all at once. We wondered whether this operational transparency would change the way customers viewed the service.

For our travel study, we recruited people to search for flights from Boston to Los Angeles on our website. After they entered their search information, we randomly varied how long people waited as the website searched for possible tickets. While waiting, some people saw a progress bar, and some were shown, in addition to the progress bar, the hidden work that the website was doing: "Now getting results from American Airlines . . . from JetBlue . . . 133 results found so far . . . Now 427 . . ." We then surveyed people about how valuable they perceived the website to be. No matter how long people had waited, they always considered the website to be more valuable when it showed the work it was doing for them. They also reported a higher willingness to pay, a perception of higher quality, and a greater desire to use the site again. What's more, they were also considerably less sensitive to their wait time when they experienced operational transparency. People who received instantaneous service perceived the service to be as valuable as people who waited 25 seconds with a progress bar, and as valuable as people who waited 55 seconds with operational transparency. That's remarkable in an era in which we have come to expect online services to be delivered in fractions of a second.

In other experiments, people who experienced operational transparency expressed more interest in using the website again in the future, even when they compared it with a faster website that returned the same results and did not show the work. We also found that people preferred websites that showed them the work over ones that did other things to distract from the wait—like providing entertaining pictures of their destination, promotional messages about other services offered by the website, or an interactive game of tic-tac-toe. None of those types of approaches made the service seem more valuable.

Why does operational transparency seem to have this unique power? We surveyed people who have (and have not) been given a glimpse behind the curtain in services as varied as restaurants, retail, and online dating to learn how operational transparency changes their perceptions. We found that when people could see the work that was going on behind the scenes, they perceived that more effort went into the delivery of the service. They also believed that the service provider had more expertise and was being more thorough. They appreciated that effort and quality, and they in turn valued the service more.

In retail, for instance, Bhavya Mohan (of the University of San Francisco), Leslie John (of Harvard Business School), and I studied what happened when an online retailer added an infographic highlighting the costs and processes involved in manufacturing various products. For example, a wallet that sold for $115.00 included costs for raw materials ($14.68), construction ($38.56), duties ($4.26), and transportation ($1.00). Revealing the costs enabled the company to showcase to customers the otherwise hidden work that went into creating the wallet. In the process, of course, it also revealed that customers were paying $115.00 for something that cost $58.50 to make. The company further informed customers that its 1.9x markup compared favorably with the 6x markup charged by competing retailers—whose prices for similarly constructed items were higher. We found that sales of the wallets with operational transparency went up by 26% relative to wallets where the costs were not shared.

In subsequent experiments, we've learned that voluntarily providing operational transparency not only increases sales but also increases people's trust and satisfaction—even in settings where trust is otherwise low, such as government services. According to the Pew Research Center, 73% of Americans in 1958 reported trusting government to do the right thing at least most of the time; today a paltry 20% do. So-called sunshine laws require a minimum level of transparency by elected officials and policy makers about certain of their activities, but those laws are not meant to spotlight the often invisible work that government does on a daily basis to create value in citizens' lives—such as disposing of trash, filling potholes, cleaning up graffiti, and fixing broken streetlights.

In 2009, Boston's local government developed a smartphone app called Citizens Connect (now BOS:311), which enables residents of the city to submit public service requests. Using the app, a resident can take a photo of a problem they want to report, such as a pothole, and the picture will automatically be geotagged using the phone's GPS and sent to the public works department. My colleagues Ethan Porter (of George Washington University), Michael Norton (of HBS), and I partnered with the City of Boston and Code for America in 2014 to study how showing the work being performed affected people's perceptions of government. We found that when people interacted with a website that showed images of the work being requested and performed, they became significantly more trusting and supportive of the government than if they interacted with a website that merely provided a tally of issues being reported and resolved. What's more, when the city took things a step further and asked employees to take photos of the work they were doing and share them with the people who submitted the original requests, users became considerably more engaged, increasing the number of requests they made on a monthly basis by 60% and reporting issues in 40% more categories. Increased citizen engagement enabled Boston's government to allocate more workers to solving problems and fewer to finding them, so more work could get done.

The thoughtful application of transparency can create value even in settings where privacy is traditionally prized, such as health care. London Business School's Kamalini Ramdas and Nazli Sonmez and I collaborated with doctors at Aravind Eye Hospital, in Pondicherry, India, to study an application of operational transparency in delivering care to patients with glaucoma—an eye disease that is the second leading cause of blindness and afflicts some 12 million Indians. Some patients in our study were given appointments with their doctors in accordance with the hospital's normal protocol. Others were given shared appointments with three or four other patients. At the shared appointments, patients were able to see what the doctor could see when examining the eyes of others and hear the questions asked by other patients. Results from our ongoing collaboration suggest that patients who have shared medical appointments are more satisfied and engaged during their experience, are more likely to ask questions, learn more from the interactions, are more compliant with their pre-scriptions, and are more likely to return for follow-up care than patients who have traditional one-on-one appointments with their doctor.

Although companies generally strive to make services appear as effortless as possible, examples of organizations beginning to experiment with various forms of operational transparency are becoming more abundant. When customers use an ATM to with-draw money from their BBVA bank accounts in Spain, the ATM's full-color screen displays visual representations of the currency being counted, sorted, and arranged for distribution. At most Starbucks drive-through locations in the United States, the intercom has been replaced with a video monitor and camera system. When customers place an order, they come face-to-face with the barista as he or she rings up the order and marks instructions on each cup. At Domino's, customers can use the company's Pizza Tracker app to watch as the kitchen workers prep, bake, and package the pizza for delivery.

NPR and the *New York Times* podcast *The Daily* are connecting listeners and readers with the otherwise obscure work involved in researching, producing, and delivering the headlines of the day. NPR posts live feeds from its studios, and *The Daily* interviews the paper's own reporters. In Detroit, the Mayor's Office has invested in the Neighborhood Improvement Tracker, a public-facing website that shows at a lot-by-lot level the many efforts being directed toward the city's recovery, such as demolitions scheduled and completed to remove urban blight and building permits issued to enhance the community.

The evidence is clear: Operational transparency can fundamen-tally reshape the ways customers understand, perceive, and engage with the organizations that serve them. But what of employees?

Closing the Loop for Employees

Pioneering studies of service industries in the early 2000s found that a primary driver of satisfaction among employees is the knowledge that their company is delivering results to happy customers. Indeed, a 2007 study led by Adam Grant, an organizational psychologist and professor at Wharton, found that when call center agents soliciting donations for college scholarships actually met some of the students their work supported, their productivity and persistence skyrocketed. But what happens when the interaction between the customer and employee occurs in real time?

In 2012, Tami Kim (of the Darden School of Business), Chia-Jung Tsay (of University College London), and I ran an experiment in the Annenberg Hall dining facility at Harvard, which serves more than 3,000 meals every day. Annenberg was built in the late 1800s at a time when it was considered uncouth for diners to be able to see the work taking place in the kitchen. In that tradition, diners at Annenberg who desire eggs, a fish sandwich, a hamburger, or some other grill item cooked their way must write their order on a piece of paper and hand it to an employee, who passes it through a small window into the kitchen, where a chef reads the order, cooks the item, and places it back in the window to be taken by an employee and given to the customer. The chefs can't see the customers, and the customers can't see the chefs.

We installed iPads with video-conferencing software—one at the order station, in view of the customers, and another in the kitchen, in view of the chefs. We then timed how long it took to make various dishes and measured both chef and diner satisfaction. When we turned on the iPads in a way that allowed only the chefs to see their customers, customer satisfaction with the food rose 14%. When we turned on the iPads so the customers could see the chefs too, satisfaction went up 22%, and the chefs worked 19% faster. One chef told us, "When [the customers] can see us [make their food], they appreciate it, and I appreciate that. It makes me want to improve."

Through surveys and additional experiments, we learned that when customers saw the chefs cooking their food, they perceived that more effort went into serving them, they appreciated the effort, and they valued the service more. When the chefs could see their customers—the people who were benefiting from their efforts—the work they were doing seemed more appreciated and impactful, making them more satisfied with their jobs and more willing to exert effort. It was a virtuous cycle.

Consider another example: the Japanese train-cleaning company, Tessei, which I researched with Ethan Bernstein for an HBS case study. Tessei is charged with the Herculean task of cleaning the Shinkansen bullet trains during their brief stops at Tokyo station—1,000 seats in seven minutes. That's the equivalent of cleaning six Boeing 737s in less than half the time it typically takes to clean one. In the early 2000s, Tessei's employees were struggling to get the job done. Part of the challenge was that the work was underappreciated: Cleaning the bullet trains was known to be dirty and difficult, and so being a cleaner at Tessei was considered shameful in Japan. Accordingly, workers did whatever they could to escape the notice of customers. In 2005, a new leader, Teruo Yabe, revitalized the service, in part by promoting operational transparency among customers and employees. After the company changed employee uniforms from an invisible pale blue (which blended in with the body of the trains) to a vibrant red, passengers began to see and appreciate the work that these crews were doing, and after more interaction was instituted between the workers and the passengers, employees felt more appreciated and found a greater sense of purpose in their work. Employees began suggesting process improvements, and customers began chipping in to help tidy up their seats. There were quantifiable performance improvements too; today a Tessei crew can clean a train in four minutes.

The India-based luxury hotel chain Oberoi Hotels takes operational transparency one step further, as I learned in my research for an HBS case study with Ananth Raman (of HBS) and Vidhya Muthuram (of the Blavatnik School of Government). Every employee in the company is preauthorized to spend up to Rs 1,500 (about US$25) to create moments of delight for guests. Whenever they learn of an opportunity to customize the service to improve a guest's experience, they're encouraged to act on it. The only stipulation is that employees must log what they have done so that the company and other employees can learn from their creativity. What has resulted is a feedback loop that fosters in employees a greater sense of purpose, helps customers feel better cared for, and improves organizational learning. Thanks in part to these efforts, Oberoi's properties routinely receive effusive reviews in customer surveys, and the company is perennially rated as one of the best luxury hotel brands in the world.

In contexts in which designing a face-to-face connection between employees and customers is impractical, technology can be used to successfully facilitate operational transparency. In 2013, Domino's piloted a feature called Domino's Live in one of its Salt Lake City locations, installing web cameras in the kitchen. Building on its Pizza Tracker app, customers ordering pizzas in Salt Lake could log on and watch a live feed of their pizzas being made. As it turned out, tens of thousands of people from around the country logged on to watch other people's pizzas get made. Recognizing the potential, Domino's promoted Domino's Live on Facebook, and anytime someone clicked the "Like" button, a "Like Light" in the kitchen went on. This gave the pizza makers a signal that someone looking on appreciated the work they were doing. Although Domino's discontinued Domino's Live, the company added a feature to Pizza Tracker that enables customers to send notes of encouragement through the app to the people who are preparing their pizzas—prespecified messages such as "I don't know what I'd do without you" and "You are my pizza-making heroes." In a similar move, Uber recently updated its app to allow riders to close the loop with drivers—prompting them to send thank-you notes, along with tips, to the drivers after the ride is over. As one driver explained, "It makes my day to know when I've made somebody else's."

The Risk of Backfire

For all its benefits, operational transparency doesn't always deliver positive results. There are circumstances when it can repel customers and undermine employees. But even in such instances, managers should think twice before opting for complete opacity. Operational transparency should be carefully considered when:

It reveals things people genuinely don't want to see
Few may desire a behind-the-scenes look at trash collection or enjoying watching the dashcam footage of a violent police altercation.

However, there's a difference between transparency that elicits the reaction "I'd rather not see that" and transparency that elicits the reaction "That should not happen." In the case of services that people aren't really interested in or find unappealing, companies should look for ways to use transparency to change the way people think about and engage with a service. For example, the city of Halifax, Nova Scotia, switched to clear trash bags in 2015 so that everyone could see what was being thrown away. Curbside waste collection fell by more than 30%, and recycling rates increased nearly 20%. When transparency causes people to object to what they see, organizations can draw on the experience to come up with alternative approaches that improve practice going forward. Dashcam footage of excessive violence by police departments has led to public outrage, but it has also improved oversight and accountability, sparked conversations that have led to policy change, and improved frontline training. "Out of sight, out of mind" may be more comfortable for everyone in the moment, but it rarely ensures the best long-term outcomes.

It engenders anxiety

Showing customers every step while their credit is being evaluated for a loan, or peering over employees' shoulders as they work, amplifies anxiety. Ethan Bernstein, of HBS, found that when curtains were put up around production lines at a Chinese cell phone manufacturer, productivity increased by 10% to 15%. Free from prying eyes, workers felt more focused and licensed to experiment with ways to improve standardized processes. What's more, workers felt safe to share ideas with one another, building team camaraderie and improving performance. When transparency makes us feel watched, it can hold us back; but when it helps us feel engaged, it can move us forward. For example, my HBS colleague Michelle Shell and I found that when customers who were transparently being evaluated for a loan were also provided with an easy way to contact a support person with questions throughout the process, the probability they would move forward with the loan, if offered, increased.

It shatters our faith in the relationship

When transparency reveals that a company isn't even-handed or that its practices violate implicit social norms, it makes customers understandably upset. Incidents of air rage—when an irate passenger causes a plane to land early—are higher on flights that have both a business class and an economy class and all passengers board from the front, forcing people in economy class to experience the disparity. This study, conducted by Katherine DeCelles (of the Rotman School of Management) and Michael Norton, found that when the plane boards in the middle, so there's less transparency, the effect goes away. Or consider the ubiquitous marketing practice of personalizing ads. Tami Kim, along with Kate Barasz (of HBS) and Leslie John, found that when companies are transparent about targeting online ads on the basis of things we've revealed about ourselves, we appreciate the personalization. But when the transparency instead shows that they customize ads according to things they've *inferred* about us, it makes us upset. Customers also bristle when it's clear instead that companies are sharing their information with third parties without permission.

It destroys the magic

Sometimes we want to suspend our disbelief, and providing too much transparency would make that impossible. Retailers that sell high-end jewelry, musical instruments, or home decor often keep redundant inventory off the floor to give the pieces we see a special, one-of-a-kind mystique. The illusion that our ring or guitar or vase is unique enhances our experience. Likewise, even when it's 95 degrees outside, the cast member playing Mickey Mouse at Disneyland should keep the heavy, stuffy head of the costume on during the parade. Nothing can ruin the experience of make-believe like too much transparency. In other cases, we're fascinated to be in on the secret. Factory tours and "how it's made" shows are ubiquitous, and we clamor to watch bloopers and outtakes from our favorite movies. In fact, Disney offers a Backstage Magic experience for those who self-select into peeking behind the curtain.

It exposes an ineffective process

When transparency reveals employees who are incapable, indifferent, or powerless to deliver on the value proposition of the firm, customers can become incensed. Think back to the last service interaction you had where two employees were visibly chatting with each other instead of helping you. Or remember the last time your simmering frustration rose to a boil when a customer service rep repeated apologies for a problem over and over but had no means or authority to remedy the situation. Meanwhile, exposing employees to disenchanted and overtly negative customers, whom they have no hope of satisfying, can be a recipe for burnout. Agent turnover in many call centers, for example, exceeds 150% per year. Often situations like these arise when transparency hasn't been designed to be reciprocal and to engender learning. Transparency that is accompanied by mechanisms to collect and learn from customer-provided feedback can accelerate, and create opportunities to celebrate, improvement.

It reveals that a company's best efforts yield poor results

When people can see that a lot of behind-the-scenes effort went into creating an inadequate outcome, it reinforces their impression that the company is bad at what it does. In an experiment I conducted with Michael Norton, participants engaged with one of two online dating websites that gave them dissatisfying results. Participants perceived that the site that showed them how hard it was working was worse than the one that delivered the same bad result but didn't show the work. The impression was, "You tried so hard, and that's the best you could do? You must not be very good at your job." That said, when mistakes are made, timely transparency is still typically the best path. Customers may punish companies that fail to be transparent about missteps or errors, questioning the organization's motives for hiding the information. "Why did Equifax wait 40 days to inform 143 million people that their confidential information had been compromised?" customers might wonder. Or "Why did Facebook wait three years to disclose that Cambridge Analytica improperly accessed the records of 50 million users?"

It shows that the company's products or services are inferior to competitors'

A fundamental tenet of business still applies: If your customers find that your products are of poor quality, overly expensive, or otherwise less attractive than your competitors' offerings, they will do business elsewhere. Shwetha Mariadassou (of Stanford), Yanchong Zheng (of MIT), and I found that such revelations are most damaging when a company's level of performance is seen as inferior to a competitor or industry benchmark. On the other hand, transparency that exposes a customer's own poor performance—for example, when your power company reports that you consume more electricity than your neighbors—can be a potent motivator of change. The effect can be especially powerful when the company reveals unflattering changes in your performance: You increased consumption by 5%, but your neighbors decreased consumption by an average of 3%.

It highlights a lack of progress

Uncertainty about our status makes our skin crawl. That's why progress bars are ubiquitous online, and why American, Delta, and United Airlines now update the status of people's bags throughout their journey, providing mobile alerts when bags have been scanned, loaded, off-loaded, placed in baggage claim, and so on. We like to have the feeling of moving forward, and transparency that demonstrates the opposite can be frustrating. For example, in a recent experiment, I found that when people who have been waiting for service can see that nobody has joined the queue behind them, they're significantly more likely to give up waiting than if they don't know whether anyone else has joined. Making visible their lack of progress from the end of the queue leaves them wondering whether continuing to wait is worthwhile. On the other hand, when people who have been waiting for service are able to see that their time waiting has resulted in advancement from the end of the queue, they're significantly more likely to stay in line.

**It reveals that the company's operations harm workers
or the environment**

News coverage of the 2013 collapse of Rana Plaza, which killed and injured thousands of Bangladeshi garment workers, and the 2010 Deepwater Horizon oil spill, which released millions of barrels of oil into the Gulf of Mexico, casts spotlights on inhumane working conditions and subpar environmental standards that reshaped corporate initiatives around supply chain sustainability. Visibility into such problems can cause a strong and swift customer backlash. To that end, transparency functions as a test of sorts: If you don't want people to see how you treat your employees or the planet, you probably need to make some changes. On the other hand, when transparency reveals that companies are operating sustainably, it can have a powerful effect.

Georgia Institute of Technology's Basak Kalkanci and I ran field experiments with Alta Gracia, an apparel manufacturer that pays a living wage to its workers in the Dominican Republic, and with Counter Culture Coffee, a North Carolina–based coffee roasting company that engages in environmentally sustainable practices. We collaborated with the Looma Project to produce a short video showing footage of working conditions inside Alta Gracia's factory and featuring interviews with workers discussing the living wage that Alta Gracia pays. We produced a similar video highlighting Counter Culture Coffee's environmental sustainability practices, such as composting the chaff from its roasting process to reduce landfill waste. Showing these videos at point-of-sale kiosks increased the probability that customers would buy the company's products by roughly 20%, relative to merely showing brand videos.

It's deceptive

Transparency is helpful when it reveals work, but when the illusion of transparency is used to deceive or manipulate, it can backfire spectacularly. When customers call AT&T or Apple to request customer support, the companies' automated systems play the sound of typing between prompts to signal that work is being done. Customers understand these cues for what they are and do not mistake them for the sound of an actual person performing a task. However, companies can easily stray into dodgy territory. For example, several years ago, a company called Premier Health Plans used software to speak on behalf of telemarketing agents who had heavy accents. Calls would typically start off with the agent identifying "herself" as Samantha West and asking an initial question, prompting customers to think they were engaging with a live customer service rep. However, awkward pauses between exchanges, the software's limited repertoire of phrases, and the mechanical word-for-word repetition that resulted during interactions caused skeptical customers to interrupt, asking, "Are you a robot?" Anticipating this possibility, the developers had included the recording of a disarming laugh and the response "I am a real person. Can you hear me OK?" Customers weren't buying it. Recordings soon emerged online of people interrogating Samantha West to expose her as a fraud.

Recently, Google announced its plans to roll out a much more sophisticated phone robot, called Google Duplex, that is fully automated and can pass as a human—calling restaurants and hair salons to make reservations and appointments on behalf of its users. The technology is breathtaking, and the potential for value creation is enormous, but unless Duplex is modified to be genuinely transparent, it's hard to imagine that those it deceives will be forgiving.

Bringing Operational Transparency to Your Organization

Given all the potential advantages and pitfalls of operational transparency, managers should be thoughtful about how they implement it. They should consider the following factors in designing their initiatives:

What to reveal?

A great place to start is to think about moments in the process that could be easily showcased with minimal effort. For example, one dessert-focused restaurant introduced operational transparency by suspending a tilted mirror from the ceiling above the pastry chefs who were plating and finishing desserts. Diners, whose views had been previously obscured by high counters and a bank of espresso machines, were captivated by their new window into the action.

Other opportunities for transparency can be found by considering what information already captured in the organization's databases would be appreciated by customers. For example, several years ago, as a part of its efforts to improve access to health care, the U.S. Department of Veterans Affairs began internally tracking how long veterans were waiting at each of its facilities to get an appointment to see a doctor. Recently, the agency made this information publicly available to patients on its website. Similarly, Quick Lane Tire and Auto Center, a nationwide auto repair company, has been experimenting with providing a digital information board in its waiting rooms that gives customers real-time updates about what's happening with their cars and the current status of the service queue.

When to reveal?

Transparency boosts value perceptions most when it reveals work as it is happening or just after it has been completed, rather than showing work that has not yet occurred. In my research, I've found that customers are more satisfied when a travel site like Kayak shows its efforts to find a flight *as it searches* dozens of airlines than when it merely tells customers before they hit the "search" button *that it will search* dozens of airlines. In addition, consumers shouldn't be force-fed transparency. Rather, they should get to decide when they want to see more. For example, UPS receives 143 million package-tracking requests on a typical business day—which converts to an average of about seven lookups per package. These requests are made by customers who are actively curious about the status of particular packages and are tracking them at times of their choosing. Imagine if UPS instead called you at its own discretion seven times per shipment with a running progress report.

How to reveal?

Transparency implementations work best when they're visual— ideally giving customers actual windows into the process so that there's no question about the credibility of what's being shown.

When this isn't possible, video or animated infographics and diagrams that provide a visual representation of the work boost the perception of value more than static imagery, which in turn outperforms text descriptions. Transparency also works best when it's voluntarily provided by companies; transparency that is wrung out of corporations as a result of regulations, investor pressure, or other factors does not build trust.

Don't forget to close the loop. Transparency is the most beneficial when it's allowed to flow in both directions—from the customers into the operation and from the employees out to the customers. Forcing employees to toil in obscurity deprives them of seeing how their work is helping customers, reducing their feeling that their work is appreciated and undermining their motivation. What's more, transparency for employees can give them the information they need to customize service and help them learn better ways of operating.

In a sense, today's businesses have become victims of the global economy's immense productivity gains over the past two centuries. Consumers today rely on a dizzying array of products that are manufactured and distributed from all around the world and on services that are delivered with an intensifying frequency. But the apparently effortless abundance and convenience also make it easy for consumers to take work for granted and for employees to lose out on the learning and motivation that customer connections afford. With that in mind, businesses should stop reflexively hiding their operations for the sake of efficiency and instead thoughtfully consider when and how to open them up to create more value for customers and employees alike.

Originally published in March–April 2019. Reprint R1902H

Disclosure: Ryan W. Buell has given paid lectures at Google and Uber in the past.

The Dual-Purpose Playbook

by Julie Battilana, Anne-Claire Pache, Metin Sengul, and Marissa Kimsey

CORPORATIONS ARE BEING PUSHED to change—to dial down their single-minded pursuit of financial gain and pay closer attention to their impact on employees, customers, communities, and the environment. Corporate social responsibility from the sidelines is no longer enough, and the pressure comes from various directions: rising and untenable levels of inequality, increasing evidence that the effects of climate change will be devastating, investors' realization that short-term profitability and long-term sustainability are sometimes in conflict. For reasons like these, a growing number of business leaders now understand that they must embrace both financial and social goals.

However, changing an organization's DNA is extraordinarily difficult. How can a company that has always focused on profit balance the two aims? It takes upending the existing business model. Not surprisingly, researchers have consistently found that companies are quick to abandon social goals in the quest for profitability.

Yet some enterprises successfully pursue both. The U.S. outdoor-clothing company Patagonia, for example, which initially prioritized financial goals, has come to pursue social good more seriously over time. Others began with social goals but must earn revenue to survive. Grameen Bank, the Nobel Prize–winning microlender in Bangladesh, is an iconic example. We've spent a decade studying how socially driven businesses succeed, and what we've learned from in-depth qualitative studies and quantitative analyses may prove useful to traditional companies that want to adopt a dual purpose.

Our research reveals that successful dual-purpose companies have this in common: They take an approach we call *hybrid organizing,* which involves four levers: setting and monitoring social goals alongside financial ones; structuring the organization to support both socially and financially oriented activities; hiring and socializing employees to embrace both; and practicing dual-minded leadership. Taken together, these levers can help companies cultivate and maintain a hybrid culture while giving leaders the tools to productively manage conflicts between social and financial goals when they emerge, making the endeavor more likely to succeed.

Setting Goals, Monitoring Progress

Dual-purpose companies need to set goals along both financial and social dimensions and monitor performance on an ongoing basis.

Setting goals

Well-constructed goals are an essential management tool. They communicate what matters and can highlight what's working and what's not. These goals should go beyond mere aspirations to clarify a company's dual purpose for employees, customers, suppliers, investors, and regulators. Companies may need to experiment their way to a goal-setting model that works for them—something Grameen Veolia Water has managed by continually recalibrating its activities around explicit aims.

The company, which provides safe water in Bangladesh, started in 2008 as a joint venture between Grameen Bank and the water services provider Veolia. Veolia, which traditionally works under government contracts, recognized that no local authorities were responsible for providing drinking water to rural areas at that time.

Idea in Brief

The Problem

Corporations are being pushed to dial down their single-minded pursuit of financial gain and pay closer attention to their impact on society. But how can a company balance the two?

The Research

The authors have studied companies around the globe that pursue financial and social goals simultaneously. They find that the successful ones build a commit-

ment to both economic and social value into their core organizational activities.

The Solution

Companies that want to do well and do good should focus on four key management practices: setting and monitoring dual goals; structuring the organization to support both goals; hiring and socializing employees to embrace them; and practicing dual-minded leadership.

The partnership aimed to fill this gap. Its board set two goals for the new business at the outset: to provide safe, affordable drinking water to the inhabitants of the rural villages of Goalmari and Padua over the long term, and to sustain operations from sales without relying on grants.

These two goals came into conflict. When managers realized how difficult it would be to break even if they sold water only to poor rural households at a very low price, they designed a new revenue-generating activity: selling water in jars to schools and businesses in nearby urban areas. At this point it might have been tempting to focus attention and resources on the profitable new market segment at the expense of the original one. But leadership did not drift. The venture's clearly stated social goal reminded board members and managers that urban sales were meant to subsidize village sales. Ultimately the former amounted to half the company's revenues, helping Grameen Veolia Water pursue its social goal.

No single playbook exists for setting social goals. But our studies point to two rules of thumb. First, *do the research.* Often leaders try to set goals without developing a deep understanding of the specific social needs they aim to address—or of how they may have contributed in the past to the buildup of problems. Just as they conduct market research to identify opportunities for profit, they should study those social needs. Their research should involve the intended beneficiaries along with other stakeholders and experts.

Prior to launching operations, Grameen Veolia Water conducted major research to understand water issues in Bangladesh, interviewing public officials and health and water experts along with community organizations. Managers discovered that some rural populations suffered not only from drinking surface water contaminated with bacteria (the researchers' initial assumption) but also from drinking water from wells built in the 1980s. Some well water, although clear and tasteless, was naturally contaminated by arsenic and was a major source of cancers in adults and cognitive impairment in children. This information led the business to focus its activity in Goalmari and Padua, which suffered from both sources of contamination. The company thus defined its goal as providing permanent access to clean water for everyone in those villages.

Second, *set goals that are explicit and enduring* (though they may have to be updated in light of a changing environment). Impact would be limited if the village residents consumed clean water for just a few years; to achieve a significant positive change in their health, they would need access to clean water over decades.

Monitoring progress

Just as important as setting goals is identifying and adapting key performance indicators (KPIs) in order to measure the achievement of specific targets, be they financial or social. While we know how to measure sales, revenue growth, and return on assets, no widely accepted metrics currently exist for many social goals (although more progress has been made on measuring environmental impact). Nonetheless, it is possible to set both financial and social KPIs successfully. Our research has found that companies succeed by dedicating substantial time and effort to developing a manageable number of trackable metrics during the goal-setting process and revisiting them regularly to assess their continuing relevance and adequacy.

At Grameen Veolia Water, managers consulted with members of the rural communities they sought to serve and with academic experts before formalizing four KPIs: the company's self-financing ratio (its ability to fund planned investments from its own resources), the number of villagers with access to its services, the rate of rural penetration, and the rate of rural regular consumption (which captures both financial and social performance). The four numbers are updated monthly to monitor operations, and the board discusses them quarterly to guide strategic decision making.

A learning mindset is essential for developing and using KPIs. A willingness to experiment and change on the basis of experience, whether their own or others', helps businesses better understand social problems and how to address them. Dimagi's approach to setting social performance metrics exemplifies this mindset. Founded in 2002 and led by Jonathan Jackson, one of its cofounders, Dimagi provides software that NGOs and governments can use to develop mobile apps for frontline health-care workers in developing countries. At first Dimagi's primary social metric was the number of active users, which was meant to indicate how many people the technology positively affected. Jackson hoped to improve this metric, because it failed to distinguish between those who actually used the data to improve service delivery to patients and those who collected but did nothing with it.

The company formed a dedicated impact team to refine the social KPI. After exploration, the team created a metric—"worker activity months"—to measure the number of health care providers who were actually applying Dimagi's technology, and it implemented internal data systems to track the metric across all projects. But Jackson soon realized that this, too, was flawed, because the outcome was beyond Dimagi's control: How workers used the software depended more on the actions of Dimagi's clients—NGOs and governments—than on its own.

After reaching out to other social enterprises for advice, Jackson reverted to the number of active users as the company's primary social barometer, yet combined it with a new entity—an impact review team—that focused on qualitative quarterly analyses and discussions about the impact of all projects. These reviews ensure that a team doesn't focus unduly on the quantifiable aspects of a project (revenue, costs, completion dates) but also explores the effectiveness of its service delivery and how that could be improved to better support frontline health-care workers. The team discusses indirect forms of impact as well, such as helping organizations assess their readiness for digitization.

Other successful businesses also complement KPIs with in-depth qualitative assessments of their social performance. For example, the Brazilian impact investing firm Vox Capital hired Jéssica Silva Rios, an executive dedicated to understanding and measuring its impact, and recently made her a full partner. Some companies also incorporate external social indicators developed by independent NGOs such as the Global Reporting Initiative, the Sustainability Accounting Standards Board, and B Lab. For example, Vox Capital monitors whether its rating from the Global Impact Investing Rating System is above average in comparison with other funds in developing markets and adjusts the fees it charges investors accordingly.

Structuring the Organization

It's virtually impossible to succeed on financial and social fronts over the long run if the company isn't designed to support both. Achieving an effective design requires that you think about which organizational activities create economic value and which create social value, how those activities relate to one another, and how you'll try to balance them.

Aligning activities and structure

Some activities create social and economic value at the same time. Others create predominantly one kind of value. For activities that create both kinds, an integrated organizational structure usually makes sense. Otherwise the activities are often best managed separately.

Revolution Foods, founded in 2006 by Kristin Richmond and Kirsten Tobey, provides nutritious lunches to low-income students in the United States. Richmond and Tobey created the company to serve a social purpose, having witnessed how poor food options hold kids back in underfunded schools. Every time they sell a healthful meal to a school, two things happen: They enhance a child's health, and they make money. Their core activity thus creates both kinds of value. As a result, they opted for an integrated structure, with a single manager in charge of operational efficiency, business growth, and the promotion of child well-being. Account managers often engage students in nutrition education (either directly or through community organizations), introducing them to new foods and collecting their feedback on taste. The exposure to healthful foods enhances the long-term wellness of students and supports sales at the same time.

In contrast, the French company ENVIE learned over time that it needed to decouple the two kinds of activities. Launched in 1984, it had the goal of reintegrating long-term unemployed people into the job market by hiring them on two-year contracts to collect and repair used appliances for sale in secondhand shops. The company also provides support and training in how to repair appliances, how to look for a job, how to write a CV, and how to interview. The resale of appliances is what creates economic value. The training to enhance individuals' ability to find jobs outside ENVIE creates social value, but it doesn't make the company more profitable—in fact, it increases costs.

In the early years, staff members were asked to do two jobs: give beneficiaries technical guidance on how to repair or dismantle appliances (economic value) and provide them with social support (social value). However, it was difficult to find supervisors with both social and technical expertise. Even when they had both, the supervisors struggled to balance the two dimensions of their jobs. ENVIE's founders accordingly decided to set up separate organizational units, one for social support and one for repair, to be overseen by social workers and technical experts respectively. This increased the company's effectiveness in generating both kinds of value.

Creating spaces of negotiation

The rub is that tensions inevitably arise—particularly in differentiated structures. Left unattended, they can bring an organization to a halt. The Bolivian microlender Banco Solidario provides a cautionary example. In the 1990s constant resentment and fighting between bankers (concerned with fees and efficiency) and social workers (concerned with the affordability of loans and the livelihoods of microentrepreneurs) essentially froze the company. Loan officers quit left and right, the number of active borrowers plummeted, and the profit margin dropped. We've found that successful dual-purpose companies avoid such paralysis by supplementing traditional organizational structures with mechanisms for surfacing and working through tensions. These mechanisms don't make the tensions disappear—rather, they bring them into the open by letting employees actively discuss trade-offs between creating economic value and creating social value. Such deliberation provides a powerful safety valve and can speed up effective resolution.

Consider Vivractif, another French work-integration company. Founded in 1993, it hires and trains the long-term unemployed at recycling facilities. Those responsible for achieving one kind of goal or the other at the company often did not see eye to eye. While production supervisors managed workers to meet recycling targets, social workers were eager to take them away from the floor for mentorship and job-search training. The company set up quarterly meetings between the two groups so that they could discuss each beneficiary's progress and bring up coordination issues. Joint work planning allowed both to share important deadlines (such as for commercial deliveries or social trainings) and to find joint solutions to scheduling conflicts. This improved productivity and furthered the company's social goals.

Spaces of negotiation can be successful in large companies as well. In one multinational cooperative bank headquartered in Europe, decision makers representing each of the local branches collectively make strategic decisions only after iterative debate, during which different groups of employees are responsible for championing either the social or the financial objectives of the organization. When individuals speak up about issues, their assigned roles prevent tensions from becoming personal.

Hiring and Socializing Employees

Embedding a dual-purpose focus in an organization's DNA requires a workforce with shared values, behaviors, and processes. Hiring and socialization are crucial to getting that right.

Hiring

Employees in a company that pursues dual goals tend to be successful when they understand and connect with both the business and the social mission. We've seen companies mobilize such people by recruiting three types of profiles: hybrid, specialized, and "blank slate."

Hybrid individuals arrive equipped with training or experience in both business and social-value fields, such as environmental science, medicine, social work, and so forth. Such people are able to understand issues in both camps and can connect with employees and other stakeholders of either orientation.

Jean-François Connan is a good example. He was recruited in the late 1980s by Adecco, one of the largest temp work groups in the world, because he had training in industrial maintenance and human resources and experience as a teacher and a mentor for at-risk youth. The company hired him to help address a long-standing problem: A large number of its temp workers lacked strong qualifications. Connan played a leading role in building a dual-purpose subsidiary for Adecco that helps the long-term unemployed reenter the job market by hiring them for temp jobs. His background lets him interact seamlessly with Adecco leaders and corporate clients as well as with local partners (such as nonprofits dedicated to youth mentorship) and those whom they seek to serve. Now he is the company's head of responsibility and social innovation.

But hybrid employees aren't always available and may not always be the best fit. Dual-purpose corporations often hire *specialized* talent, which allows them to tap into deep expertise and networks in each area. The main weakness of this approach is that it is more likely to result in conflict between groups, which may not understand each other's norms, vocabularies, and constraints—especially if the organization separates economic activities from social ones. As a result, tensions and turnover in these companies tend to be higher than in those with an integrated structure, producing a negative effect on the bottom line.

To mitigate this at Dimagi, Jackson explains the primacy of the organization's social purpose on his very first recruitment call with a technical expert (such as a software developer). After hiring, he creates opportunities for the expert to learn about the social business through formal talks, informal office interactions, and even face-to-face fieldwork in the underserved communities with which Dimagi works. Vox Capital, too, has hired managers with technical capabilities (such as fund management) and no experience in a social-mission-driven environment. Yet it systematically screens applicants for their ability to embrace and thus adapt to the company's hybrid culture.

When companies recruit *blank slate* individuals, who have experience in neither business nor the social sector, they put them in entry-level jobs and help them acquire dual values and skills. The Bolivian microcredit lender Los Andes S.A. Caja de Ahorro y Préstamo, founded in 1995, took this approach, hiring university graduates with hardly any professional experience to become loan officers. The sense was that they would embrace a hybrid organizational culture more readily than experienced employees might. Of course, this approach has limitations. Taking inexperienced staffers into an organization may lower productivity. It also requires a considerable investment in training.

Although recruitment strategies obviously must be adapted to specific HR needs, we have observed that hybrid employees tend to be particularly well-suited for managerial and coordination positions; specialists can contribute useful expertise as middle managers in differentiated structures; and blank slates do best in entry-level jobs, where training won't be too challenging.

Socialization
Once people are on board, socializing them can be daunting. Every employee needs to understand, value, and become capable of contributing to both financial and social goals in some form.

Formal approaches to socialization may include companywide events such as annual general assemblies and retreats where dual goals and values are explained, discussed, assessed, and put into perspective. Dedicated trainings can remind employees—particularly those who specialize in just one sector—of the interconnectedness of revenue-generating and social-value-creating activities. Job-shadowing programs and other forms of experiential training can also purposefully bring different groups together. At Vivractif social workers spend at least one day a year alongside recycling supervisors, and vice versa, so that each can learn and relearn about the company from the other perspective.

Another example comes from Oftalmología salauno, a Mexican company cofounded in 2011 by Javier Okhuysen and Carlos Orellana to provide high-quality, low-cost eye care to people who can't otherwise afford it. Although the pair saw economic goals and social goals as connected, they observed that some doctors focused only on patient care, and some managers considered only costs. So they formulated a set of core tenets and shared them at a daylong training for all employees, which clarified the interrelatedness of the company's financial and social aspects and gave employees a shared language for discussing tensions. Okhuysen and Orellana later instituted such sessions for new hires and continue to reinforce the training content in day-to-day interactions.

Spaces of negotiation can be valuable informal socialization opportunities, too. At Vox Capital a weekly time slot allows anyone to pose a question if he or she feels that the company's practices don't align with the organizational mission and values or is witnessing financial-social tradeoffs. Employees haven't shied away from tough topics. Some have asked whether its investment portfolio sufficiently emphasizes the social missions of the businesses, while others have questioned whether the company's approach to raising capital is ethical.

Such conversations pushed cofounder Daniel Izzo to think critically about Vox's principles. "First I thought, It doesn't matter as long as [investors] don't have a say in what we do," he says. "But then someone asked, 'Would you take a drug lord as an investor?' Of course not. So there is a line. But where do we draw it? Do you take money from companies involved in corruption scandals in Brazil? Or from sons and daughters of top executives in those companies?"

Similarly, Bernardo Bonjean, who founded the Brazilian micro-finance organization Avante in 2012, instituted a monthly breakfast where employees could come together and ask him questions. He also shares what's on his mind in letters to employees, discussing everything from the company's KPIs to his concerns about cash flow in the coming months. Okhuysen and Orellana put posters showing a matrix of Oftalmología salauno's four core tenets—commitment, service, reach, and value—in every meeting room. They can refer to these tenets when decision points arise, supporting a shared language among employees.

To encourage questions from employees, it's important to create an environment where people feel safe raising contentious issues. And when employees see changes in thinking and processes result from these discussions, they know that what they say is valued.

Events and conversations aren't the only ways to socialize employees. Promotion and compensation are also important. At the multinational cooperative bank mentioned above, being promoted to general director of a local branch requires excelling in business development, cost reduction, and profit making while also demonstrating a clear adherence to the company's social goals and a willingness to work collaboratively. One candidate for promotion commented, "I have seen many brilliant people fail because they did not embrace our values enough."

Vox Capital, like several other companies we studied, bases individual bonuses on both financial and social performance. Furthermore, Izzo is clear that he does not want the economic inequality that Vox is trying to redress in Brazil reproduced inside the company itself, so the maximum difference between employees' highest and lowest salaries and bonuses is capped at a multiple of 10. (In the United States in 2017 the average ratio of CEO-to-worker compensation was 312:1, according to the Economic Policy Institute.) Other companies, such as Revolution Foods, use shared ownership to motivate employees and increase their commitment to dual performance. Any full-time employee can become a shareholder through stock options. Richmond and Tobey believe that sharing ownership with employees, many of whom live in the low-income communities the company serves, is integral to their social mission.

Practicing Dual-Minded Leadership

Leaders must manage the tensions that inevitably crop up on the path to achieving dual goals. These tensions often involve competition for resources and divergent views about how to reach those goals. Leaders must affirm, embody, and protect both the financial and the social side and address tensions proactively.

Making decisions

Strategic decisions should embody dual goals. Whereas goals reflect aspirations, decisions provide real evidence of leaders' commitment to achieving specific aims. The experience of François-Ghislain Morillon and Sébastien Kopp is a good example.

Morillon and Kopp created Veja in 2004 to sell sneakers made under fair trade and environmentally friendly conditions in small cooperatives in Brazil. When they realized that advertising accounted for 70% of the cost of a typical major brand's sneakers, they made the bold decision not to advertise at all. That allowed them to sell sneakers at a price comparable to what their bigger competitors asked despite having production costs five to seven times as high. To make up for the absence of traditional advertising, the company formed strategic partnerships with high-end fashion brands such as agnès b. and Madewell and stores such as the Galeries Lafayette to increase media exposure, grow sales, and become profitable.

At first Veja's clients—shoe retailers accustomed to the marketing of major sneaker brands—were skeptical. So Veja trained salespeople to educate them about the benefits of its product for people and the environment. Clients and the media now view the "zero ads" decision as evidence of the founders' commitment to their social goals, ultimately both giving the company social impact and making it profitable.

Morillon and Kopp also decided to temper the company's growth, despite increasing consumer demand in the United States. They refused to lower their fair trade and environmental standards to sell more shoes. Instead they decided to set production targets in keeping with the capacity of their fair trade partners while working closely with them to increase that capacity, ensuring a growth rate compatible with financial sustainability. That decision demonstrated, to employees in particular, the genuine commitment of Veja's leaders to their dual goals. In making bold decisions, the cofounders both emphasized the company's priorities and created the conditions for achieving them. They also showed that it's possible to avoid one of the most common pitfalls for dual-purpose companies: prioritizing profits over society when the pressure is on.

Profit allocation is another important area of strategic decision making. Dividends can be capped to ensure that financial goals don't overshadow social ones. When founding Oftalmología salauno, Okhuysen and Orellana pledged to reinvest 100% of their profits for at least seven years, so the investors they selected—a social impact fund, the World Bank, and a private wealth-management fund—knew that no dividends would be paid during that time. Okhuysen explains: "Our investors ultimately expect both financial and social returns on their capital. But the alignment between us around reinvesting profits to improve and grow our network of eye-care clinics has helped ensure that financial goals do not take precedence over our social purpose."

Engaging the board

In successful hybrid companies, board members serve as guardians of the dual purpose. Thus they must collectively bring a combination of business and social expertise to the table. Diversity on the board is important for drawing the organization's attention to both social and financial goals, yet it increases the risk of conflict, because members with different perspectives are more likely to differ as to the best course of action. We have seen some companies experience near-paralyzing governance crises when socially and commercially minded board members with similar levels of influence strongly disagree.

Yet other companies have managed to avoid such crises because a chair or an executive director systematically bridged gaps between the two groups. By fostering regular interactions and information sharing between them, such leaders enabled the groups to develop mutual understanding. Recall the subsidiary Jean-François Connan founded at Adecco. He invited representatives from prominent local nonprofits to join the board as minority shareholders, enabling the company to benefit from their social expertise, networks, and legitimacy and helping to protect the company's social mission. His hybrid experience put Connan in a good position to bridge the gap between the two groups of directors, fostering common ground by constantly reminding each of the importance of the other.

Some major roadblocks to dual-purpose organizing are outside a company's control. Chief among them is that the business ecosystem is still set up to prioritize the creation of shareholder wealth. The Global Reporting Initiative, the Sustainability Accounting Standards Board, and B Lab, among others, have taken steps to overcome some of these barriers. Each of them has created metrics for tracking companies' impact on the lives of employees and customers, the communities served, and the environment, providing organizations with benchmarks. What is at stake is ensuring that companies don't pick and choose areas of social focus on the basis of convenience.

Rating agencies are only one part of the ecosystem, however. Although more changes are under way—such as awarding legal status to public benefit corporations in the United States, community interest companies in the United Kingdom, and *società benefit* in Italy—the regulations, educational standards, investment models, and norms that govern the production of economic value and social value are still mostly distinct from one another. As an increasing number of companies engage in hybrid organizing, the systems that support business also need to change.

But changing organizations and the ecosystem that surrounds them is difficult. Companies must fight the inertia of inherited ways of thinking and behaving. Trade-offs and tensions are inevitable, and success is more likely when leaders address them head-on. The four levers we have outlined are meant to help.

Originally published in March–April 2019. Reprint R1902K

How CEOs Manage Time

by Michael E. Porter and Nitin Nohria

IN THE LEXICON OF MANAGEMENT, the CEO is the epitome of leader-ship. Yet surprisingly little is known about this unique role. While CEOs are the ultimate power in their companies, they face chal-lenges and constraints that few others recognize.

Running a large global company is an exceedingly complex job. The scope of the organization's managerial work is vast, encom-passing functional agendas, business unit agendas, multiple orga-nizational levels, and myriad external issues. It also involves a wide array of constituencies—shareholders, customers, employees, the board, the media, government, community organizations, and more. Unlike any other executive, the CEO has to engage with them all. On top of that, the CEO must be the internal and external face of the organization through good times and bad.

CEOs, of course, have a great deal of help and resources at their disposal. However, they, more than anyone else in the organization, confront an acute scarcity of one resource. That resource is *time*. There is never enough time to do everything that a CEO is respon-sible for. Despite this, CEOs remain accountable for *all* the work of their organizations.

The way CEOs allocate their time and their presence—where they choose to personally participate—is crucial, not only to their own effectiveness but also to the performance of their companies. Where and how CEOs are involved determines what gets done and signals priorities for others. It also affects their legitimacy. A CEO who doesn't spend enough time with colleagues will seem insular and out of touch, whereas one who spends too much time in direct decision making will risk being seen as a micromanager and erode employees' initiative. A CEO's schedule (indeed, any leader's schedule), then, is a manifestation of *how* the leader leads and sends powerful messages to the rest of the organization.

A crucial missing link in understanding the time allocation of CEOs—and making it more effective—has been systematic data on what they actually do. Research on that has tended either to cover a small handful of CEOs, like the 1973 study in which Henry Mintzberg closely observed five chief executives (some of whom led nonprofits) for five days each, or to rely on large surveys that cover short periods (such as our HBS colleague Raffaella Sadun's 2017 study based on daily phone surveys with 1,114 CEOs from a wide variety of companies in six countries over one week).

Our study, which we launched in 2006, offers the first comprehensive and detailed examination of CEO time use in large, complex companies over an extended period. To date, we have tracked the time allocation of 27 CEOs—two women and 25 men—for a full quarter (three months) each. Their companies, which are primarily public, had an average annual revenue of $13.1 billion during the study period. These leaders were all participants in the New CEO Workshop, an intensive program that every year brings newly appointed CEOs of large companies to Harvard Business School in two cohorts of 10 to 12 each. In total just over 300 CEOs have attended it.

In the study each CEO's executive assistant (EA) was trained to code the CEO's time in 15-minute increments, 24 hours a day and seven days a week, and to regularly verify that coding with the CEO. The resulting data set reveals where, how, and with whom the CEO spent his or her time and on what activities, topics, and tasks. Because it also covers what CEOs do outside of work, we have visibility into how CEOs balance work and personal life. In all, we collected and coded data on nearly 60,000 CEO hours.

After CEOs completed the time-tracking phase, we shared their data with them, comparing it with anonymized data of the other CEOs we

Idea in Brief

The Problem

Managing the immense demands on their time is one of the biggest challenges CEOs face. Yet knowledge about how CEOs actually use time is almost nonexistent.

The Study

The authors tracked the activities of CEOs at 27 large companies 24/7 for 13 weeks and then held intensive debriefs with them. The resulting data set offers deep insights not just into time management but into the CEO's role itself.

The Findings

Leaders must learn to simultaneously manage seemingly contradictory dualities—integrating direct decision making with indirect levers like strategy and culture, balancing internal and external constituencies, proactively driving an agenda while responding to unfolding events, exercising leverage while being mindful of constraints, focusing on tangible decisions and the symbolic significance of every action, and combining formal power and legitimacy.

had studied up to that point. These intensive debriefings often included the CEOs' reflections on the pressures they faced in managing time, and on their mistakes and lessons learned. We also shared our accumulated data with the participants in each New CEO Workshop. In our discussions, CEOs routinely described managing time as one of their greatest challenges. The observations, questions, and personal approaches to allocating time they shared further enriched our understanding.

In this article we will do three things:

First, we'll provide a descriptive analysis of the data. How much time do CEOs spend at work versus on personal activities? How much do they spend in meetings versus thinking and reflecting alone? How much do they rely on email versus face-to-face conversation? Do they spend more time inside the company or outside, more with customers or investors? We'll answer those questions—and many more.

Second, we will offer prescriptions for how CEOs can manage their time more effectively across their many responsibilities. One of our most striking observations is that the way leaders allocate their time varies considerably. (See the exhibit "Looking Beyond the Averages.") Some of this variation reflects differences in their businesses and management practices. However, many time allocation decisions, such as participation in company rituals that offer limited return, reflect legacy norms and cultures, as well as a CEO's own habits. In our debriefings the CEOs all acknowledged that there were important areas where they could be using their time better. On the basis of these discussions and those with the hundreds of other CEOs in our workshops, we are convinced that every leader can improve his or her time management.

Finally, we will reflect on what our rich data reveals about the overall role of the CEO. A CEO has to simultaneously manage multiple dimensions of influence, which all contain dualities, or seeming contradictions, that effective CEOs must integrate. Understanding this broader view of the role is essential to success and also provides an important perspective for managing time well.

While our research focuses on the CEO role in large, complex companies, its findings have implications for all leaders (including executives of nonprofits) looking for ways to use their time and influence more effectively.

The Job Is All-Consuming

CEOs are always on, and there is always more to be done. The leaders in our study worked 9.7 hours per weekday, on average. They also conducted business on 79% of weekend days, putting in an average of 3.9 hours daily, and on 70% of vacation days, averaging 2.4 hours daily. As these figures show, the CEO's job is relentless.

About half (47%) of a CEO's work was done at company headquarters. The rest was conducted while visiting other company locations, meeting external constituencies, commuting, traveling, and at home. Altogether, the CEOs in our study worked an average of 62.5 hours a week.

Why such a grueling schedule? Because it is essential to the role. Every constituency associated with a company wants direct contact with the person at the top. As much as CEOs rely on delegation, they can't hand off everything. They have to spend at least some time with each constituency in order to provide direction, create alignment, win support, and gather the information needed to make good decisions. Travel is also an absolute must. You can't run a domestic company, let alone a global one, from headquarters alone. As a CEO, you have to be out and about.

Making time for personal well-being

Given that work could consume every hour of their lives, CEOs have to set limits so that they can preserve their health and their relationships with family and friends. Most of the CEOs in our study recognized that. They slept, on average, 6.9 hours a night, and many had regular exercise regimens, which consumed about 9% of their nonwork hours (or about 45 minutes a day). To sustain the intensity of the job, CEOs need to train—just as elite athletes do. That means allocating time for health, fitness, and rest.

We paid special attention to the 25% of time—or roughly six hours a day—when CEOs were awake and not working. Typically, they spent about half those hours with their families, and most had learned to become very disciplined about this. Most also found at least some hours (2.1 a day, on average) for downtime, which included everything from watching television and reading for pleasure to hobbies like photography.

The CEO's job is mentally and physically demanding. Activities that preserve elements of normal life keep CEOs grounded and better able to engage with colleagues and workers—as opposed to distant, detached, and disconnected. CEOs also have to make time for their own professional renewal and development (which our data showed was often the biggest casualty of a packed schedule). And they must be careful, as our colleague Tom DeLong puts it, not to become "like race car drivers and treat home like a pit stop."

They Work Face-to-Face

The top job in a company involves primarily face-to-face interactions, which took up 61% of the work time of the CEOs we studied. Another 15% was spent on the phone or reading and replying to written correspondence. The final 24% was spent on electronic communications.

Face-to-face interaction is the best way for CEOs to exercise influence, learn what's really going on, and delegate to move forward the multiple agendas that must be advanced. It also allows CEOs to best support and coach the people they work closely with. How a CEO spends face-to-face time is viewed as a signal of what or who is important; people watch this more carefully than most CEOs recognize.

Avoiding the lure of email

In theory, email helps leaders cut down on face-to-face meetings and improve productivity. In reality, many find it ineffective and a dangerous time sink—but one they have trouble avoiding. Email interrupts work, extends the workday, intrudes on time for family and thinking, and is not conducive to thoughtful discussions. CEOs are endlessly copied on FYI emails. They feel pressure to respond because ignoring an email seems rude.

CEOs should recognize that the majority of emails cover issues that needn't involve them and often draw them into the operational weeds. Conversely, emails from the CEO can create a downward spiral of unnecessary communication and set the wrong norms, especially if the CEO sends them late at night, on weekends, or on holidays. It then becomes easy for everyone in an organization to fall into the bad habit of overusing electronic communications.

That's why setting proper expectations and norms for what emails the CEO needs to receive—and when he or she will respond—is essential. Norms are necessary for the others in the organization as well, to prevent email from having a cascading effect on everyone, wasting precious hours and intruding on personal time. One way for the CEO to stay ahead of the digital avalanche is to have an adept EA filter messages and delegate many of them to others before the CEO even sees them. In the end, though, there is no substitute for being disciplined about resisting the siren call of electronic communications. This is a topic our CEOs were often animated about, and best practices in this area are still emerging.

Some CEOs in our study have begun to use videoconferencing as an alternative to face-to-face meetings, especially to cut down on travel for themselves and for team members who might otherwise have to come to see them. Although such efficiencies should surely be sought, CEOs must never forget that at its core their job is a face-to-face one.

They Are Agenda Driven

CEOs oversee a large number of organizational units and work streams and countless types of decisions. Our research finds that they should have an explicit personal agenda and that most do. A clear and effective agenda optimizes the CEO's limited time; without one, demands from the loudest constituencies will take over, and the most important work won't get done.

A good agenda sets priorities for the CEO's personal involvement over the coming period. But it is not unidimensional; rather, it is a matrix including both broader areas for improvement and specific matters that need to be addressed, and it combines time-bound goals with more open-ended priorities.

In our study we asked each CEO to describe the agenda he or she was pursuing during the quarter being tracked and to highlight the hours devoted primarily to advancing it. Every executive provided an agenda. We found that the CEOs invested significant time—43%, on average—in activities that furthered their agendas. Some were far more disciplined about this than others: Time devoted to the core agenda varied widely, ranging from 14% to 80% of leaders' work hours. Most CEOs we talked with agreed that the more time they spent on their agendas, the better they felt about their use of time.

Overall, we found that an explicit agenda is one of the CEO's most important tools for making progress on multiple work streams simultaneously, addressing differences in the rate of progress across priorities, and using time effectively despite the need to respond personally to unforeseen events.

Advancing the agenda

Keeping time allocation aligned with CEOs' top priorities is so crucial that we suggest that every quarter CEOs make a point of looking back at whether their schedule for the previous period adequately matched up with their personal agenda. They should also update the agenda to reflect current circumstances.

Four Behaviors of Great Executive Assistants

EXECUTIVE ASSISTANTS PLAY A VITAL ROLE in shielding CEOs from distractions and unnecessary activities and ensuring that leaders' limited time is used well. We often hear CEOs say that a highly skilled EA can dramatically increase their efficiency and effectiveness, and our research supports that view.

EAs often feel conflicting pressures, however, that can result in poor scheduling choices. For instance, although they may recognize that CEOs need time alone, our study shows that many EAs believe that a full CEO calendar signals that they're doing their job. They tend to book back-to-back appointments, limiting time for spontaneous communications or solitary reflection. In addition, while EAs recognize that protecting a CEO's time is one of their most important duties, some have a human reluctance to say no to people (especially colleagues in the organization). That allows unessential meetings to creep into the CEO's day. Conversely, other EAs take their traditional role as gatekeeper too far, maintaining such tight control over access that their bosses risk being seen as aloof or inaccessible.

Finding the right balance in managing the CEO's time requires judgment and emotional intelligence. It also requires strong communication skills, because an EA speaks for the CEO and can affect how a leader comes across. In our research we have identified four key behaviors that drive better performance:

1. **Understand the leader's agenda.** CEOs should have a written agenda detailing their top priorities (updated quarterly) and should spend much of their time on activities that advance the agenda. It's critical

---

CEOs can benefit from making their personal agenda explicit to others. Their EAs and leadership teams both need to know and understand it so that they can stay aligned with it. (See the sidebar "Four Behaviors of Great Executive Assistants.") This understanding will help team members assume ownership of the goals and priorities of the work the CEO needs them to drive.

Dealing with unfolding developments

A good portion of our CEOs' time (about 36%, on average) was spent in a reactive mode, handling unfolding issues, both internal and external. For many chief executives, it is not immediately clear when

that the EA internalize this agenda and use it as a lens through which each meeting request is viewed. The CEO's responsibility is to ensure that the EA knows the agenda and the importance of keeping the schedule aligned with it.

2. **Include all the relevant players.** Managers at all levels tend to complain about having too many meetings. One solution is to try keeping meetings small and inviting only those whose attendance is essential. However, good CEOs delegate well, and to do so they need their direct reports and affected managers to be present. Otherwise, extra rounds of communication and follow-up will be needed after meetings. Good EAs avoid that problem by getting the right players in the room to begin with.

3. **Recognize the value of spontaneity.** Most CEOs are overbooked. They would benefit from more time to walk the hallways and initiate unplanned interactions. They also need room to react to events that can't be anticipated; leaving some open time in the leader's day will help EAs avoid frequently canceling and rescheduling appointments.

4. **Zealously protect personal and family time.** EAs should recognize that the long hours, travel, and stress of the CEO job can take a toll. Time with family and friends, regular exercise, and opportunities to recharge and reflect are crucial to effectiveness and avoiding burnout. EAs' daily scheduling choices play an important part in helping CEOs maintain the balance they need to succeed over the long haul.

and how to address such issues or how much time to devote to them. Say that a member of the CEO's senior leadership team leaves a meeting looking upset. Should the CEO follow up with that person right away to make sure everything is OK? Should the CEO just wait and let the team member cool off? Sometimes emerging problems seem small at first but balloon into larger distractions if the CEO doesn't attend to them. In other instances a CEO's intervention makes an issue bigger than it might have been. It's essential for CEOs to figure out appropriate responses to these unfolding situations.

Every now and then, CEOs find themselves dealing with a sudden, full-blown crisis—a product or safety failure, a hostile activist's bid, a serious cyberattack, or even an external catastrophe such as a tsunami or a terrorist attack. Most of our CEOs (89%) spent some time on crises. Though on average it was small (1% of work time during the quarter we tracked), the total amount spent varied a great deal among the leaders in our study. Crises can create make-or-break moments in a CEO's leadership. In dealing with them, CEOs need to be highly visible and personally involved; the response to such events can't be delegated. Showing genuine concern for the people affected, avoiding defensiveness, holding everyone together, and creating confidence that the organization will not only survive but emerge stronger are some of the things CEOs need to do during these times.

Limiting routine responsibilities

A surprisingly significant fraction (11%, on average) of our CEOs' work time was consumed by routine duties. Such activities varied considerably across CEOs, running the gamut from review meetings to board meetings, earnings calls, and investor days.

Operating reviews are a major component of a CEO's routine tasks. Their number, frequency, and length ranged widely across the leaders we studied, and our discussions suggested that some CEOs—especially those who had been COOs—overinvested in reviews that could be delegated to direct reports.

The ability of CEOs to control what we term "have-to-dos" was also quite variable. Have-to-dos include rituals such as giving welcome talks to new employees. These can play an important symbolic role and help reinforce the company's values and culture. By thoughtfully choosing which of these events to attend, CEOs can set the tone of their relationship with the organization. Yet a CEO must be disciplined about ensuring that feel-good activities don't collectively take up more time than he or she can afford.

Our discussions suggest that CEOs need to take a hard look at every activity that falls into the routine and have-to-do categories. They must ask whether it serves an important purpose or is simply a company habit, something instituted by the predecessor, or a carry-over from the CEO's previous role.

They Rely Heavily on Their Direct Reports

A CEO's direct reports are the company's most senior executives and include some of its most skilled managers. They span all the key elements of the business and offer CEOs the greatest opportunity for leverage. The leadership team, working together, can be the glue that helps the CEO integrate the company and get the work done.

In our study about half (46%) of a CEO's time with internal constituencies was spent with one or more direct reports, and 21% of it was spent only with direct reports. The total time spent with direct reports ranged from a low of 32% of time with internal constituencies to a high of 67%. When we explored that variation, we found that CEOs were more likely to spend time with their reports present when they had greater confidence in them.

We found that it's critical for each member of the leadership team to have the capabilities to excel and earn the CEO's full trust and support. Any weaknesses in this group significantly reduce the CEO's effectiveness, because dealing with work that reports should have handled, and cleaning up after them, eats up valuable time. In fact, when our CEOs gathered as a group across cohorts to see how things were going after they had been in office awhile, their number one regret was not setting high-enough standards in selecting direct reports. Many CEOs told us this was because they focused too much on the present and not enough on the future when they first stepped into the role. Direct reports who could manage the status quo were often not the ones who could help the CEO take the company to a new level.

The more CEOs can delegate to their leadership team, the better they generally feel about their use of time. It eases the burden of needing to get personally engaged, following up, and asking others to report back. Since CEOs see their direct reports so frequently, it is also easy to stay in touch with how things are going with matters they are handling.

Staying connected to other managers

The CEOs in our study also spent considerable time (32% of their time with internal constituencies, on average) with a broader group of senior leaders, often called the top 100 (plus or minus). Many in this group report to the CEO's direct reports. We found that time with this next level of leadership was well spent. The top 100 are often the driving force for execution in the organization, and direct contact with the CEO can help align and motivate them. These leaders are also key to succession planning: Some will be candidates to replace the company's most senior executives. Given that the people at this level are often a generation younger, a few may eventually even be candidates to succeed the CEO. So getting to know them personally can be very useful.

Not surprisingly, the CEOs in our study spent less time with lower-level managers (14%, on average) and even less time with rank-and-file employees (about 6%, on average). However, our research suggests that effective CEOs need to be careful to maintain a human face in the organization. They must stay approachable and find ways to meaningfully engage with employees at all levels. This not only keeps them in touch with what is really going on in the company but helps them model and communicate organizational values throughout the workforce.

Direct human contact with the rank and file also grounds CEOs and helps them understand employees' reality. CEOs face a real risk of operating in a bubble and never seeing the actual world their workers face. Relationships with employees at multiple levels also build a CEO's legitimacy and trustworthiness in the eyes of employees, which is essential to motivating them and winning their support.

Knowing what is going on

Spending time with the rank and file, and with savvy external frontline constituencies, is also an indispensable way to gain reliable information on what is really going on in the company and in the industry. This is a major CEO challenge. Some CEOs get frontline contact by walking the hallways and factory floors, and using mechanisms like periodic lunches, unscheduled visits, and carefully designed field trips to customer and company sites. Others use group interactions, such as town halls, to foster genuine and open conversations with a large cross section of employees (rather than present slide decks). Our data indicates that CEOs have varying success in carving out time for such steps, however.

They Manage Using Broad Integrating Mechanisms

CEOs must avoid trying to do too much themselves. It just isn't possible for them to make or even ratify most decisions directly. Instead, effective CEOs put in place well-designed structures and processes that help everyone else in the organization make good choices. These inform, support, enable, and integrate the work of others while building the organization's capabilities.

The most powerful integrating mechanisms include strategy (on which CEOs in our study spent an average of 21% of their work time), functional and business unit reviews (25% of their time), developing people and relationships (25% of their time), matching organizational structure and culture with the needs of the business (16% of their time), and mergers and acquisitions (4% of their time).

Harnessing strategy

The CEO's single most powerful lever is ensuring that every unit—and the company as a whole—has a clear, well-defined strategy. Strategy creates alignment among the many decisions within a business and across the organization. By spending time on strategy, a CEO provides direction for the company, helps make its value proposition explicit, and defines how it will compete in the marketplace and differentiate itself from rivals. Strategy also provides clarity on what the company will *not* do. A compelling strategy—if well understood throughout the organization—is motivating and energizing. And without clarity on strategy, the CEO will be drawn into too many tactical decisions.

In large, complex firms, CEOs can almost never spend enough time on strategy—they must constantly be working to shape it, refine it, communicate it, reinforce it, and help people recognize when they may be drifting from it. CEOs must also ensure that the strategy is renewed from time to time and based on changes in the environment. Portfolio choices such as divestitures, mergers, and acquisitions are critical to strategy, and a CEO must be personally involved with them.

Aligning organizational structure and culture

To foster appropriate decisions across the company, the organization's structure needs to be aligned with its strategy. Otherwise, the CEO will be drawn into endless adjudication among units. It can also become a big drain on the CEO and others if the organization is constantly lurching from one structure to another.

Culture—which encompasses an organization's values, beliefs, and norms—is another key CEO lever for reinforcing strategy and influencing how the organization as a whole goes about doing its work. CEOs can shape a company's culture in many ways, from the time they spend talking about it at various forums, to personally living the valued behaviors, to recognizing, rewarding, and celebrating those who exemplify the desired culture while taking corrective action with those who don't. It is the CEO's job to champion the organization's culture and constantly look for opportunities to strengthen it.

Designing, monitoring, and improving processes

CEOs must ensure that the company's strategy is being well executed. This will occur when the organization has rigorous processes through which work—such as marketing plans, pricing, product development, and strategy development itself—is done. Good processes bring together the best organizational knowledge and keep the CEO from continually having to override decisions.

Formal reviews are essential to monitoring whether the company is delivering the required process performance. Though these consume a quarter of a CEO's total work time, they allow CEOs to track progress, provide regular feedback, uphold high standards, and ensure timely course corrections. Reviews are also necessary to make sure that lessons learned are used to enhance the various processes through which work gets done.

However, excessive participation in reviews can get the CEO too involved in the company's operations and mired in unnecessary details. We talked a lot with the CEOs in our study about this problem. We have found, again and again, that many have a hard time shedding the COO or president roles they may have previously held.

Some also forget that their senior team should bear the primary responsibility for many reviews and keep the CEO informed on a regular basis.

When CEOs fail to delegate reviews to direct reports who can handle them, they erode the autonomy and accountability of their management teams. That doesn't help CEOs get the best out of others.

Developing people and relationships

Building the company's leadership pipeline is an important CEO function in its own right. We have found that CEOs must be personally committed to and be involved in improving the quality of the company's leaders. They cannot just leave this task to HR. Leadership choices are also pivotal in shaping the company's culture. Who gets hired, promoted, or fired signals what is truly valued by the CEO and the company.

CEOs need to get the most out of an organization's talent, and to do that, they must forge personal connections. Our CEOs spent another quarter of their total work time in meetings that focused on building relationships. When trust is mutual, delegation comes more naturally, agreement is easier to reach, and less monitoring and follow-up are necessary. Good relationships also make people more likely to give you the benefit of the doubt when you need it— and to tell you the truth, which is invaluable at the top.

The time CEOs spend building social capital through a network of personal relationships has many benefits and is time well spent.

They Are Always in Meetings

CEOs attend an endless stream of meetings, each of which can be totally different from the one before and the one that follows. Their sheer number and variety is a defining feature of the top job. On average, the leaders in our study had 37 meetings of assorted lengths in any given week and spent 72% of their total work time in meetings.

Looking beyond the averages

How much do CEOs' practices differ? We've ranked the variation in their uses of time from the lowest to the highest.

	Degree of variation (standard deviation/mean)	
Meeting time	0.14	
Face-to-face interactions	0.14	
Time with internal constituencies	0.14	
Total workweek obligations	0.14	
One-hour meetings	0.21	Low
Scheduled time	0.22	
One-on-one meetings	0.24	
CEO-initiated meetings	0.28	
Weekend days worked	0.31	
Core agenda time	0.36	
Meetings per week	0.36	
Electronic communication	0.38	
Time with direct reports	0.39	
Functional and business-unit review time	0.41	Medium
People and relationship time	0.44	
Strategy time	0.48	
Time on organizational structure and culture	0.54	
Spontaneous time	0.59	
Have-to-do time	0.59	
Time with other outside commitments	0.59	
Two-hour-plus blocks of alone time	0.70	High
Time with rank-and-file employees	0.71	
Exercise time	0.89	
Time with investors	0.95	
Time with customers	1.10	

Making meetings shorter and more effective

CEOs need to regularly review which meetings are truly needed and which can be delegated, and to let go of ones they were accustomed to in previous roles.

They should also take a hard look at meeting length. In our study, meetings that lasted an hour accounted for 32% of a CEO's meetings, on average. Meetings that were longer accounted for 38%, and shorter meetings, 30%. We found that the length of meetings was often a matter of organizational or personal habit or both—a default length (like one hour) was the norm.

"Standard" meeting times should be revisited with an eye toward shortening them. Doing this can significantly enhance a CEO's efficiency. In our debriefs, CEOs confessed that one-hour meetings could often be cut to 30 or even 15 minutes. Another good way to streamline things is to reset meeting norms: Every meeting should have a clear agenda, and to minimize repetition, attendees should come prepared. Effective CEOs spread these meeting norms throughout the organization.

Some CEOs were worried that they might appear standoffish if someone asked for an hour and the CEO (or the EA) offered 30 minutes. But we have found that meeting length is worth confronting. "Whatever they ask for, cut it in half," said one CEO.

Another important meeting attribute is the number and composition of attendees. One-on-one meetings were the most common (accounting for 42% of CEOs' meetings, on average), followed by meetings with two to five participants (21%). Although every CEO had meetings involving large groups of 50 or more—like town halls, leadership off-sites, or all-company meetings—these were infrequent (5% of meetings).

The emphasis on one-on-one and small group meetings makes sense for enabling delegation and relationship building, and allows confidentiality. But leaders should also look for opportunities to bring the right people together. An essential part of the CEO's role is to align various internal and external constituencies around a common understanding of issues, decisions, and action agendas. Having the right people in the room is a powerful way to build that alignment and avoid the need for repetitive, time-consuming inter-actions to bring everyone along.

Allowing for accessibility and spontaneity

The vast majority of our CEOs' time (75%, on average) was sched-uled in advance. The CEOs initiated more than half (51%) of their meetings themselves.

While controlling the nature and number of meetings is essential, we also found that CEOs need to regularly set aside time for more spontaneous interaction (which represented 25% of their work time in our study). This frees up space for same-day appointments ini-tiated by others, for opportune conversations or meetings, and for responding to unfolding events.

The amount of time our CEOs allowed for spontaneous meetings varied considerably, ranging from 3% to 61%. In our debriefings, CEOs who discovered that they had left little room for spur-of-the-moment meetings were often surprised and quick to recognize the need for change.

Spontaneity and accessibility enhance a CEO's legitimacy. Lead-ers whose schedules are always booked up or whose EAs see them-selves as gatekeepers and say no to too many people risk being viewed as imperious, self-important, or out of touch. EAs play a key role in finding the right balance here.

Carving out alone time

It's also vital for CEOs to schedule adequate uninterrupted time by themselves so that they can have space to reflect and prepare for meetings. In our study, CEOs spent 28% of their work time alone, on average—but again, that varied a great deal, from a low of 10% to a high of 48%. Unfortunately, too much of this alone time (59% of it) was fragmented into blocks of an hour or less; too little (18%) was in blocks of two hours or longer. CEOs need to cordon off mean-ingful amounts of alone time and avoid dissipating it by dealing with immediate matters, especially their in-boxes. This proved to be a common problem among the CEOs in our study, who readily acknowledged it.

Given that time in the office is easily eaten up, alone time outside the office is particularly beneficial. Long-distance travel out of contact with the office often provides critical thinking time, and many CEOs swear by it. To capitalize on it, CEOs should avoid traveling with an entourage.

They Juggle Many External Constituencies

While the CEOs we studied spent the majority of their time (70%, on average) dealing with internal constituencies, a good chunk (30%, on average) was spent with outsiders: 16% with business partners (such as customers, suppliers, bankers, investors, consultants, lawyers, PR firms, and other service providers), 5% with the company's board of directors, and 9% on other outside commitments (service on other boards, industry groups, dealing with the media and the government, and community and philanthropic activities).

External constituencies can be just as demanding as internal ones. Everyone wants to talk to the CEO, and dealing with external stakeholders is time-consuming. It often involves longer workdays and time away from headquarters and from home. There is a risk of drifting toward outside commitments less tied to company success.

Finding time for customers

Most of our CEOs were dismayed to discover how little time they spent with their customers—just 3%, on average. It surprised some even more to learn that this was less than the amount they spent with consultants. The scant time devoted to customers is partly a function of the huge scope of internal responsibilities: As an executive ascends from managing a line of business (which involves more-frequent customer contact) to the job of leading the entire company, it is natural for customer-facing time to decline.

Nonetheless, the CEOs in our study clearly felt that 3% was too low. Customers are a key source of independent information about the company's progress, industry trends, and competitors. In the B2B space, meeting with customers' CEOs is highly valuable, since peer conversations can be very candid. In B2C companies, there are also rich opportunities for customer contact. For retail CEOs, for example, store visits—especially unannounced ones—are an indispensable way to talk to regular customers, not just the company staff.

Some CEOs systematically schedule time with customers. The CEO of a financial services firm in our study, for instance, aims to meet face-to-face with one customer a day. A manufacturing CEO allocates two days a month to customer visits. Other CEOs try to build customer visits into their travel. A habit of some type seems to be the most reliable way to ensure enough customer time.

Limiting time with investors

On average, our CEOs spent only 3% of their total work time on investors. Most of them found this surprising; they tended to believe they spent more. But while more time is likely to be better when it comes to customers, the same is not true with investors. Too many meetings with investors can easily become a time sink and can draw the CEO into trying to manage the stock price rather than focusing on business fundamentals. Staying in touch with a few key buy-side investors, doing quarterly calls, and holding an annual investor day may be all a CEO needs to do—unless, of course, the company is dealing with serious investor unrest or activism. By and large, the CEOs in our study seem to have discovered such focus over time, after getting caught up early in their tenures in too much investor relations.

Limiting unrelated outside commitments

There is a real risk that CEOs will get distracted by outside activities not directly connected to the business, where they are in high demand and which often involve worthy community and social issues. Such activities consumed an average of almost 2% of the work time of the CEOs in our study. While CEOs should give back to their communities and play the role of business statespeople, they should carefully restrict the hours they personally spend on such activities and on participating in business groups. Though the CEO's presence can be important, overseeing and managing such work does not require the CEO and can be delegated to direct reports, for whom it is motivational and provides professional development opportunities.

Finding time for directors

All our CEOs understood the importance of spending time with their boards. In our study, interacting with directors accounted for 5% of CEOs' total work time, or 41 hours a quarter, on average. But again we saw significant variation: One CEO spent six hours with directors; another spent 165.

A CEO must never forget that the board is his or her boss and that "managing up" is vital to success. However, that involves more than board meetings, committee meetings, and board retreats; CEOs must find time to build meaningful one-on-one relationships with individual directors. This is essential to take advantage of each board member's particular expertise and perspective. At board meetings, it's often not clear where each director is coming from, but that knowledge is crucial in crises and when dealing with controversial topics. CEOs also need to keep the directors well informed and engage with them between meetings through newsletters and updates. A common understanding and alignment with the board is important in periods of stress or market challenge.

Dimensions of the CEO's Role and Influence

The data on CEOs' time use reveals that the sheer complexity of their role—the myriad types of work, activities, and constituencies—is much greater than has previously been documented or perhaps even understood.

In examining the CEO's role, we have come to see that their work entails six dimensions of influence. Each involves a duality—a seeming contradiction, akin to yin and yang—that CEOs must manage simultaneously in order to be effective. (See the exhibit "Managing the Dimensions of CEO Influence.")

First, CEOs clearly have *direct* influence over many issues and decisions, as their numerous reviews and one-on-one meetings reveal. However, the inherent limits on CEOs' time and knowledge

Managing the dimensions of CEO influence

Chief executives exert influence along six dimensions, each of which involves a duality, or seeming contradiction akin to yin and yang. Managing these dualities simultaneously is a hallmark of effective CEOs.

Direct

The CEO is directly involved in numerous agendas and makes many decisions.

Indirect

The CEO also exerts much influence over the work of others, using integrative mechanisms, processes, structures, and norms.

Internal

The CEO works with the senior team and with employees at all other levels to get all the organization's work done.

External

The CEO also engages myriad external constituencies, serving as the face of the company, and must bring these external perspectives to the organization.

Proactive

The CEO must articulate a sense of purpose, have a forward-looking vision, and lead the company to greater success.

Reactive

The CEO must also respond to events as they unfold, from daily issues to full-blown crises that will prove to have a major impact on the company's success.

Leverage

CEOs' position and control of resources give them immense clout.

Constraints

CEOs are constrained by the need to build buy-in, bring others along, and send the right message.

Tangible

The CEO makes many decisions about concrete things like strategic direction, structure, resource allocation, and the selection of key people.

Symbolic

Much of CEOs' influence proves to be intangible and symbolic; their actions set the tone, communicate norms, shape values, and provide meaning.

Power

CEOs hold formal power and authority in the company that is reinforced by their competence and track record.

Legitimacy

CEOs' influence also rests on legitimacy that comes from their character and the trust they earn from employees through their demonstrated values, fairness, and commitment to the organization.

mean that much of their influence must also be *indirect*. Good CEOs are very much in charge but work through others using strategy, culture, and effective organizational processes that drive sound analysis and alignment across the organization. CEOs need to learn how to marry direct and indirect influence.

Second, much of a CEO's work necessarily involves *internal* constituencies and managerial tasks, and our data verifies the overwhelming amount of such work to be done. However, CEOs are unique in the degree to which they must also engage and influence numerous *external* constituencies and represent the company to the world. Effective CEOs connect their internal and external roles by bringing outside perspectives into the work of the company. They also need to make sure outside constituencies understand the company's work and value.

Third, much of a CEO's work is inherently *proactive*: It involves anticipating problems, gathering the facts, conducting analyses, and making sound and timely choices. Here, the CEO sets and drives the agenda. However, *reacting* well to unplanned and unforeseen events and crises is some of the most important work CEOs do. Choices here, and the CEO's personal presence or lack of presence, can have major consequences both outside and within the organization. Such periods can make or break a company and the CEO's own capacity to lead.

Fourth, while CEOs have a great deal of *leverage* to exert because of their position in the hierarchy and access to resources, they also face numerous—and often unrecognized—*constraints* and complexities in exercising that leverage. They are constrained in how often they can overturn decisions that have been brought to them for approval or how quickly they can drive changes without securing the support and buy-in of their senior team and board of directors. They must identify the group or people who are needed to bring about a change and then figure out how to win over the leader that will mobilize them. CEOs must find the right balance between taking full advantage of the leverage they possess, while being equally sensitive to the constraints they must navigate and the constituencies they must bring along. Otherwise, resistance will emerge and come back to bite them.

Fifth, while much of the CEO's influence is highly *tangible,* involving decisions about things like strategic priorities, budget targets, and people selection, some of the CEO's greatest influence is *symbolic.* This comes from the meaning people attach to a CEO's actions. What CEOs do (and don't do), including everyday things like how they dress, what cars they drive, where they park, where they eat, and whom they talk to and how—always sends implicit messages to the company and its constituencies. Everything a CEO does affects what the organization focuses on, its norms of behavior, and its culture and values. The symbolic effects of CEOs' choices can reach even further than their specific actions.

Sixth, CEOs hold a great deal of formal *power* and authority, and exercise it in the many ways we have described. However, power, authority, competence, and even results are insufficient to truly ensure their success. Effective CEOs combine formal power and authority with *legitimacy.* CEOs achieve legitimacy when employees believe in them as people and as leaders. They earn legitimacy in multiple ways—by demonstrating values, ethics, fairness, and a selfless commitment to the company and its people, among other things. Legitimacy gives rise to motivation that goes far beyond carrying out orders and can lead to extraordinary organizational performance. CEO time allocation, then, is not simply a matter of what

What Do CEOs Actually Do?

WHILE WE REALIZE THAT CORPORATE leaders are really busy, we know surprisingly little about their day-to-day schedules. To fill that gap, in 2006 Harvard Business School professors Michael Porter and Nitin Nohria began asking participants of their New CEO Workshop to track their use of time, 24/7, for 13 weeks. The data on these pages, which were created with assistance from Harvard Business School research associate Sarah Higgins, summarizes the information gathered on how 27 CEOs spent a total of nearly 60,000 hours. Here is how they allocated their time, on average, among various activities, places, priorities, meetings, and constituencies.

Work vs. personal time

	Personal	Vacation		Sleep
31%	10	25	5	29
Work	Commute and transit			

Where they work

47%	6	47
HQ	Non-HQ site	Outside

Mode of communication

61%	15	24
Face-to-face	Phone and letter	Electronic

Core agenda vs. other activities

43%	36	21
Core agenda	Important unfolding developments	Have-to-do

Content of work

| | Organization | People and |
Strategy	and culture	relationships
21%	16	25	25

Functional and business unit reviews	M&A	4
	Operating plans	4
	Professional development	3
	Crisis management	1

Length of meetings

	30m		1–2h		>5h
7%	23	32	21	13	4
<15m		1h		2–5h	

Scheduled vs. spontaneous time

75%	25
Scheduled	Spontaneous

Meetings vs. alone time

72%	28
Meeting time	Alone time

Time with key constituencies

Insiders

Direct reports	33
Other senior managers	22
Other managers	10
Other employees	5

Business partners

Consultants	5
Customers	3
Investors	3
Bankers	2
Suppliers	1
Legal/ accounting	1
Other	1

Board

Full board	2
Individual board members	2
Committees	1

70%	16	9	5

Other outside commitments

Industry groups	5
Philanthopy	2
Media	1
Government/regulators	1

happens in meetings and decision-making processes. It reflects the far broader set of ways in which the CEO as an individual engages with the organization and its people.

In managing across these six dimensions of influence, it is easy for CEOs to overlook the less direct, less top-down, less tangible, and more human aspects of their work. Without this awareness, though, CEOs give up some of their most powerful levers for driving change.

Why Good Leaders Matter

Countless concepts, tools, and metrics have been developed to help leaders manage well. However, our study of what the CEOs of large, complex organizations actually do—as manifest in how they spend their time—opens a new window into what leadership is all about and into its many components and dimensions. Being the CEO is a highly challenging role, and it is difficult to do it well.

The success of CEOs has enormous consequences—good or bad— for employees, customers, communities, wealth creation, and the trajectory of economies and even societies. Being a CEO has gotten harder as the size and scope of the job continue to grow, organizational complexity rises, technology advances, competition increases, and CEO accountability intensifies. The ideas we have introduced here aim to provide current and future leaders, who must bear this enormous responsibility, with a broader understanding of their role and how to best use their most important resource: their time.

Originally published in July–August 2018. Reprint R1804B

When No One Retires

by Paul Irving

BEFORE OUR EYES, THE WORLD is undergoing a massive demographic transformation. In many countries, the population is getting old. Very old. Globally, the number of people age 60 and over is projected to double to more than 2 billion by 2050 and those 60 and over will outnumber children under the age of 5. In the United States, about 10,000 people turn 65 each day, and one in five Americans will be 65 or older by 2030. By 2035, Americans of retirement age will eclipse the number of people aged 18 and under for the first time in U.S. history.

The reasons for this age shift are many—medical advances that keep people healthier longer, dropping fertility rates, and so on—but the net result is the same: Populations around the world will look very different in the decades ahead.

Some in the public and private sector are already taking note—and sounding the alarm. In his first term as chairman of the U.S. Federal Reserve, with the Great Recession looming, Ben Bernanke remarked, "In the coming decades, many forces will shape our economy and our society, but in all likelihood no single factor will have as pervasive an effect as the aging of our population." Back in 2010, Standard & Poor's predicted that the biggest influence on "the future of national economic health, public finances, and policymaking" will be "the irreversible rate at which the world's population is aging."

The world is getting older

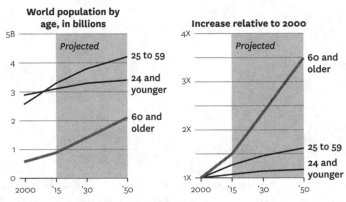

World population by age, in billions

5B

Projected

4

25 to 59

24 and younger

3

2

60 and older

1

0

2000   '15   '30   '50

Increase relative to 2000

4X

Projected

60 and older

3X

2X

25 to 59

24 and younger

1X

2000   '15   '30   '50

Source: United Nations, "World Population Prospects: The 2015 Revision."

This societal shift will undoubtedly change work, too: More and more Americans want to work longer—or have to, given that many aren't saving adequately for retirement. Soon, the workforce will include people from as many as five generations ranging in age from teenagers to 80-somethings.

Are companies prepared? The short answer is "no." Aging will affect every aspect of business operations—whether it's talent recruitment, the structure of compensation and benefits, the development of products and services, how innovation is unlocked, how offices and factories are designed, and even how work is structured—but for some reason, the message just hasn't gotten through. In general, corporate leaders have yet to invest the time and resources necessary to fully grasp the unprecedented ways that aging will change the rules of the game.

What's more, those who *do* think about the impacts of an aging population typically see a looming crisis—not an opportunity. They fail to appreciate the potential that older adults present as workers and consumers. The reality, however, is that increasing longevity contributes to global economic growth. Today's older adults

Idea in Brief

Before our eyes, the world is undergoing a massive demographic transformation. In many countries, the population is aging rapidly. In the United States, about 10,000 people turn 65 each day, and one in five Americans will be 65 or older by 2030. This societal shift will affect every aspect of business operations, but corporate leaders have not yet grasped the unprecedented ways that an aging workforce will change the rules of the game. Those who *do* think about the impacts typically see a looming crisis—not an opportunity. This article helps companies develop a "longevity strategy" for fostering a vibrant multigenerational workforce.

are generally healthier and more active than those of generations past, and they are changing the nature of retirement as they continue to learn, work, and contribute. In the workplace, they provide emotional stability, complex problem-solving skills, nuanced thinking, and institutional know-how. Their talents complement those of younger workers, and their guidance and support enhance performance and intergenerational collaboration. In encore careers, volunteering, and civic and social settings, their experience and problem-solving abilities contribute to society's well-being.

In the public sector, policy makers are beginning to take action. Efforts are under way in the United States to reimagine communities to enhance "age friendliness," develop strategies to improve infrastructure, enhance wellness and disease prevention, and design new ways to invest for retirement as traditional income sources like pensions and defined benefit plans dry up. But such efforts are still early stage, and given the slow pace of governmental change they will likely take years to evolve.

Companies, by contrast, are uniquely positioned to change practices and attitudes *now*. Transformation won't be easy, but companies that move past today's preconceptions about older employees and respond and adapt to changing demographics will realize significant dividends, generating new possibilities for financial return and enhancing the lives of their employees and customers. I spent many years in executive management, corporate law, and board

The Big Idea: The Aging Workforce

"When No One Retires" is the lead article of HBR's **The Big Idea: The Aging Workforce.** Read the rest of the series at hbr.org/aging:

- "Rethinking Retraining," by Willy C. Shih, Howard Rudnick, and Colleen Tapen
- "Caring for Your Company's Caregivers," by Sarita Gupta and Ai-Jen Poo
- "Retirement-Proof Your Company," by Peter Berg and Matt Piszczek
- "Just How Old Are We Getting?" by Ramsey Khabbaz and Matt Perry
- "What Happens to Younger Workers When Older Workers Don't Retire," by Nicola Bianchi, Jin Li, and Michael Powell

service. Based on this experience, along with research conducted with Arielle Burstein, Kevin Proff, and other members of our staff at the Milken Institute Center for the Future of Aging, I have developed a framework for building a "longevity strategy" that companies can use to create a vibrant multigenerational workforce. Broadly, a longevity strategy should include two key elements: internal-facing activities (hiring, retention, and mining the talents of workers of all ages) and external-facing ones (how your company positions itself and its products and services to customers and stakeholders). In this article, I'll address the internal activities companies should be engaging in.

But first, let's examine why leaders seem to be overlooking the opportunities of an aging population.

The Ageism Effect

There's broad consensus that the global population is changing and growing significantly older. There's also a prevailing opinion that the impacts on society will largely be negative. A Government Accountability Office report warns that older populations will bring slower growth, lower productivity, and increasing dependency on society. A report from the Congressional Budget Office projects that higher entitlement costs associated with an aging population will drive up expenses relative to revenues, increasing the federal deficit. The World Bank foresees fading potential in economies across the globe, warning in 2018 of "headwinds from ageing populations in both advanced and developing economies, expecting decreased labour supply and productivity growth." Such predictions serve to further entrench the belief that older workers are an expensive drag on society.

What's at the heart of this gloomy outlook? Economists often refer to what's known as the dependency ratio: the number of people not typically in the workforce—those younger than 15 and older than 65—in a population divided by the number of working-age people. This measure assumes that older adults are generally unproductive and can be expected to do little other than consume benefits in their later years. Serious concerns about the so-called silver tsunami are justified if this assumption is correct: The prospect of a massive population of sick, disengaged, lonely, needy, and cognitively impaired people is a dark one indeed.

This picture, however, is simply not accurate. While some older adults do suffer from disabling physical and cognitive conditions or are

The global aging phenomenon

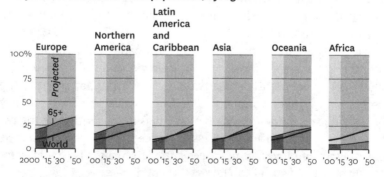

Projected breakdown of world population, by region

Note: Northern America consists of Canada and the United States.
Source: United Nations, "World Population Prospects: The 2015 Revision."

otherwise unable to maintain an active lifestyle, far more are able and inclined to stay in the game longer, disproving assumptions about their prospects for work and productivity. The work of Laura Carstensen and her colleagues at the Stanford Center on Longevity shows that typical 60-something workers today are healthy, experienced, and more likely than younger colleagues to be satisfied with their jobs. They have a strong work ethic and loyalty to their employers. They are motivated, knowledgeable, adept at resolving social dilemmas, and care more about meaningful contributions and less about self-advancement. They are more likely than their younger counterparts to build social cohesion and to share information and organizational values.

Yet the flawed perceptions persist, a byproduct of stubborn and pervasive ageism. Positive attributes of older workers are crowded out by negative stereotypes that infect work settings and devalue older adults in a youth-oriented culture. Older adults regularly find themselves on the losing end of hiring decisions, promotions, and even volunteer opportunities. Research from AARP found that approximately two-thirds of workers ages 45 to 74 said they have seen or experienced age discrimination in the workplace. Of those, a remarkable 92% said age discrimination is very, or somewhat, common. Research for the Federal Reserve Bank of San Francisco backs this up. A study involving 40,000 made-up résumés found compelling evidence that older applicants, especially women, suffer consistent age discrimination. A case in point is IBM, which is currently facing allegations of using improper practices to marginalize and terminate older workers.

There's more: Deloitte's 2018 Global Human Capital Trends study found that 20% of business and HR leaders surveyed viewed older workers as a competitive disadvantage and an impediment to the progress of younger workers. The report concludes that "there may be a significant hidden problem of age bias in the workforce today." It also warns that "left unaddressed, perceptions that a company's culture and employment practices suffer from age bias could damage its brand and social capital."

The negative cultural overlay about aging is reinforced by media and advertising that often portray older adults in clichéd, patronizing ways. A classic example is Life Alert's ad from the 1980s for its medical alert necklace, immortalizing the phrase "I've fallen, and I can't get up!" Recent ads by E*TRADE and Postmates have also drawn criticism as ageist. A more subtle, but just as damaging example is the trumpeting of "anti-aging" benefits on beauty products as a marketing tool, suggesting that growing older is, by definition, a negative process.

Some companies are pushing back: In a recent video, T-Mobile's John Legere took on the topic of ageist stereotypes while promoting a T-Mobile service for adults age 55-plus. He chided competitors for what he called their belittling treatment of older adults in marketing campaigns that emphasize large-size phone buttons and imply that boomers are tech idiots. "Degrading at the highest level," Legere calls it. "The carriers assume boomers are a bunch of old people stuck in the past who can't figure out how the internet works. News flash, carriers: Boomers invented the internet."

Yet for the most part, employers continue to invest far more in young employees and generally do not train workers over 50. In fact, many companies would rather not think about the existence of older workers all. "Today it is socially unacceptable to ignore, ridicule, or stereotype someone based on their gender, race, or sexual orientation," points out Jo Ann Jenkins, the CEO of AARP. "So why is it still acceptable to do this to people based on their age?"

Over the past decades, companies have recognized the economic and social benefits of women, people of color, and LGBT individuals in the workforce. These priority initiatives must be continued—obviously, we're not even close to achieving genuine equality in the corporate world; at the same time, the inclusion of older adults in the business diversity matrix is long overdue. Patricia Milligan, senior partner and global leader for Mercer's Multinational Client Group, observes, "At the most respected multinational companies, the single class not represented from a diversity and inclusion perspective is older workers. LGBT, racial and ethnic diversity, women, people with physical disabilities, veterans—you can find an affinity group in a corporation for everything, except an older worker."

The U.S. labor force is getting older, too

**Projected average annual growth rate
by age group, 2014 to 2024**

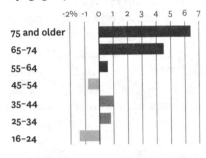

**Breakdown by age group,
1970 to 2024**

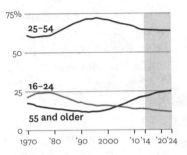

Source: U.S. Bureau of Labor Statistics.

Managing a Multigenerational Workforce

How can companies push past stereotypes and other organizational impediments to tap into a thriving and talented population of older workers? A range of best practices have been emerging, and some companies are making real progress. Each points to specific changes companies should be considering as they develop their own strategies.

Redefine the workweek

To start, you need to reconsider the out-of-date idea that all employees work Monday through Friday, from 9 to 5, in the same office. The notion that everyone retires completely by age 65 should also be jettisoned. Companies instead should invest in opportunities for creative mentorship, part-time work, flex-hour schedules, and sabbatical programs geared to the abilities and inclinations of older workers. Programs that offer preretirement and career transition support, coaching, counseling, and encore career pathways can also make employees more engaged and productive. Many older workers say they are ready to exchange high salaries for flexible schedules and phased retirements. Some companies have already embraced nontraditional work programs for employees, creating a new kind of environment for success. The CVS "Snowbird" program, for example, allows older employees to travel and work seasonally in different CVS pharmacy regions. Home Depot recruits and hires thousands of retired construction workers, making the most of their expertise on the sales floor. The National Institutes of Health, half of whose workforce is over 50, actively recruits at 50-plus job fairs and offers benefits such as flexible schedules, telecommuting, and exercise classes. Steelcase offers workers a phased retirement program with reduced hours. Michelin has rehired retirees to oversee projects, foster community relations, and facilitate employee mentoring. Brooks Brothers consults with older workers on equipment and process design, and restructures assignments to offer enhanced flexibility for its aging workforce.

Reimagine the workplace
Your company should also be prepared to adjust workspaces to improve ergonomics and make environments more age-friendly for older employees. No one should be distracted from their tasks by pain that can be prevented or eased, and even small changes can improve health, safety, and productivity. Xerox, for example, has an ergonomic training program aimed at reducing musculoskeletal disorders in its aging workforce. BMW and Nissan have implemented changes to their manufacturing lines to accommodate older workers, ranging from barbershop-style chairs and better-designed tools to "cobot" (collaborative robot) partners that manage complicated tasks and lift heavier objects. The good news is that programs that improve the lives of older workers can be equally valuable for younger counterparts.

Mind the mix
Lastly, you need to consider and monitor the age mixes in your departments and teams. Many companies will need to manage as many as five generations of workers in the near future, if they aren't already. Some pernicious biases can make this difficult. For example, research

shows that every generation wants meaningful work—but that each believes everyone else is just in it for the money. Companies should emphasize workers' shared value. "Companies pursuing Millennial-specific employee engagement strategies are wasting time, focus, and money," Bruce Pfau, the former vice chair of human resources at KPMG, argues. "They would be far better served to focus on factors that lead all employees to join, stay, and perform at their best."

By tapping ways that workers of different generations can augment and learn from each other, companies set themselves up for success over the long term. Young workers can benefit from the mentorship of older colleagues, and a promising workforce resource lies in intergenerational collaboration, combining the energy and speed of youth with the wisdom and experience of age.

PNC Financial Group uses multigenerational teams to help the company compete more effectively in the financial markets through a better understanding of the target audience for products. Pharma giant Pfizer has experimented with a "senior intern" program to reap the benefits of multigenerational collaboration. In the tech world, Airbnb recruited former hotel mogul Chip Conley to provide experienced management perspective to his younger colleagues. Pairing younger and older workers in all phases of product and service innovation and design can create opportunity for professional growth. And facilitating intergenerational relationships, mentoring, training, and teaming mitigate isolation and help break down walls.

To begin this process, start talking to your employees of all ages. And get them to talk with each other about their goals, interests, needs, and worries. Young and old workers share similar anxieties and hopes about work—and also have differences that need to be better understood companywide. Look for opportunities for engagement between generations and places where older and younger workers can support one another through skill development and mentorship. After all, if everyone needs and wants to work, we're going to have to learn to work together.

To be clear, all of these changes—from flexible hours to team makeup—will require a recalibration of company processes, some of which are deeply ingrained. Leaders must ask, do our current health insurance, sick leave, caregiving, and vacation policies accommodate people who work reduced hours? Do our employee performance-measurement systems appropriately recognize and reward the strengths of older workers? Currently, most companies focus on individual achievement as opposed to team success. This may inadvertently punish older employees who offer other types of value—like mentorship, forging deep relationships with clients and colleagues, and conflict resolution—that are not as easily captured using traditional assessment tools. Here, too, initiatives aimed at older workers can benefit other workers as well. For instance, research suggests that evaluating team performance also tends to boost the careers of employees from low-income backgrounds.

Turning a Crisis into an Opportunity

I'm admittedly bullish about the positive aspects of working longer and believe that company leaders can harness the opportunity of an aging population to gain competitive advantage. But I'm not oblivious to the challenges a longevity strategy poses. We're talking about initiating a massive culture change for firms—a change that must come from the top.

But ignoring the realities of the demographic shift under way is no longer an option. CEOs and senior executives will need to put the issue front and center with HR leaders, product developers, marketing managers, investors, and many other stakeholders who may not have it on their radar screens. This will take guts and persistence: Leaders must bravely say, "We reject the assumption that people become less tech-savvy as they get older" and "We will fight the impulse to put only our youngest employees on new initiatives." To genuinely make headway on this long-range issue, companies will have to make tough, and sometimes unpopular, decisions, especially in a world where short-term results and demands dominate leaders' agendas. But isn't that what great leaders do?

The business community has a chance to spearhead a broad movement to change culture, create opportunity, and drive growth. In doing so, companies will improve not only mature lives, but lives of all ages, and the prospects of workers for generations to come. This transformative movement to realize the potential of the 21st century's changing demography is the next big test for corporate leadership.

The Longevity Opportunity

by Paul Irving

AS THE GLOBAL POPULATION AGES, new consumer opportunities and markets will emerge. Every company should have a strategy for tapping into the needs, wants, and buying power of older customers.

In my previous article, I outlined the beginnings of an internal, employee-focused "longevity strategy" that organizations can use to reap the benefits of an aging workforce. In this one, I'll discuss its external, consumer-facing complement.

The market for products and services for older adults is already strong, and it will become even stronger. With distinct consumption habits and service needs, Americans over 50 accounted for $7.6 trillion in direct consumer spending and related economic activity in 2015, and controlled more than 80% of household wealth, according to a 2016 joint report from Oxford Economics and AARP. Further, a 2010 AARP survey reveals that 90% of older adults say they want to be able to remain in their own homes as they age. Envisioning how communities will respond to the needs of aging people will keep many more of them in their homes and contributing to the economy. Bank of America Merrill Lynch projects that the global spending power of those age 60 and over will reach $15 trillion annually by 2020.

But the potential for forward-thinking companies goes beyond just an interesting business opportunity. Older adults are poised to shape consumer and capital markets in the years ahead. The McKinsey Global Institute concludes that the 60-plus population, one of the few engines of global economic growth, is on track to generate half of all urban consumption growth between 2015 and 2030. "The Longevity Economy is redrawing economic lines, changing the face of the workforce, advancing technology and innovations, and busting perceptions of what it means to age," states the Oxford Economics/AARP report.

Across industries, there are multiple avenues for offering products and services that make a difference in people's lives. In the health sector, "gray is the new black," a Reuters piece observed. New offerings in biotechnology, devices, pharmaceuticals, and care services all target older consumers.

Research reveals that older adults dominate spending in 119 of 123 consumer packaged goods categories, spend more in grocery stores and purchase more new cars than any other age group, and account for 80% of luxury travel. The demographic is eager to spend on transportation, entertainment, food, and alcohol, representing an immense target market for fresh ideas and innovations.

The financial services industry has always catered to older people—primarily those planning for retirement. As customers and clients prepare for longer lives, retirement remains a powerful growth driver. But a financial market for older workers and entrepreneurs is rapidly expanding too. Driven by financial assets controlled by older investors, this segment of the longevity market simply cannot be ignored. People age 60 and over hold the majority of wealth worldwide and 70% of the disposable income in the U.S.

For most companies, longevity marketing is still in its early days. That must change. You need a strategy for older consumers, and identifying new opportunities and markets is just the first step. You and your employees also need to reconsider what you "know" about this population to avoid ageist and outdated messaging. Incorporate older employees into product planning, design, and communications to benefit from their experience and understanding. Use focus groups that include older participants to test products and services before they make it to market.

While most companies are in the early stages of developing their strategies, it's worth exploring what some industry leaders are up to.

Philips and Nestlé have fundamentally shifted their businesses to capitalize on trends that are driven in many ways by the aging population. Both global companies have focused their futures on health and wellness, recognizing the massive opportunities ahead. In partnership with the Global Social Enterprise Initiative at Georgetown University's McDonough School of Business, Philips is developing new technologies that can meet the needs of its older customers, including connected care solutions, safety applications, and cognitive health innovations. Patients and their doctors will be able to see, monitor, and share vital health information through secure devices, for example. Nestlé is investing in personalized diet and nutrition initiatives, and is broadening its portfolio by buying or acquiring stakes in health supplement and pharmaceutical companies.

Best Buy, with its recent acquisition of GreatCall, the provider of connected health and personal emergency services to the aging population, is focused on building relationships with older consumers. By gaining access to GreatCall's customer base, Best Buy can further penetrate the health services and monitoring business and grow through its supply chain efficiencies and marketing reach. Several analysts hailed the acquisition, praising Best Buy for recognizing the market's size and potential and the opportunity for a services business line to diversify the company's offerings and counterbalance the margin pressures on electronics products.

Bank of America Merrill Lynch is training its customer-facing workforce to understand the needs of its aging clients. The bank recognizes that increasing longevity leads to new health care choices, housing issues, and questions about retirement and financial security. In partnership with the USC Leonard Davis School of Gerontology (which I'm affiliated with), the company's longevity training program teaches financial advisers about older people's experiences, priorities, and goals.

Uber and Lyft have developed programs to provide rides for older adults through age-friendly web tools, apps, and phone systems. Recognizing the importance of mobility to health and well-being, both ride-hailing companies are creating partnerships and scaling up efforts to facilitate access and ease of use for older adults and their families and caregivers. For example, both companies are working with call services (Lyft with GreatCall and Uber with RideWith24) to make it easier for older adults to book rides.

Intel is working on internet-of-things software that flags health concerns, and projects such as enabling wearables to analyze and communicate health data faster than ever through 5G internet connections. And Nest has begun modifying its line of smart home products to help older adults continue to live independently.

These are just a few examples of the longevity market's prospects and possibilities.

Finally, as longevity strategies are developed and implemented, companies must consider not only how their products and services are designed but also how they are promoted. The power of media and advertising should be used to reflect realistic images of older adults instead of stereotypes. Older consumers do not want to be patronized, but they do want their needs acknowledged, and companies can do this while emphasizing both positive and real aspects of aging. While many companies have a long way to go, some are getting it right. On the positive side, Unilever's Dove successfully employed its Pro-Age campaign, realizing significant market share increases. The smart marketing for Dannon's Activia yogurt is focused on the common issue of digestive health. And in 2017 *Allure* Magazine showed leadership when it announced that it would no longer use the term "anti-aging" to describe skin care or makeup.

We're still in the early stages of understanding what older consumers' needs are and how to address them. The aging population is diverse, and the answers are not simple; one size certainly does not fit all. But we do know that there's already a clear demand for products and services that can help people live longer, more-comfortable, and more-meaningful lives—and that are promoted without stigma or stereotype. This demand will grow rapidly in the coming decades, and companies that start meeting it now can reap a sizable dividend. It's a huge opportunity, one that will have benefits both to their bottom lines and to society.

Originally published on hbr.org in November 2018. Reprint BG1806

Why Design Thinking Works

by Jeanne Liedtka

OCCASIONALLY, A NEW WAY of organizing work leads to extraordinary improvements. Total quality management did that in manufacturing in the 1980s by combining a set of tools—kanban cards, quality circles, and so on—with the insight that people on the shop floor could do much higher-level work than they usually were asked to. That blend of tools and insight, applied to a work process, can be thought of as a *social technology*.

In a recent seven-year study in which I looked in depth at 50 projects from a range of sectors, including business, health care, and social services, I have seen that another social technology, design thinking, has the potential to do for innovation exactly what TQM did for manufacturing: unleash people's full creative energies, win their commitment, and radically improve processes. By now most executives have at least heard about design thinking's tools—ethnographic research, an emphasis on reframing problems and experimentation, the use of diverse teams, and so on—if not tried them. But what people may not understand is the subtler way that design thinking gets around the human biases (for example, rootedness in the status quo) or attachments to specific behavioral norms ("That's how we do things here") that time and again block the exercise of imagination.

In this article I'll explore a variety of human tendencies that get in the way of innovation and describe how design thinking's tools and clear process steps help teams break free of them. Let's begin by looking at what organizations need from innovation—and at why their efforts to obtain it often fall short.

The Challenges of Innovation

To be successful, an innovation process must deliver three things: superior solutions, lower risks and costs of change, and employee buy-in. Over the years businesspeople have developed useful tactics for achieving those outcomes. But when trying to apply them, organizations frequently encounter new obstacles and trade-offs.

Superior solutions

Defining problems in obvious, conventional ways, not surprisingly, often leads to obvious, conventional solutions. *Asking a more interesting question* can help teams discover more-original ideas. The risk is that some teams may get indefinitely hung up exploring a problem, while action-oriented managers may be too impatient to take the time to figure out what question they should be asking.

It's also widely accepted that solutions are much better when they incorporate *user-driven criteria*. Market research can help companies understand those criteria, but the hurdle here is that it's hard for customers to know they want something that doesn't yet exist.

Finally, bringing *diverse voices* into the process is also known to improve solutions. This can be difficult to manage, however, if conversations among people with opposing views deteriorate into divisive debates.

Lower risks and costs

Uncertainty is unavoidable in innovation. That's why innovators often build a *portfolio of options*. The trade-off is that too many ideas dilute focus and resources. To manage this tension, innovators must be willing to let go of bad ideas—to "call the baby ugly," as a manager in one of my studies described it. Unfortunately, people often find it easier to kill the creative (and arguably riskier) ideas than to kill the incremental ones.

Idea in Brief

The Problem

While we know a lot about what practices stimulate new ideas and creative solutions, most innovation teams struggle to realize their benefits.

The Cause

People's intrinsic biases and behavioral habits inhibit the exercise of the imagination and protect unspoken assumptions about what will or will not work.

The Solution

Design thinking provides a structured process that helps innovators break free of counterproductive tendencies that thwart innovation. Like TQM, it is a social technology that blends practical tools with insights into human nature.

Employee buy-in

An innovation won't succeed unless a company's employees get behind it. The surest route to winning their support is to involve them in the process of generating ideas. The danger is that the involvement of many people with different perspectives will create chaos and incoherence.

Underlying the trade-offs associated with achieving these outcomes is a more fundamental tension. In a stable environment, efficiency is achieved by driving variation out of the organization. But in an unstable world, variation becomes the organization's friend, because it opens new paths to success. However, who can blame leaders who must meet quarterly targets for doubling down on efficiency, rationality, and centralized control?

To manage all the trade-offs, organizations need a social technology that addresses these behavioral obstacles as well as the counterproductive biases of human beings. And as I'll explain next, design thinking fits that bill.

The Beauty of Structure

Experienced designers often complain that design thinking is too structured and linear. And for them, that's certainly true. But managers on innovation teams generally are not designers and also aren't used to doing face-to-face research with customers, getting deeply

Shaping the innovator's journey

What makes design thinking a social technology is its ability to counteract the biases of innovators and change the way they engage in the innovation process.

Problem	Design thinking	Improved outcome
Innovators are:		
Trapped in their own expertise and experience	**Provides immersion** in the user's experience, shifting an innovator's mindset toward. . .	A better understanding of those being designed for
Overwhelmed by the volume and messiness of qualitative data	**Makes sense** of data by organizing it into themes and patterns, pointing the innovator toward. . .	New insights and possibilities
Divided by differences in team members' perspectives	**Builds alignment** as insights are translated into design criteria, moving an innovation team toward. . .	Convergence around what really matters to users
Confronted by too many disparate but familiar ideas	**Encourages the emergence** of fresh ideas through a focused inquiry, shifting team members toward. . .	A limited but diverse set of potential new solutions
Constrained by existing biases about what does or doesn't work	**Fosters articulation** of the conditions necessary to each idea's success and transitions a team toward. . .	Clarity on make-or-break assumptions that enables the design of meaningful experiments
Lacking a shared understanding of new ideas and often unable to get good feedback from users	**Offers preexperiences** to users through very rough prototypes that help innovators get. . .	Accurate feedback at low cost and an understanding of potential solutions' true value
Afraid of change and ambiguity surrounding the new future	**Delivers learning in action** as experiments engage staff and users, helping them build. . .	A shared commitment and confidence in the new product or strategy

immersed in their perspectives, co-creating with stakeholders, and designing and executing experiments. Structure and linearity help managers try to adjust to these new behaviors.

As Kaaren Hanson, formerly the head of design innovation at Intuit and now Facebook's design product director, has explained:

"Anytime you're trying to change people's behavior, you need to start them off with a lot of structure, so they don't have to think. A lot of what we do is habit, and it's hard to change those habits, but having very clear guardrails can help us."

Organized processes keep people on track and curb the tendency to spend too long exploring a problem or to impatiently skip ahead. They also instill confidence. Most humans are driven by a fear of mistakes, so they focus more on preventing errors than on seizing opportunities. They opt for inaction rather than action when a choice risks failure. But there is no innovation without action—so psychological safety is essential. The physical props and highly formatted tools of design thinking deliver that sense of security, helping would-be innovators move more assuredly through the discovery of customer needs, idea generation, and idea testing.

In most organizations the application of design thinking involves seven activities. Each generates a clear output that the next activity converts to another output until the organization arrives at an implementable innovation. But at a deeper level, something else is happening—something that executives generally are not aware of. Though ostensibly geared to understanding and molding the experiences of customers, each design-thinking activity also reshapes the experiences of the *innovators themselves* in profound ways.

Customer Discovery

Many of the best-known methods of the design-thinking discovery process relate to identifying the "job to be done." Adapted from the fields of ethnography and sociology, these methods concentrate on examining what makes for a meaningful customer journey rather than on the collection and analysis of data. This exploration entails three sets of activities:

Immersion

Traditionally, customer research has been an impersonal exercise. An expert, who may well have preexisting theories about customer preferences, reviews feedback from focus groups, surveys, and, if available, data on current behavior, and draws inferences about needs. The better the data, the better the inferences. The trouble is, this grounds people in the already articulated needs that the data reflects. They see the data through the lens of their own biases. And they don't recognize needs people have *not* expressed.

Design thinking takes a different approach: Identify hidden needs by having the innovator live the customer's experience. Consider what happened at the Kingwood Trust, a UK charity helping adults with autism and Asperger's syndrome. One design team member, Katie Gaudion, got to know Pete, a nonverbal adult with autism. The first time she observed him at his home, she saw him engaged in seemingly damaging acts—like picking at a leather sofa and rubbing indents in a wall. She started by documenting Pete's behavior and defined the problem as how to prevent such destructiveness.

But on her second visit to Pete's home, she asked herself: What if Pete's actions were motivated by something other than a destructive impulse? Putting her personal perspective aside, she mirrored his behavior and discovered how satisfying his activities actually felt. "Instead of a ruined sofa, I now perceived Pete's sofa as an object wrapped in fabric that is fun to pick," she explained. "Pressing my ear against the wall and feeling the vibrations of the music above, I felt a slight tickle in my ear whilst rubbing the smooth and beautiful indentation . . . So instead of a damaged wall, I perceived it as a pleasant and relaxing audio-tactile experience."

Katie's immersion in Pete's world not only produced a deeper understanding of his challenges but called into question an unexamined bias about the residents, who had been perceived as disability sufferers that needed to be kept safe. Her experience caused her to ask herself another new question: Instead of designing just for residents' disabilities and safety, how could the innovation team design for their strengths and pleasures? That led to the creation of living spaces, gardens, and new activities aimed at enabling people with autism to live fuller and more pleasurable lives.

Sense making

Immersion in user experiences provides raw material for deeper insights. But finding patterns and making sense of the mass of qualitative data collected is a daunting challenge. Time and again, I have seen initial enthusiasm about the results of ethnographic tools fade as nondesigners become overwhelmed by the volume of information and the messiness of searching for deeper insights. It is here that the structure of design thinking really comes into its own.

One of the most effective ways to make sense of the knowledge generated by immersion is a design-thinking exercise called the Gallery Walk. In it the core innovation team selects the most important data gathered during the discovery process and writes it down on large posters. Often these posters showcase individuals who have been interviewed, complete with their photos and quotations capturing their perspectives. The posters are hung around a room, and key stakeholders are invited to tour this gallery and write down on Post-it notes the bits of data they consider essential to new designs. The stakeholders then form small teams, and in a carefully orchestrated process, their Post-it observations are shared, combined, and sorted by theme into clusters that the group mines for insights. This process overcomes the danger that innovators will be unduly influenced by their own biases and see only what they want to see, because it makes the people who were interviewed feel vivid and real to those browsing the gallery. It creates a common database and facilitates collaborators' ability to interact, reach shared insights together, and challenge one another's individual takeaways—another critical guard against biased interpretations.

Alignment

The final stage in the discovery process is a series of workshops and seminar discussions that ask in some form the question, If anything were possible, what job would the design do well? The focus on possibilities, rather than on the constraints imposed by the status quo, helps diverse teams have more-collaborative and creative discussions about the design criteria, or the set of key features that an ideal innovation should have. Establishing a spirit of inquiry deepens dissatisfaction with the status quo and makes it easier for teams to reach consensus throughout the innovation process. And down the road, when the portfolio of ideas is winnowed, agreement on the design criteria will give novel ideas a fighting chance against safer incremental ones.

Consider what happened at Monash Health, an integrated hospital and health care system in Melbourne, Australia. Mental health clinicians there had long been concerned about the frequency of patient relapses—usually in the form of drug overdoses and suicide attempts—but consensus on how to address this problem eluded them. In an effort to get to the bottom of it, clinicians traced the experiences of specific patients through the treatment process. One patient, Tom, emerged as emblematic in their study. His experience included three face-to-face visits with different clinicians, 70 touchpoints, 13 different case managers, and 18 handoffs during the interval between his initial visit and his relapse.

The team members held a series of workshops in which they asked clinicians this question: Did Tom's current care exemplify why they had entered health care? As people discussed their motivations for becoming doctors and nurses, they came to realize that improving Tom's outcome might depend as much on their sense of duty to Tom himself as it did on their clinical activity. Everyone bought into this conclusion, which made designing a new treatment process—centered on the patient's needs rather than perceived best practices—proceed smoothly and successfully. After its implementation, patient-relapse rates fell by 60%.

Idea Generation

Once they understand customers' needs, innovators move on to identify and winnow down specific solutions that conform to the criteria they've identified.

Emergence

The first step here is to set up a dialogue about potential solutions, carefully planning who will participate, what challenge they will be given, and how the conversation will be structured. After using the design criteria to do some individual brainstorming, participants gather to share ideas and build on them creatively—as opposed to simply negotiating compromises when differences arise.

When Children's Health System of Texas, the sixth-largest pediatric medical center in the United States, identified the need for a new strategy, the organization, led by the vice president of population health, Peter Roberts, applied design thinking to reimagine its business model. During the discovery process, clinicians set aside their bias that what mattered most was medical intervention. They came to understand that intervention alone wouldn't work if the local population in Dallas didn't have the time or ability to seek out medical knowledge and didn't have strong support networks— something few families in the area enjoyed. The clinicians also realized that the medical center couldn't successfully address problems on its own; the community would need to be central to any solution. So Children's Health invited its community partners to codesign a new wellness ecosystem whose boundaries (and resources) would stretch far beyond the medical center. Deciding to start small and tackle a single condition, the team gathered to create a new model for managing asthma.

The session brought together hospital administrators, physicians, nurses, social workers, parents of patients, and staff from Dallas's school districts, housing authority, YMCA, and faith-based organizations. First, the core innovation team shared learning from the discovery process. Next, each attendee thought independently about the capabilities that his or her institution might contribute toward addressing the children's problems, jotting down ideas on sticky notes. Then each attendee was invited to join a small group at one of five tables, where the participants shared individual ideas, grouped them into common themes, and envisioned what an ideal experience would look like for the young patients and their families.

Champions of change usually emerge from these kinds of conversations, which greatly improves the chances of successful implementation. (All too often, good ideas die on the vine in the absence of people with a personal commitment to making them happen.) At Children's Health, the partners invited into the project galvanized the community to act and forged and maintained the relationships in their institutions required to realize the new vision. Housing authority representatives drove changes in housing codes, charging inspectors with incorporating children's health issues (like the presence of mold) into their assessments. Local pediatricians adopted a set of standard asthma protocols, and parents of children with asthma took on a significant role as peer counselors providing intensive education to other families through home visits.

Articulation

Typically, emergence activities generate a number of competing ideas, more or less attractive and more or less feasible. In the next step, articulation, innovators surface and question their implicit assumptions. Managers are often bad at this, because of many behavioral biases, such as overoptimism, confirmation bias, and fixation on first solutions. When assumptions aren't challenged, discussions around what will or won't work become deadlocked, with each person advocating from his or her own understanding of how the world works.

In contrast, design thinking frames the discussion as an inquiry into what would have to be true about the world for an idea to be feasible. (See "Management Is Much More Than a Science," by Roger L. Martin and Tony Golsby-Smith, HBR, September–October 2017.) An example of this comes from the Ignite Accelerator program of the U.S. Department of Health and Human Services. At the Whiteriver Indian reservation hospital in Arizona, a team led by Marliza Rivera, a young quality control officer, sought to reduce wait times in the hospital's emergency room, which were sometimes as long as six hours.

The team's initial concept, borrowed from Johns Hopkins Hospital in Baltimore, was to install an electronic kiosk for check-in. As team members began to apply design thinking, however, they were asked to surface their assumptions about why the idea would work. It was only then that they realized that their patients, many of whom were elderly Apache speakers, were unlikely to be comfortable with computer technology. Approaches that worked in urban Baltimore would not work in Whiteriver, so this idea could be safely set aside.

At the end of the idea generation process, innovators will have a portfolio of well-thought-through, though possibly quite different, ideas. The assumptions underlying them will have been carefully vetted, and the conditions necessary for their success will be achievable. The ideas will also have the support of committed teams, who will be prepared to take on the responsibility of bringing them to market.

The Testing Experience

Companies often regard prototyping as a process of fine-tuning a product or service that has already largely been developed. But in design thinking, prototyping is carried out on far-from-finished products. It's about users' iterative experiences with a work in progress. This means that quite radical changes—including complete redesigns—can occur along the way.

Pre-experience

Neuroscience research indicates that helping people "pre-experience" something novel—or to put it another way, *imagine* it incredibly vividly—results in more-accurate assessments of the novelty's value. That's why design thinking calls for the creation of basic, low-cost artifacts that will capture the essential features of the proposed user experience. These are not literal prototypes—and they are often much rougher than the "minimum viable products" that lean start-ups test with customers. But what these artifacts lose in fidelity, they gain in flexibility, because they can easily be altered in response to what's learned by exposing users to them. And their incompleteness invites interaction.

Such artifacts can take many forms. The layout of a new medical office building at Kaiser Permanente, for example, was tested by hanging bedsheets from the ceiling to mark future walls. Nurses and physicians were invited to interact with staffers who were playing the role of patients and to suggest how spaces could be adjusted to better facilitate treatment. At Monash Health, a program called Monash Watch—aimed at using telemedicine to keep vulnerable populations healthy at home and reduce their hospitalization rates—used detailed storyboards to help hospital administrators and government policy makers envision this new approach in practice, without building a digital prototype.

Learning in action

Real-world experiments are an essential way to assess new ideas and identify the changes needed to make them workable. But such tests offer another, less obvious kind of value: They help reduce employees' and customers' quite normal fear of change.

Consider an idea proposed by Don Campbell, a professor of medicine, and Keith Stockman, a manager of operations research at Monash Health. As part of Monash Watch, they suggested hiring laypeople to be "telecare" guides who would act as "professional neighbors," keeping in frequent telephone contact with patients at high risk of multiple hospital admissions. Campbell and Stockman hypothesized that lower-wage laypeople who were carefully selected, trained in health literacy and empathy skills, and backed by a decision support system and professional coaches they could involve as needed could help keep the at-risk patients healthy at home.

Their proposal was met with skepticism. Many of their colleagues held a strong bias against letting anyone besides a health professional perform such a service for patients with complex issues, but using health professionals in the role would have been unaffordable. Rather than debating this point, however, the innovation team members acknowledged the concerns and engaged their colleagues in the codesign of an experiment testing that assumption. Three hundred patients later, the results were in: Overwhelmingly positive patient feedback and a demonstrated reduction in bed use and emergency room visits, corroborated by independent consultants, quelled the fears of the skeptics.

As we have seen, the structure of design thinking creates a natural flow from research to rollout. Immersion in the customer experience produces data, which is transformed into insights, which help teams agree on design criteria they use to brainstorm solutions. Assumptions about what's critical to the success of those solutions are examined and then tested with rough prototypes that help teams further develop innovations and prepare them for real-world experiments.

Along the way, design-thinking processes counteract human biases that thwart creativity while addressing the challenges typically faced in reaching superior solutions, lowered costs and risks, and employee buy-in. Recognizing organizations as collections of human beings who are motivated by varying perspectives and emotions, design thinking emphasizes engagement, dialogue, and learning. By involving customers and other stakeholders in the definition of the problem and the development of solutions, design thinking garners a broad commitment to change. And by supplying a structure to the innovation process, design thinking helps innovators collaborate and agree on what is essential to the outcome at every phase. It does this not only by overcoming workplace politics but by shaping the experiences of the innovators, and of their key stakeholders and implementers, at every step. *That* is social technology at work.

Originally published in September–October 2018. Reprint R1805D

Time for Happiness

by Ashley Whillans

ADAM (REAL STORY, FAKE NAME) was a good employee who was given a plum project he believed could get him a promotion and a raise. Taking it seemed like the proverbial no-brainer: Work hard, nail the assignment, get more pay. He knew he'd have to put in long days and some hours on weekends, which meant he'd be sacrificing time with his young family. He knew the deadlines would be stressful, as would managing the people and the expectations involved. But he also knew that at the end, he'd be rewarded, and he could make up for the lost time.

Except that he wasn't rewarded. Though his project was a success, the promotion and the raise went to someone on another project, who also was deserving. After receiving accolades for a job well done, Adam continued to run his project successfully, but he wasn't happy. At night, he sat in bumper-to-bumper traffic, brooding over what had happened, calculating all the hours he had put in, and for what? He couldn't help feeling he had wasted—no, that he had *lost*—valuable time.

While Adam is right, the research shows that even if he *had* gotten the promotion and the raise, he might have felt just as discontented. No matter what the outcome of our efforts, we all feel increasingly strapped for time, and often the things that we think will make us happy—the accomplishments we work so hard for—don't. They most certainly do not give us back moments with our families and friends or more hours to ourselves.

A preponderance of evidence shows that the feeling of having enough time—"time affluence"—is now at a record low in the United States. When my team and I analyzed a survey of 2.5 million Americans by the Gallup Organization, we found that 80% of respondents did not have the time to do all they wanted to each day. This situation is so severe it could even be described as a "famine"—a collective cultural failure to effectively manage our most precious resource, time.

Time poverty exists across all economic strata, and its effects are profound. Research shows that those who feel time-poor experience lower levels of happiness and higher levels of anxiety, depression, and stress. They experience less joy. They laugh less. They exercise less and are less healthy. Their productivity at work is diminished. They are more likely to get divorced. And in our analysis of the Gallup survey data, my team and I even found that time stress had a stronger negative effect on happiness than being unemployed did.

On a broader level, time poverty directly accounts for billions of dollars in productivity costs to companies each year, and secondary costs multiply that number many times over. Public health officials rank it as one of the top contributors to rising obesity. Researchers put the health care costs of time stress at $48 billion a year.

The irony is, despite the perception that people today work longer hours, the data reveals that most of us have more discretionary time than ever before. How can we feel so starved for time?

The answer seems to be money. Just like Adam, most of us fall into a trap of spending time to get money, because we believe money will make us happier in the long run.

Our thinking is backward. In fact, research consistently shows that the happiest people use their *money* to buy *time*. My colleagues and I have conducted correlational, longitudinal, and experimental research with nearly 100,000 working adults from all over the world. We consistently find that people who are willing to give up money to gain more free time—by, say, working fewer hours or paying to outsource disliked tasks—experience more fulfilling social relationships, more satisfying careers, and more joy, and overall, live happier lives.

Idea in Brief

People today feel increasingly starved for time, and the fallout is profound: Higher anxiety and depression. Poor health. Divorce. Lower productivity.

Yet according to the data, people actually have more discretionary time than they did 50 years ago. So why is everyone so stressed out? Because we fall into the trap of using our time to get more money, in the belief that it will make us happier. We've got it backward. Study after study shows that the happiest people consistently use their money to buy time.

Because both our cognitive biases and work performance incentives rig us to prioritize money, it's not easy to break our habits. But there are concrete steps individuals and employers can take to promote time-savvier choices. Time is our most precious resource, and if we learn how to value it properly, we'll make trade-offs that significantly improve our well-being.

If there's one resolution that you keep this year, it should be to focus on making choices based on time, not money. It's not easy; our entire world and even our brains are rigged to make us value money first. But it can be done, and in this article, I'll share some smart strategies you can start employing today.

Why We Value Money over Time

The most obvious explanation for today's time famine is that we simply spend more hours doing routine chores and working. But there is very little evidence that supports this idea. Some of the best time diary research suggests that in the United States, men's leisure time has increased by six to nine hours a week over the past 50 years, and women's leisure time has risen four to eight hours a week. And according to the OECD, in 1950, people in the U.S. worked an average of 37.8 hours a week; in 2017 they worked an average of 34.2 hours a week.

Instead, the evidence points to other culprits for time poverty: wealth and financial insecurity. In studies of middle- and upper-income people across diverse cultural contexts in Europe, Asia, and North America, individuals who earn more money report feeling

The Big Idea: Time Poor and Unhappy

"Time for Happiness" is the lead article of HBR's **The Big Idea: Time Poor and Unhappy.** Read the rest of the series at hbr.org/time:

- "Can You Identify the Hidden Time Traps?" by Gretchen Gavett and Karen Player
- "Why Money Manages Us," by Kathleen D. Vohs
- "Don't Feel Guilty About Wanting Your Time Back," by *Harvard Business Review* staff
- "Accounting for Time," by Ashley Whillans and Hanne Collins
- "Treat Your Weekend Like a Vacation," by Cassie Mogilner Holmes

more pressed for time. In a survey of over 30,000 respondents from Australia, for example, higher levels of time stress were correlated with higher incomes, and the longer work hours correlated with greater pay could not explain this effect. Considering that wealthier people can afford to, say, hire house cleaners and take cabs instead of public transportation, their greater time poverty may seem counterintuitive.

But it makes more sense if you understand commodity theory, which holds that when any resource is perceived as valuable, it is also perceived as scarce. So, the more we get paid for our time, the more we value it, and the more intensely we feel the loss of any moment.

Feelings of financial insecurity (regardless of actual wealth) may also prompt people to experience more intense time poverty. That's because individuals who feel unsure that they'll have the same job or earn the same level of pay in the future are more likely to prioritize having more money at the expense of having more time.

Despite the inverse relationship between wealth and time affluence, most of us keep striving to make more money. In my team's research, only 48% of respondents reported that they would rather have more time than more money. Even the majority of people in the group that was the most time-impoverished—parents who had full-time jobs and young children—shared this preference. The very wealthy didn't always prioritize time over money, either.

Nearly half of the 818 millionaires we surveyed said that they didn't spend anything to delegate disliked tasks to others. In addition, when we asked 98 working adults how they would spend a windfall of $40 to maximize happiness, only two said that they would make a time-saving purchase. When we asked 300 adults in romantic relationships how they would spend $40 to maximize their partners' well-being, only three said they would use it to save their partners time.

It's not that people can't think of ways to save time: In one study, 99% of respondents could name a chore they wanted to pay to offload. But across several additional studies, just 17% of respondents spent money to do so. And it's not that people can't think of anything better to do, either: Most could name several activities, such as pursuing a hobby, that they'd like to have time for, even as very few bought the time to do them.

The core challenge to reducing time poverty and unhappiness is not financial but psychological: the erroneous belief that wealth will make our lives better. Even individuals with a net worth of $10 million think they need to increase their wealth dramatically to be happier.

Research shows, for instance, that employees frequently overestimate the value of cash rewards and salary when considering what jobs to accept. They believe that pay, insurance, and other financial benefits like retirement plans will determine job satisfaction. And they underestimate the value of flexibility regarding their work schedules.

When my team and I analyzed 42,721 employee responses from a Glassdoor survey, we found that noncash benefits such as social experiences and the opportunity to take leaves had a greater impact on job satisfaction than money did. In one analysis, all else being equal, benefits such as generous parental leaves, flextime, and sick days had a larger effect on job satisfaction than receiving an additional $60,000 in annual salary (on top of an average salary of

$48,000) did. These results held even after controlling for income, age, gender, education, industry, employer type, firm size, and firm revenue.

Research shows that once people make more than enough to meet their basic needs, additional money does not reliably promote greater happiness. Yet over and over, our choices do not reflect this reality.

Why We *Should* Value Time over Money

It's important to note that some people—particularly those who are struggling to make ends meet or who feel uncertain about their financial future—often do feel happier when they choose money over time. But it's still clear that those of us who are more fortunate may need to rethink our priorities.

To understand which people are happy and how they make time-money trade-offs, my team and I presented thousands of participants with the following two descriptions of individuals (whose names always matched the gender of the respondents):

> **Tina** values her **time** more than her money. She is willing to sacrifice money to have more time. For example, Tina would rather work fewer hours and make less money than work more hours and make more money.

> **Maggie** values her **money** more than her time. She is willing to sacrifice time to have more money. For example, Maggie would rather work more hours and make more money than work fewer hours and have more time.

We then asked our respondents which person they resembled most. Just by knowing their answers, we could predict what decision they would make when given the choice of a cheaper flight with a longer layover or a more expensive direct flight, and of a house-cleaning voucher or a cash prize.

We also learned that people who valued time more (the Tinas) were older, worked fewer hours, were more likely to volunteer, and were more civically engaged. Most important, they were happier by about 0.5 point on a 10-point happiness scale. This difference is equal to about half the happiness bump people experience, on average, from being married.

From this and many, many other studies we can also assert:

Time yields happiness

The Tinas' reports of greater overall well-being cannot be explained by income, education, age, marital status, number of children living at home, or number of hours worked per week. Their broad tendency to prioritize time was what made the difference.

When my colleagues and I surveyed more than 6,000 working adults living in the Netherlands, Denmark, the United States, and Canada we found that people who spent money on time-saving services reported greater satisfaction with their lives. Purchasing them helped respondents deal with stress and feel less overwhelmed by their to-do lists. This was true even with relatively small, onetime purchases.

Time is social

Across three studies that I conducted with professor Elizabeth Dunn from the University of British Columbia, people who valued time over money socialized more with peers. In one study, they spent 18% more time interacting with a new peer than people prioritizing money did. This is important because even fleeting social interactions with others can play a surprisingly large role in reducing stress and promoting happiness, as other researchers have found.

In another study of nearly 40,000 Americans, when people made time-saving purchases on Saturday or Sunday (versus those who did not), they spent about 30 minutes more socializing with friends and family. That in turn promoted greater end-of-day happiness. The people who made those purchases were happier not only because they socialized more but because they derived greater joy from doing it.

Across nine studies with 4,300 Americans in committed romantic relationships, my colleagues and I saw that prioritizing time over money brought couples closer. Those who spent money on time-saving services reported spending more quality time together and derived greater satisfaction from their relationships. When couples were under stress, the benefits were stronger for time-saving purchases (like ordering takeout) than for experiential purchases (like going out to a nice dinner, which involves more planning, decision making, and travel). Time-saving purchases even erased some of the unhappiness produced by having an unsupportive spouse. In other words, paying for a house cleaner might do as much for your marriage as learning to be a better listener!

A focus on time builds more-rewarding careers

People who value their time are more likely to pursue careers that they love. In another study, Elizabeth Dunn and I found that graduating college students who prioritized time were more likely to choose careers that offered intrinsic rewards and as a result, were significantly happier one year later. And that didn't mean they were working fewer hours. When people have jobs they truly enjoy and thus are happier, they are less negatively affected by stress and more productive and creative. They also are less likely to quit.

Why It's Hard

If the solution to time poverty is so simple—just make choices that give you more time—then why are we all still stressed?

I'm a happiness researcher. I should know better than to sacrifice all my leisure hours to work and making money. Yet I feel as if I must be on call constantly to keep up with the demands of work. To cope, I email or talk on the phone while commuting to the office, while exercising, while on beaches, and even while on a safari. From time to time, I have been spotted typing on my laptop in a gym locker room. And I confess I spent one and a half hours working (not so secretly) during my wedding reception.

What years of studying time-money trade-offs have revealed to me is that I'm not alone in making suboptimal decisions about how to use my time. It's not easy to make better choices. It may not even be our natural inclination.

The Long View

WE SHOULD ALSO THINK ABOUT how our money and time decisions might have consequences for our happiness farther down the road. If we choose a job in which we make a lot of money but work 80 hours a week, our personal relationships and happiness could suffer in the long term. My data suggests that college students who choose career paths that enable them to have more money (versus more time) experience significant decreases in happiness one to two years after graduation. And over the span of many years, the negative effects of such major life decisions could really add up.

It is crucial to think about the other goals (besides earning money) you want to achieve in the next five to 10 years. Are you planning to have children? If so, you may try choosing time over money more often, to minimize work-life conflict. Your values will also shift over the course of your lifetime. My data suggests that as people age and have objectively less time left in their lives, they naturally start to favor more time over more money in their decisions. Other researchers have found that as people get older they start to focus on having more meaningful experiences (versus earning more money).

There are any number of reasons for our misguided pursuit of wealth, but they fall into two categories:

Behavioral factors
Several cognitive biases make money seem like a more appealing choice than time. Americans, for example, think being busy signals higher status. The desire to feel important is a powerful motivator that may undermine our best interests.

My research suggests that people also feel guiltier about spending money to have more time than they do about spending money on material goods. Paying someone to complete tasks we ourselves don't like can make us feel lazy, so we opt out to avoid that feeling.

And because we overestimate the amount of time needed to enjoy an experience, we end up wasting small pockets of free time that we could use more effectively. Five minutes spent socializing with a colleague or 20 minutes on an elliptical machine often have more powerful mood benefits than we expect.

Last, we suffer from something called future time slack—the belief that we'll have more time in the future than we do in the present. So, we decide to make some sacrifices now with the promise of enjoying more time later. Of course, when the future comes, we don't have more time. We just repeat the same mistake.

Organizational factors

HR departments may think that how employees choose between time and money has little to do with them, but a large body of research shows that organizational factors shape the way employees perceive their time and can increase their feelings of stress and undermine social connections and happiness.

We know from decades of research, for example, that financial incentives increase people's efforts to perform better. But we now also know that they make workers obsessed with money. Across six studies, NYU professor Julia Hur found that employees who were paid for better performance reported a greater desire for money and put in dramatically more effort to earn additional compensation. They also became more self-focused and less willing to donate to charity, a sign that they were turning away from activities that we know lead to happiness.

Building on this research, Julia, my student Alice Lee-Yoon, and I analyzed a publicly available data set to see how performance incentives changed attitudes *outside* work. We found that employees who were paid for performance spent significantly less time socializing with friends and family and significantly more time socializing with their customers and coworkers. This was true no matter how many hours the employees worked or what industry they were in.

Those findings were supported by additional studies we conducted. They, too, revealed that employees who were paid for their performance were more willing to spend time with work connections instead of friends and family, because they perceived work ties to be more "productive" and "helpful" for getting ahead. But the employees didn't enjoy this time with professional connections more. Regardless of their pay level or job type, employees who were paid for their performance said they derived greater happiness from spending time with friends. But they didn't get to do it much.

Policies that make workers think about the monetary value of their time also create time stress. Employees paid by the hour are more likely to think of their time as money and be more concerned about wasting time, saving time, and using their time profitably. In one experiment, Berkeley professor Dana Carney and Stanford professor Jeff Pfeffer found that simply asking employees to calculate their hourly wage significantly increased their levels of cortisol—a hormone associated with stress. In related research, UCLA Anderson professor Sanford DeVoe and his former graduate student Julian House found that asking people to calculate the economic value of their time made them more impatient—and undermined both their ability to savor their leisure time and their desire to volunteer to help others. And in another study, Elizabeth Dunn and I found that asking people to calculate it made them less likely to go two seconds out of their way to help the environment by recycling.

How to Start

Although your brain and your organization may be conspiring to make you choose money over time, a few daily actions could help you shift your mindset. The following simple strategies can reduce your time poverty and help you reclaim your schedule.

1. Personal activities

Plan your future time. When it comes to leisure time, our preliminary data suggests that people have a natural bias toward spontaneity: We don't want to feel our free time is too scheduled. So we do things like leaving weekends up to chance—and then end up wasting much of them. But we're actually happier if we make plans and don't passively fritter away time.

Be more active. Personal pursuits like volunteering, socializing, and exercising can have a transformative effect on people. Our research shows that *active* leisure is profoundly better at combating time stress than *passive* leisure (such as watching TV or just relaxing) is. When my colleagues—professor Paul Smeets at Maastricht

University, professor Rene Bekkers at Vrije Universiteit Amsterdam, and professor Michael Norton at Harvard Business School—and I conducted a study in the Netherlands comparing millionaires with people who had an average net worth of $37,500, we found that the millionaires were happier—but not just because they had more money. They spent 30 more minutes a day engaged in active leisure and 40 fewer minutes engaged in passive leisure.

Spend more time eating. When Romain Cadario, a professor at IÉSEG School of Management in Paris, and I recently surveyed 12,000 French and American adults about their dining habits, we found that on average, the French spent significantly more time eating. Americans spent more time choosing their meals than actually enjoying them. Because they savored their food more, the French derived greater satisfaction from it—which in turn reduced their stress.

Meet new people and help others. Although initiating a conversation with someone you don't know is hard, casual social interactions with strangers significantly boost happiness. And volunteering is not only linked to greater happiness but also increases your feelings of time affluence. This seems backward, because volunteering consumes your time, but the act of giving time away makes you feel more in control of it.

Spend more time experiencing awe. Awe is a positive emotion we feel when encountering something vast and expansive, like a panoramic view of the Pacific Ocean. It can increase our sense of time affluence—which is yet another reason that scenic hikes, tropical vacations, or just a few moments of looking up into the sky can rejuvenate us.

Take more vacation time. This is almost too obvious, but in America especially, vacation days are underutilized. This probably relates to our sense that missing work or being able to *afford* vacation time signals lower status; important people are too busy for that. But initial research that my student Hanne Collins and I did showed that employees who took more vacation days reported greater life satisfaction. These results held even after we controlled for age, gender, marital status, and current work hours. And yet 15% of employees reported taking *no* vacation days in the past year, and only 40% said they'd taken all their paid vacation.

2. Buying time

When considering how we can use money to increase our happiness, most of us think of investing it in positive experiences like Hawaiian vacations. But it's also important to think about how to eliminate negative experiences from our day. My research suggests that people have a lot of trouble doing this, but here are some ideas to get you started.

Outsource your chores. In the sharing economy, companies like Angie's List, Rent the Runway Unlimited, and TaskRabbit make it possible and affordable for consumers to "buy" time by hiring out tasks they dislike. Today you can hire people to walk your dog, assemble your furniture, pick out your clothes, chauffeur your kids to their sports practices, declutter your home, and even wait in line for tickets for you. Yet using such services is a big leap for many, who see them as extravagant or unaffordable. It's the money-first mindset that makes them believe that. In fact, spending money on time-saving services—like shopping, cleaning, and laundry—can reduce stress and increase happiness, even for people with low incomes. (See the sidebar "Time, Money, Privilege, and Guilt.") One caveat: My ongoing research suggests that outsourcing *too* much can make people feel that their schedules are out of control, which undermines contentment.

But understand what specifically you want to offload. We often dislike certain aspects of a chore but enjoy others. In new research conducted with the smartphone application Joy, for instance, Elizabeth Dunn and I found that consumers gained greater satisfaction from food subscription services (like Blue Apron and HelloFresh)

Time, Money, Privilege, and Guilt

ISN'T TRADING MONEY FOR TIME just for rich people? Not really. Of course, people who are just making ends meet or are financially struggling are unlikely to face such trade-offs frequently. Yet in developed countries a large proportion of people have a nontrivial amount of discretionary income to play with. More important, what my team and I find across our studies is that spending as little as $40 to save time can increase happiness (more than spending that same $40 buying random stuff for ourselves). Consider that in 2017, Americans spent an average of $1,110 each, or about $3 a day, buying coffee. So, simply by sacrificing coffee for two weeks, they could each afford to buy about one hour of housecleaning through TaskRabbit.

Even so, many people still associate hiring that kind of help with being privileged and feel guilty doing it. We also feel bad about asking others for help—even when we're paying for it! My data suggests when we outsource tasks we dislike, we feel as if we are burdening the people we hire even though it is their job. We also don't want others to know that we pay for daily services—like cleaning and cooking—since it appears to signal that we aren't managing things well on our own. Yet, as my data suggests, when we find simple ways to get more time, our happiness and productivity benefit.

And if you *still* feel guilty about buying time this way, try asking for time as a gift.

If on the other hand you're looking for a present for someone, take note: Gifts that save people time are perceived to be more thoughtful and are more appreciated than gifts that save money. One word of caution: If time-saving gifts highlight the fact that your partner is always doing more of the chores than you are, they can backfire. They are also more appreciated in professional contexts and for activities that the recipient doesn't enjoy. For instance, if someone likes ironing, he will be less enthusiastic about a dry-cleaning service that saves time than someone who doesn't like laundry.

Still, in our studies, people who made the least amount of money gained the greatest happiness from time-saving purchases (in the off chance they made them). We believe that this is because people who are struggling to make ends meet may spend more time commuting, working multiple jobs, and waiting than people who are well off. Counter to conventional wisdom, time-saving purchases may be especially beneficial for people living at or below the poverty line.

If I still haven't convinced you that buying time isn't just for rich people, here's a bit more evidence: In collaboration with Colin West of the UCLA Anderson School of Management, I've been conducting a large-scale study in one of the largest, poorest slums in the world, Kibera in Nairobi, Kenya. There working women spend 40 hours every week on chores and other forms of unpaid labor. Hand-washing laundry and watching it dry (so that it doesn't get stolen) can take up to 10 hours a week. Yet, even in this slum, where women earn an average of $5 (US) a day, there is a market for time-saving services. Women sometimes pay others to do their laundry or take clothes to a local laundromat. They also will pay others to purchase vegetables for them to save the hours it takes to walk to and from the market. In this study, we're testing whether the women of Kibera are happier and more productive after they receive vouchers for time-saving services (meals and laundry) than after receiving vouchers for non-time-saving goods (ingredients for meals). We believe that the time-saving vouchers will be most effective. This idea fits with the idea that time poverty often coincides with material poverty.

Yet time-saving services for the poor are often undervalued by policy makers. When Colin and I asked a group of 40 students at the Harvard Kennedy School's program in public policy whether an aid initiative that would save working women time or an initiative that would provide them with cash would be most likely to improve women's welfare, only 10% of these aspiring policy makers said the time-saving initiative would be most effective.

There is also debate about whether the gig-economy marketplaces treat workers well enough to encourage consumers to purchase such services. While my research doesn't speak to those ethical questions, it does find evidence that customers are sensitive to how well their service providers are paid. When consumers feel confident the providers enjoy their jobs and receive good benefits, they feel much less guilt about hiring them and are much more likely to buy time. In one experiment, more consumers clicked on an ad to buy a time-saving service when it highlighted the benefits that the service gave providers than on an ad that highlighted the benefits to consumers. This suggests that companies that offer service providers good working conditions and competitive wages will win more business.

than from food delivery services. We speculate that this is because most people like cooking; they just find it tiresome to figure out what to make and to run to the store to buy just the right amount of each ingredient. This brings us back to a broader point: Focus on outsourcing the tasks or aspects of tasks that you find most disagreeable. That way, you can spend more minutes engaged in the part that you enjoy about any daily activity.

Do less comparison shopping. The amount of time it takes to find the best price is often more valuable than whatever savings you gain. Driving farther for cheaper gas or going from store to store to find the same outfit at the lowest cost probably isn't worth the effort. Booking the most affordable travel option isn't always, either. Flights with layovers eat up lots of time, especially if your connection is missed or delayed, but often save very little money. Reset your thinking so that price isn't the only consideration. It's OK to spend more to free up time.

Buy better time. Once you have outsourced chores, devote your new free time to things that are most likely to promote happiness, like activities with your friends and family. Don't spend all your time on the couch. And each time you open your wallet, ask yourself: Will this purchase change my use of time in positive ways? If the answer is no, you may want to rethink your purchase.

3. Work activities
Though work may seem like an arena where it's hard to gain time, there are a surprising number of ways to change your daily professional life to do so.

Buy back your commute time. Consider taking public transit or an Uber to work once a week. Instead of sitting in traffic, you can spend that time in a leisure activity like reading. Or, if you use it to work, you can leave the office earlier and have more time with friends and family. Even an hour a week adds up significantly over a year.

Ask for more time. A major source of time poverty is tight work deadlines. A simple yet powerful solution is to ask to move them back. Yet across 10 studies involving thousands of employees and managers, Harvard Business School doctoral student Jaewon Yoon, Ohio Fisher College professor Grant Donnelly, and I found that time-stressed employees avoided requesting extensions even when deadlines were adjustable. Employees, and women in particular, worry that if they ask for more time, they'll be seen as less competent and motivated—even though our data suggests that this is not always the case and that employees overestimate any negative reaction their managers might have.

When employees felt squeezed but failed to ask for more breathing room, they ended up submitting suboptimal work, feeling dissatisfied, and disappointing their managers (the very thing they were trying to avoid). These results suggest that you should ask for more time if you need it when your deadlines are adjustable. Your manager will likely grant it to you unbegrudgingly. More important, the extension will give you the chance to put your best foot forward. And if you're the manager, think about how you can help your reports request the time they need to do the best job without worrying about harsh judgment.

Learn how to say no, but don't use time as an excuse. It may be tempting to start turning down requests at work (and life) as a strategy for combating time pressure. It might be even more tempting to refuse by telling others you're too busy. But time-related excuses have a high social cost. Grant Donnelly, HBS doctoral student Anne Wilson, HBS professor Michael Norton, and I have found in new research that people who make them are seen as less likable and less trustworthy. This is because time is perceived as personally controllable. (We all have 24 hours in a day, right?) Our research suggests that people respond much more favorably to individuals who decline requests with excuses related to money or provide no excuse at all. If in reality you don't have the time, try to make it clear that the reason is something outside your personal control, such as family obligations or unexpected travel.

How Employers Can Help

HR departments have great opportunities to improve talent recruitment and retention by helping employees be time savvier and showing prospective hires that they promote time affluence for workers.

Reward employees with time, not money

My research, as well as studies done by others, suggests that employers benefit from this approach because workers who take time off are more engaged, creative, and productive. Yet people often don't take all the days off they're allowed, and when given the choice between time-saving and material rewards, most employees prefer the latter.

I recently obtained data from 207 companies—representing more than 200,000 U.S. employees—that had performance-recognition programs. Thirty-seven percent of those organizations allowed employees to redeem rewards points for time-saving services like housecleaning. Only 3.2% of employees did, whereas 67% of employees redeemed points for material items, such as books from Amazon. (In addition, 16.5% redeemed their points for experiences, and 13.3% donated their points to charity.)

Limiting employees' choices may help. Researchers at Stanford University conducted a pilot study in which doctors were rewarded with vouchers only for time-saving services. Those who received them reported higher work-life balance and lower intentions to quit than other doctors did. So if organizations want to make the most of time-saving rewards, they probably should avoid making them optional.

Give time-based rewards a cash value

Another strategy is to appeal to that money-first mindset and make time savings *seem* financial. As one Silicon Valley HR leader suggested to me, "To better motivate people to apply for jobs that tend to have lower pay and more vacation time, we should show the total compensation package, not just the salary, putting a value on health care, child care, public transportation subsidies, vacation, and sick leave, and calculating it for all. That way, employees will know what they are truly paid."

To test whether putting a dollar figure on noncash rewards increases employees' interest in them, my colleagues and I conducted eight studies with more than 3,000 Americans. Unsurprisingly, when prospective employees were faced with nearly identical jobs—one paying $100,000, with two weeks of vacation, and the other paying $90,000, with three weeks of vacation—the clear majority (75%) chose the higher-paying job. However, when the same decision was presented and the vacations were given a monetary value, the number of employees who chose the higher-paying salary dropped to 50%.

In another study, prospective employees were offered the choice of two jobs—each paying $100,000. Job A included four benefits, and Job B only three benefits. Not surprisingly, more than 80% of respondents in the control condition chose Job A. Yet when the monetary value of Job B's benefits was presented but that of A's was not, 50% of respondents chose Job B—the position with fewer benefits and equal pay! (One caveat: For jobs with low starting salaries, there was no advantage to highlighting the cash value of time benefits, a finding consistent with other research.)

Marketing time as money could be a crucial talent recruitment strategy, as across all these studies the monetized benefits positively shifted perceptions about organizations: Job seekers reported that they thought those employers truly cared about employees and were more considerate of work-life balance. And companies could enjoy an additional upside: increased diversity. Women often see high-powered jobs as equally attainable but less desirable. This simple and costless intervention could draw more women into the applicant pool by making a company seem more family-friendly.

It's been nearly 20 years since HBS professor Leslie Perlow popularized the term "time famine." Since then, we've learned a lot about the psychology of time poverty. Now it is up to each of us to put those lessons into practice. As HBS professor Michael Porter and dean Nitin Nohria wrote in a recent HBR article that appears earlier in this volume, "Time is the scarcest resource that leaders have.

Where they allocate it matters—a lot." I would argue that one critical determinant of whether we allocate our time optimally is the value we place on it relative to money.

Time is hard to account for—it's easily consumed, squandered, and lost. But it receives far less attention than money does. Few of us carefully budget how we'll spend our next small windfall of time. We worry about wasting money on a cup of coffee every day, and how that adds up, when we should be just as concerned about all those minutes we frittered away that could have been used to make us happier. And very few of us strategize about how to gain a large chunk of time in the future, perhaps to devote to a rewarding project or to enjoy a family vacation.

This year let's all resolve to be as deliberate about time as we are about money and work. Before spending your next cent, think about whether that purchase will enhance your use of time. Before making your next work-related decision, think about the impact it will have on your time with your family, and how much you will enjoy being with them. Remind yourself that it's not true that there will always be more time later. There won't!

As a manager, think about the signals that performance rewards and incentives send to your people. Ask yourself whether you make it easier for your employees to ask for more time to complete projects, to spend less time stuck in traffic, to waste less time taking cheaper indirect flights, to reduce their stress and improve their productivity. As the data I've collected over many years and across many countries suggests, your happiness and health and the health of your organization could depend on the trade-offs you make (and help your employees make) each day.

While our overarching focus on financial gain has created economic growth, it has had a cost. All of us—employees and managers alike—should consider giving up money to have more and better time. Time is a precious resource. Rethinking how we value it will help us answer the more fundamental question of how to maximize individual and societal well-being—and help all of us escape the stress traps of everyday life.

Originally published on hbr.org in January 2019. Reprint BG1901

About the Contributors

JULIE BATTILANA is the Joseph C. Wilson Professor of Business Administration at Harvard Business School and the Alan L. Gleitsman Professor of Social Innovation at Harvard Kennedy School.

ADAM BRANDENBURGER is the J.P. Valles Professor at the Stern School of Business, Distinguished Professor at the Tandon School of Engineering, and faculty director of the Shanghai Program on Creativity + Innovation at New York University.

ALISON WOOD BROOKS is an assistant professor at Harvard Business School.

RYAN W. BUELL is the UPS Foundation Associate Professor of Service Management at Harvard Business School.

PAUL R. DAUGHERTY is Accenture's chief technology and innovation officer. He is a coauthor of *Human + Machine: Reimagining Work in the Age of AI* (Harvard Business Review Press, 2018).

ROBIN J. ELY is the Diane Doerge Wilson Professor of Business Administration at Harvard Business School and the faculty chair of the HBS Gender Initiative.

JOSHUA GANS is the Jeffrey S. Skoll Chair of Technical Innovation and Entrepreneurship at the University of Toronto's Rotman School of Management and serves as chief economist in the Creative Destruction Lab.

PAUL IRVING is chairman of the Milken Institute Center for the Future of Aging, chairman of the board of Encore.org, and a distinguished scholar in residence at the University of Southern California, Davis School of Gerontology.

LESLIE K. JOHN is an associate professor at Harvard Business School.

MARISSA KIMSEY is a research associate at Harvard Business School.

KATRINA LAKE is the CEO of Stitch Fix.

JEANNE LIEDTKA is a professor at the University of Virginia's Darden School of Business.

ANDY NOBLE is a partner in Bain's Boston office, specializing in retail and organization.

NITIN NOHRIA is the dean of Harvard Business School.

ANNE-CLAIRE PACHE is the Chaired Professor in Philanthropy at ESSEC Business School.

MICHAEL E. PORTER is a University Professor at Harvard, based at Harvard Business School.

DARRELL K. RIGBY is a partner in the Boston office of Bain & Company. He heads the firm's global innovation and retail practices and is the author of *Winning in Turbulence* (Harvard Business Review Press, 2009).

ERIN L. SCOTT is a senior lecturer in the Technological Innovation, Entrepreneurship, and Strategic Management Group at the MIT Sloan School of Management.

METIN SENGUL is an associate professor of strategy at Boston College's Carroll School of Management.

SCOTT STERN is the David Sarnoff Professor of Management at the MIT Sloan School of Management and serves as faculty director of the Martin Trust Center for MIT Entrepreneurship.

JEFF SUTHERLAND is a co-creator of the scrum form of agile innovation and the CEO of Scrum Inc., a consulting and training firm.

CATHERINE H. TINSLEY is the Raffini Family Professor of Management at Georgetown University's McDonough School of Business and the faculty director of the Georgetown University Women's Leadership Institute.

ASHLEY WHILLANS is an assistant professor at Harvard Business School.

H. JAMES WILSON is a managing director of information technology and business research at Accenture Research. He is a coauthor of *Human + Machine: Reimagining Work in the Age of AI* (Harvard Business Review Press, 2018).

Index

AARP, 169, 174–175
Acquisti, Alessandro, 7
Activia, 177
Adecco, 129, 135
Agassi, Shai, 72
ageism, 166–169
agendas, CEOs and, 143–146
agility
  benefits of, 102
  building across the business,
    97–101
  getting started with, 91–97
  large-scale initiatives, 96–97
  leading, 88–91
  operating architectures and,
    98–100
  scaling, 87–102
  sequencing the transition to,
    93–96
  talent acquisition and motivation
    and, 100–101
aging population, 163–177
AI (artificial intelligence), 20–21,
    43–59
  amplifying with, 47, 51
  assistants, 45–46
  embodying, 47, 52
  employee skills for working with,
    58–59
  fashion personalization and, 61–70
  humans assisting machines,
    45–47
  humans explaining to, 45, 46
  humans sustaining, 45, 47
  interacting with, 47, 51–52
  machines assisting humans,
    47–52
  operational transparency and,
    103–120
  reimagining your business for,
    52–58
  at Stitch Fix, 69–70

Aida virtual assistant, 51–52
Airbnb, 172
air rage incidents, 114
Alibaba, 20
Allure Magazine, 177
Alta Gracia, 117
Amazon, 85
  agility at, 88
  Alexa, 46
  automation at, 104
  initiative profitability at, 95
  Nest Labs and, 20
  operating architecture at, 98
  technology choices at, 74
Apple
  AI data collection by, 47, 59
  Nike and, 20
  Siri, 46
  Watch, 20
Aravind Eye Hospital, 108–109
architectural strategy, 81–82
architectures, operating, 98–100
Aron, Arthur, 8
assumptions
  about aging workforce,
    166–169
  about women in the workplace,
    28–29, 31–32, 33, 37, 39–41
  in agility and annual planning,
    101
  articulating, 188–189
  identifying for strategy innova-
    tion, 17–19
  questioning, 39–41
ATMs, 103, 109
AT&T, 59
Audi, 23
Aulet, Bill, 83
authority, 160
Autodesk, 48, 51
Avante, 132
awe, experiencing, 204

baggage tracking, 116
Bain, 100
Balliet, Daniel, 31
Banco Solidario, 127–128
Bank of America Merrill Lynch, 174, 176
Barasz, Kate, 12, 114
Barclays Bank, 103
Barden, Mark, 23
Battilana, Julie, 121–136
BBVA, 109
A Beautiful Constraint (Morgan & Barden), 23
Bernanke, Ben, 163
Bernstein, Ethan, 110–111, 113
Best Buy, 176
Better Place, 72
Bezos, Jeff, 74, 95
bias
    ageism, 166–169
    closed questions in introducing, 5, 7
    cognitive, about time vs. money, 201–202
    gender difference perceptions and, 27–42
    judgment of mistakes and, 35–36
    mistakes by women vs. men and, 32–33, 35–36
    multigenerational workforces and, 171–172
biomimetics, 24
B Lab, 126, 135
black-box problem, 46
blank slate individuals, 130
Blockbuster, 17–18, 63, 79
blockchain, 20
BMW, 20, 171
board members
    CEO time with, 157
    engaging, 134–135
Bonjean, Bernardo, 132

Bonobos, 22–23
Bosch, 90–91, 98
Boston government, 108
Brandenburger, Adam, 15–26
brand loyalty, 70
Brandt, Anthony, 19
Branson, Richard, 72
"Break Free from the Product Life Cycle" (Moon), 16
Brescoll, Victoria, 36
"Bringing Science to the Art of Strategy" (Lafley, Martin, Rivkin, & Siggelkow), 83
Brooks, Alison Wood, 1–13
Brooks Brothers, 171
budgeting cycles, 101
Buell, Ryan W., 103–120
bundling/unbundling, 18–19
Burstein, Arielle, 166
Business Model Generation (Osterwalder & Pigneur), 83
Byrnes, James, 32

Cable, Dan, 3–4
Cadario, Romain, 204
call centers, 109–110, 115
Cambridge Analytica, 115
Campbell, Don, 190
cancer treatment, human/AI collaboration and, 48
capabilities, 74
career development
    agility and, 100–101
    CEOs in, 151
    dual-purpose strategy and, 132–133
    focus on time in, 200
    multigenerational workforce and, 170–171
    for women vs. men, 29–30, 37–38, 39–40

Carnegie, Dale, 2
Carney, Dana, 203
Carnival Corporation, 50, 58
Carstensen, Laura, 168
casino management, human/AI
    collaboration and, 49
CEOs
    accessibility of, 154
    agenda driven, 143–146
    all-consuming job of, 140–141
    alone time for, 154–155
    constituency management by,
        155–156
    constraints and challenges facing,
        137
    direct reports to, reliance on,
        147–148
    executive assistants and, 144–145
    face-to-face interactions with,
        141–143
    importance of successful, 162
    influence of, 157–160
    management mechanisms of,
        149–151
    reactive, 144–145
    role of, 140, 157–161
    routine duties of, 146
    time in meetings, 151–155
    time management by, 137–162
    time with investors, 156–157
    workday length of, 140
change
    champions of, 187–188
    resistance to, 19
    strategy innovation and, 19
Children's Health System of Texas,
    187–188
chores, outsourcing, 205–208
Chun, Jinseok, 11
Citizens Connect, 108
cobots, 52, 171
co-creation, human/AI, 53

cognitive biases, 201–202
cognitive distance, 16
cognitive errors, 33
collaboration
    human/AI, 43–59
    intellectual property and, 76–78
    questioning in, 5, 6
    start-up strategy and, 76
Collins, Hanne, 205
Colson, Eric, 66–67
combination strategy, 16, 19–21
communication
    email, 142–143
    goals of, 2–3, 5, 6
    group dynamics and, 10–11
    listening in, 2
    power of questions in, 1–13
commute time, 208
comparison shopping, 208
competition
    architectural strategy for, 81–82
    decisions about for start-ups,
        74, 75
    disruption strategy and, 78–80
    intellectual property and, 76–78
    questioning in, 5, 6
    trade-offs and strategy for, 76–77
    value chain strategy for, 80–81
confidence
    feedback and development of, 38
    myths about women and, 31–32,
        34–35
confirmation bias, 33
conflict management, 127–128
Congressional Budget Office,
    166–167
Conley, Chip, 172
Connan, Jean-François, 129, 135
constraints
    CEOs and, 159
    strategy innovation and, 16, 21–23
consumer protection, 46, 47

context
    strategy innovation and, 16–17,
        24–25
    for women vs. men in the work-
        place, 30, 33, 38–40
contrast, strategy innovation and,
    16, 17–19
Co-opetition (Nalebuff & Branden-
    burger), 20
corporate social responsibility,
    121–136
    setting goals and monitoring
        progress in, 122–128
Cortana, 45–46, 51
Counter Culture Coffee, 117
creativity. *See also* innovation
    human/AI collaboration and, 51
    identifying assumptions and,
        17–19
    strategy and, 15–26
    tools to foster, 15–16
customers
    agility and, 101
    CEOs and finding time for,
        155–156
    decisions about for start-ups, 74,
        75
    discovery of, innovation and,
        183–186
    disruption strategy and, 79
    focusing on experience of, 95–96
    operational transparency and,
        103–104, 107–109
customer service, human/AI collab-
    oration and, 49
CVS, 171

The Daily (podcast), 109
Daimler, 20
Dannon, 177
Danske Bank, 55

data science, at Stitch Fix, 65–70
Daugherty, Paul R., 43–59
deadlines, 209
DeCelles, Katherine, 114
decision making
    with dual-purpose strategy,
        133–134
    human/AI collaboration and, 49,
        51, 56–57
    for start-ups, 74–75
    in strategy selection, 83–84
Deepwater Horizon oil spill, 117
delegation, 140–141, 147, 151, 153
Deloitte, 168
DeLong, Tom, 141
de Mestral, George, 24
demographic transformation,
    163–177
Denner, Volkmar, 90–91
dependency ratio, 167
design thinking, 179–191
    articulating assumptions in,
        188–189
    customer discovery and, 183–186
    employee buy-in and, 181
    idea generation in, 186–189
    structure and, 181–183
Detroit Neighborhood Improvement
    Tracker, 109
DeVoe, Sanford, 203
differentiation, 81
digital twins, 57
Dimagi, 125–126, 130
Disciplined Entrepeneurship
    (Aulet), 83
disease prediction, human/AI col-
    laboration and, 49
Disneyland, 114
disruption strategy, 78–80
diversity. *See also* women
    aging workforce and, 163–177
    on boards, 134–135

judgment of mistakes and, 36
problem solving and, 180
promotion and retention rates
and, 39–40
Dolby Laboratories, 77–78, 85
Domino's, 109, 112
Donnelly, Grant, 209
DonorsChoose.org, 18
Dove, 177
Dreamcatcher, 51
dual-purpose strategy, 121–136
employees for, 129–133
engaging the board in,
134–135
leadership for, 133–135
organizational structure and,
126–128
roadblocks to, 135
setting goals and monitoring
progress in, 122–128
Duhigg, Charles, 16
Dunn, Elizabeth, 199, 200, 203,
205, 208
Dwyer, Peggy, 32

Eagleman, David, 19
effect size, 40–41
Einstein, Albert, 13, 19
Ely, Robin J., 27–42
email, 142–143
emotional intelligence, questions in
improving, 1
employees
aging population and, 163–177
buy-in and innovation by, 181
CEO contact with, 148
for dual-purpose strategies,
129–133
multigenerational, 170–173
operational transparency and,
109–112

skills for collaboration with AI,
58–59
socialization of, 130–133
entrepreneurial strategy compass,
72–77
definition of, 72
the four decisions in, 72–75
ENVIE, 127
environmental issues, 117
Equifax, 115
equipment maintenance, human/AI
collaboration and, 49, 57
ergonomic workplaces, 171
ethics. *See also* dual-purpose
strategy
AI and, 47
dual-purpose strategy and,
131–132
human/AI collaboration and, 59
operational sustainability and,
116–118
E*TRADE, 169
executive assistants, 144–145
extreme-user strategies, 24–25

Facebook, 81–82, 115, 182–183
failure, treatment of women vs.
men for, 32–33, 35–36
family
assumptions about women vs.
men and, 28–29
CEOs and time for, 145
fashion industry
disruption strategy in,
79–80
guideshops in, 22–23
human/AI collaboration in, 50
personalization in, 61–70
Stitch Fix, 61–70
Federal Reserve Bank of San
Francisco, 168

feedback, to women vs. men, 32–33, 36–37

financial insecurity, 195–197

financial services
agility in, 88
aging population and, 175
fraud detection, 48, 55
human/AI collaboration and, 49, 51–52
operational transparency in, 109

Fleiss, Jennifer, 79–80

flexibility, human/AI collaboration and, 48, 54–55

Frankenstein (Shelley), 21

fraud detection, human/AI collaboration and, 48, 55

fusion skills, 58–59

future time slack, 201–202

Gallery Walk, 185

Gallup Organization, 194

Gans, Joshua, 71–85

Gaudion, Katie, 184

Gavetti, Giovanni, 16

gender and gender differences, 27–42
explanations for, 32–37
in leisure time, 195
persistence of belief in, 33
popular myths about, 31–32
science on, 28–29
Stitch Fix and, 65

General Data Protection Regulation (GDPR), 46, 47

General Electric (GE), 49, 57

Getty Images, 78

GGH Morowitz, 49

Gigster, 48

Gino, Francesca, 2–3

Glassdoor, 197–198

Global Human Capital Trends, 2018, 168

Global Impact Investing Rating System, 126

Global Reporting Initiative, 126, 135

Global Social Enterprise Initiative, 176

GNS Healthcare, 53

goals, setting social, 122–126

Gong.io, 9

Google, 81–82, 104, 118

Google Docs, 65

Google Duplex, 118

government, trust in, 107–108

Government Accountability Office, 166

Grameen Bank, 122

Grameen Veolia Water, 122–123, 125–126

Grant, Adam, 109–110

graphical user interface (GUI), 24

GreatCall, 176

group dynamics, questioning and, 10–11

guideshops, 22–23

guilt, 206–207

Halifax, Nova Scotia, 113

Hanson, Kaaren, 182–183

happiness, 193–212
barriers to, 200–203
buying time and, 205–208
how employers can help with, 210–211
money vs. free time and, 194–200
organizational factors and, 202–203
personal activities and, 203–205
work activities and, 208–209

Hastings, Reed, 79

have-to-dos, 146

HAX, 25
health, time for, 141
health care
    agility in, 94
    cancer treatment, 48
    disease prediction in, 49
    human/AI collaboration in, 48,
        49, 50, 53
    operational transparency in,
        108–109, 119
Hieronymi, Felix, 90–91
Hill, Colin, 53
hiring
    for agility, 100–101
    asking questions in, 3–4
    for dual-purpose strategy, 129–130
Home Depot, 171
Horelik, Nick, 71–72
House, Julian, 203
"How Strategists Really Think:
    Tapping the Power of Analogy"
    (Gavetti & Rivkin), 16
How to Win Friends and Influence
    People (Carnegie), 2
HR (human resources)
    hiring, asking questions in, 3–4
    human/AI collaboration in,
        49–56
    recruiting for fusion skills, 58–59
    talent acquisition and motivation
        and, 100–101
    taxonomy of teams and, 93
HSBC, 48, 55
Hsiung, Brandon, 98–100
Huang, Karen, 2–3
Hur, Julia, 202
Hybrid Designs, 68
hybrid individuals, 129, 130
hybrid organizations
    definition of, 122
    setting goals and monitoring
        progress in, 122–128

Hyman, Jennifer, 79–80
Hyundai, 52

IBM, 82
Icahn School of Medicine at Mount
    Sinai, 49
idea generation, 186–189
identity, 74
    disruption strategy and, 79
IDEO, 26
Ignite Accelerator, 188
impression management, 2–3
influence, 142, 157–160
information
    CEOs' access to, 148
    management, AI and, 46, 47
    networks, connection to for
        women vs. men, 32, 34–35
    questions for sensitive, 7, 8
ING Netherlands, 94
initiatives
    large-scale, mastering, 96–97
    operational transparency in,
        118–120
    ownership of, 90
    sequencing, 93–96
innovation
    agile, scaling up, 87–102
    agile teams in, 88–91
    alignment and, 185–186
    challenges of, 180–181
    combination approach to, 19–21
    constraints approach to, 16, 21–23
    context approach to, 16–17, 24–25
    contrast approach to, 16, 17–19
    customer discovery and, 183–186
    by data science, 68–69
    design thinking and, 179–191
    idea generation and, 186–189
    questions in encouraging, 1
    in strategy, 15–26

innovation (*continued*)
  structure and, 181–183
  testing, 189–190
Intel, 24, 177
intellectual property, 76–78
intelligence
  collaborative, 43–59
  emotional, 1
interviews, asking questions in, 3–4
investors, 156–157
Irving, Paul, 163–177
Izzo, Daniel, 131–132

Jackson, Jonathan, 125, 130
Jenkins, Jo Ann, 169
Jewel-Osco, 80–81
Jobs, Steve, 16
job shadowing, 131
John, Leslie K., 1–13, 107
Johns Hopkins Hospital, 188
Joy, 205, 208

Kaiser Permanente, 189
Kalkanci, Basak, 117
Kayak, 105–106
key performance indicators (KPIs),
  financial and social, 124–126
Kim, Tami, 110, 114
Kimsey, Marissa, 121–136
Kingwood Trust, 184
Kling, Kristen, 31–32
Koko, 46
Kopp, Sébastien, 133–134
KPIs. *See* key performance
  indicators (KPIs)
KPMG, 172

Lafley, A. G., 83
Lake, Katrina, 61–70

Lane, Julie, 11
leaders and leadership
  agile, 88–91
  agile teams and, 98
  aging workforce and, 173
  CEOs, time management by,
    137–162
  dual-purpose strategy, 133–135
  operational transparency and, 104
  pipeline for, 151
  staying connected with other,
    147–148
Leader Ventures, 62–63
lead-user strategies, 24–25
The Lean Startup (Ries), 83
learning
  agility, 91–92, 95–96, 102
  easy wins and, 95–96
  innovation and, 190
  with KPIs, 125
  promoting continual, 40–41
  questions in encouraging, 1, 2–3
Lee-Yoon, Alice, 202
Legere, John, 169
legitimacy, 160
Lehman Brothers, 32
leisure
  active vs. passive, 203–204
  time, by gender, 195
leverage, 159
Liebert, Carl, 93
Liedtka, Jeanne, 179–191
Life Alert, 169
listening, 2
Livingston, Robert, 36
Loewenstein, George, 7
longevity strategy, 166, 173–177
Looma Project, 117
Los Andes S.A. Caja de Ahorro y
  Préstamo, 130
Lyft, 176–177

machine learning. *See* AI (artificial intelligence)
management. *See also* time management by CEOs
  of agile teams, 88–91
  with broad integrating mechanisms, 149–151
  of multigenerational workforces, 170–173
  by trust and empowerment vs. command and control, 99–100
  of women vs. men, 39–41
Mariadassou, Shwetha, 116
Martin, Michael, 71–72
Martin, Roger L., 83
Mason, Malia, 11
maternity leave, 29–30
Mazei, Jens, 31
McKinsey Global Institute, 26, 174–175
meetings
  CEO time in, 151–155
  management of, 145
  number and composition of attendees in, 153–154
  videoconferencing vs., 142–143
  women compared to men in, 35–36
Mercedes-Benz, 48, 54–55
Mercer's Multinational Client Group, 169
mere exposure effect, 33
meta-analysis, 40–41
metrics, 150–151
  for social goals, 124–126
  at Stitch Fix, 69
Michelin, 171
Microsoft, 45–46, 51, 82
Milken Institute Center for the Future of Aging, 166
Millennials, 172
Milligan, Patricia, 169
Minson, Julia, 2–3, 7

MIT Media Lab, 46
mobile payment platforms, 19–20
Mohan, Bhavya, 107
Monash Health, 189–190
Moon, Youngme, 16
Morgan, Adam, 23
Morgan Stanley, 49
Morillon, François-Ghislain, 133–134
motivation, 191
Musk, Elon, 17, 72, 98
Muthuram, Vidhya, 111

Nalebuff, Barry, 20
National Institutes of Health, 171
negotiation
  on deadlines, 209
  myths about women and, 31–32
  questioning in, 7
  spaces of, dual-purpose strategy and, 127–128, 131–132
  transparency vs. secrecy in, 11–12
Neiman Marcus, 80
Nest Labs, 20, 177
Nestlé, 176
Netflix, 18, 63, 67, 79
  agility at, 87–88
networks, connection to for women vs. men, 32, 34–35
New CEO Workshop, 138–139, 160–161
New Nordic Food manifesto, 23
New York Times, 109
Nike, 20
Nike+ iPod Sport Kit, 20
911 services, 71–72, 75, 83–84
Nissan, 171
Noble, Andy, 87–102
Nohria, Nitin, 137–162, 211
Noma, 23
norms, gender, 33

Norton, Michael, 12, 105–106, 108, 114, 115, 209
"no," saying, 209
NPR, 109

Oberoi Hotels, 111–112
Ocean Medallion, 58
Oftalmología salauno, 131, 132, 134
Okhuysen, Javier, 131, 132, 134
online dating websites, 115
OpenTable, 75, 82
operating architectures, 98–100
operational transparency, 103–120
  anxiety from, 113
  backfires in, 112–118
  benefits of, 105–109
  deceptive, 117–118
  definition of, 104–105
  employees and, 109–112
  how to reveal, 119–120
  magic destroyed by, 114
  relationships damaged by, 114
  what to reveal in, 118–119
  when to reveal, 119
opportunities, for women vs. men, 32, 34–35
Orellana, Carlos, 131, 132, 134
organizational culture
  aligning structure and, 150
  data science in, 62, 68–69
  decisions about for start-ups, 74, 75
  treatment of women vs. men and, 27–42
organizational structure
  agile teams and, 89–90, 97–98
  CEO time management and, 149–151
  dual-purpose strategy and, 126–128
  treatment of women vs. men and, 27–42

Osterwalder, Alexander, 83
outsourcing chores, 205–208
Oxford Economics, 174–175

Pache, Anne-Claire, 121–136
Pandora, 57–58
Parthenon Group, 62
Patagonia, 121–122
PayPal, 17
Peapod, 80–81
performance
  human/AI collaboration and, 43–44, 48–50
  questions in improving, 1
performance appraisals
  agility and, 100–101
  multigenerational workforce and, 173
  of women vs. men, 30
Perlow, Leslie, 211
personality traits, 33
personalization
  of ads, 114
  human/AI collaboration in, 50, 57–58
  at Stitch Fix, 61–70
Pew Research Center, 107
Pfau, Bruce, 172
Pfeffer, Jeff, 203
Pfizer, 50, 172
Philips, 176
Pigneur, Yves, 83
Pizza Tracker, 109, 112
planning, agility and, 101
PNC Financial Group, 172
Porter, Ethan, 108
Porter, Michael E., 137–162, 211
portfolios of options, 180
Postmates, 169
power, 160
Predix, 57

pre-experiences, 189–190
Premier Health Plans, 118
priorities
    agility sequencing and, 91–92
    sequencing initiatives and,
        93–96
privacy
    answering questions and, 11–13
    human/AI collaboration and, 47,
        59
    operational transparency and,
        108–109
privilege, 206–207
processes
    CEO time management and,
        149–151
    human/AI collaboration in,
        52–58
    ineffective, operational transpar-
        ency and, 115
    organization of, innovation and,
        182–183
    strategy innovation and, 25
productivity
    human/AI collaboration and,
        43–44
    time poverty and, 194
products
    designing, human/AI collabora-
        tion and, 48
    operational transparency and
        inferior, 116
    strategically combining/connect-
        ing, 19–21
Proff, Kevin, 166
profitability
    agility and, 95
    dual-purpose strategy and,
        121–136
    strategy innovation and, 21
profit allocation, 134
prototyping, 189–190

public safety, human/AI
    collaboration and, 48
purpose, strategy choice and, 84

Qualcomm, 78
questions and questioning, 1–13
    answering, 11–13
    benefits of good, 2–4
    encouraging employee, 132
    follow-up, 5
    full-switch, 5
    group dynamics in, 10–11
    innovation and, 180
    introductory, 5
    mirror, 5
    new Socratic method for, 4–7
    open-ended vs. closed, 5, 7
    in sales, 9
    sequence in, 8–11
    tone in, 9–10
    types of, 5
Quick Lane Tire and Auto Center, 119

Raman, Ananth, 111
Ramdas, Kamalini, 108–109
Rana Plaza, Bangladesh, 117
Randolph, Marc, 79
RapidSOS, 71–72, 75, 83–84
R&D, context and innovation in, 25
recognition programs, 101, 132–133,
        210–211
recruiting
    for agility, 100–101
    for fusion skills, 58–59
    human/AI collaboration and, 49, 56
Reeves, Martin, 20–21
relationships. *See also* family
    CEOs in developing, 151
    human/AI collaboration and,
        47, 51–52

relationships (*continued*)
    meetings and, 153–154
    operational transparency and, 114
    questioning in developing, 2, 4, 8–9
    time for, 199–200
    transparency and, 11–12
Rent the Runway, 79–80
research
    in customer discovery, 183–186
    market, 73
    meta-analysis in, 40–41
    for setting social goals, 123–124
Revolution Foods, 126–127, 132–133
reward systems, 210–211
Richmond, Kristin, 126–127, 133
Ries, Eric, 83
Rigby, Darrell K., 87–102
Rios, Jéssica Silva, 126
Riot Games, 98–100
risk
    innovation and, 180
    myths about women and, 31, 32
    questions in mitigating, 1
Rivera, Marliza, 188
Rivkin, Jan W., 16, 83
Roberts, Peter, 187–188
robots, 52
Roche, 48
Rogers, Todd, 12–13
Rosette, Ashleigh, 36
Rumsfeld, Donald, 53
The Runaway Species (Brandt & Eagleman), 19

Saab, 96–97
Sadun, Raffaella, 138
sales
    operational transparency and, 107
    power of questions in, 9

SAP, 95
scale
    agile at, 87–102
    human/AI collaboration and, 49, 54, 55–56
    personalization and, 61–70
Schwarz, Norbert, 8–9
Schweitzer, Maurice, 7
Scott, Erin L., 71–85
SEB, 51–52
secrecy, 11–13
Sengul, Metin, 121–136
sense making, 184–185
Shell, Michelle, 113
Shelley, Mary Wollstonecraft, 21
Sidky, Ahmed, 99–100
Siggelkow, Nicolaj, 83
silver tsunami, 167
Singapore government, 48
Slepian, Michael, 11
Smarter Faster Better (Duhigg), 16
Smeets, Paul, 203–204
social capital, 151
socialization of employees, 130–133
socializing, time for, 199–200, 202. *See also* relationships
social responsibility. *See* dual-purpose strategy
social technology, 179, 191
software development, human/AI collaboration and, 48
solutions, superior, 180
Sonmez, Nazli, 108–109
SpaceX, 18, 102
Sparrow, Tammy, 95
specialized talent, 129–130
speed, 55
spontaneity, 145, 154
Spotify, 87–88
Standard & Poor's, 163
Starbucks, 58

start-ups
    architectural strategy for, 81–82
    choosing strategy for, 83–84
    competitive trade-offs and, 76–77
    context for learning and growth
        for, 25
    disruption strategy for, 78–80
    entrepreneurial strategy compass
        for, 72–77
    exploration and commercializa-
        tion by, 71–72
    intellectual property and, 76–78
    strategy for, 71–85
    value chain strategy for, 80–81
Steelcase, 171
Stern, Scott, 71–85
Stitch Fix, 50, 61–70
    algorithms at, 65–70
    human stylists at, 69–70
    style profiles at, 66–67
Stockman, Keith, 190
Stop & Shop, 81
strategy
    analytical tools for, 15, 26
    architectural, 81–82
    CEO time management and, 149
    choosing, 83–84
    combination approach to, 16,
        19–21
    competitive trade-offs and, 76–77
    constraint approach to, 16, 21–23
    context approach to, 16–17, 24–25
    contrast approach to, 16, 17–19
    creativity and, 15–26
    disruption, 78–80
    dual-purpose, 121–136
    identifying assumptions in, 17–19
    on intellectual property, 76–78
    longevity, 166
    for start-ups, 71–85
    value chain, 80–81
stress, 194, 203

sunshine laws, 107
supply chain sustainability, 116–117
SurveyMonkey, 65
surveys, 7
Sustainability Accounting Standards
    Board, 126, 135
sustainers, 45, 47
Sutherland, Jeff, 87–102
SWOT analysis, 22–23
symbolic influence, 160

taxonomy of teams, 92–93
teams
    agile, 88–91
    interaction of with the organiza-
        tion, 97–101
    multigenerational, 171–172
    readiness of, 96
    taxonomy of, 92–93
    values and principles for, 97–98
technology
    architectural strategy and, 81–82
    collaborative intelligence with,
        43–59
    combinatorial possibilities in
        new, 20–21
    customer perceptions of value
        and, 103–104
    decisions about for start-ups, 74,
        75
    human combinations with, 20–21
    humans assisting machines,
        45–47
    humans explaining to, 45, 46
    humans sustaining, 45, 47
    machines assisting humans,
        47–52
    operational transparency and,
        103–120
Templeton, Chuck, 82
Tencent, 19–20

Tesla, 22, 72, 98
Tessei, 110–111
3M Health Information Systems, 94, 95
time affluence, 194
time management by CEOs, 137–162
  agendas in, 143–146
  constituency management and, 155–156
  crises and, 144–146
  delegation and, 140–141, 147, 151, 153
  face-to-face interactions and, 141–143
  happiness and, 193–212
  management mechanisms and, 149–151
  meetings and, 151–155
  for personal activities, 203–205
  personal well-being and, 141
  reliance on direct reports and, 147–148
  research on, 138–139
  routine duties and, 146
time poverty, 194, 195–196
Tinsley, Catherine H., 27–42
T-Mobile, 169
Tobey, Kirsten, 126–127, 133
tone, of questions, 9–10
total quality management, 179
Toyota, 98
train-cleaning service, 110–111
training
  agility and, 100–101
  for dual-purpose strategy, 131
  of machines by humans, 45–46
  for women vs. men, 38
transparency
  answering questions and, 11–13
  operational, 103–120
trash collection, 113
travel, 141

TravelFinder, 105–106
trust
  operational transparency and, 107
  questions in encouraging, 1
Tsay, Chia-Jung, 110

Uber, 112, 176–177
Ueda, Daichi, 20–21
Unilever, 49, 56, 177
unknown unknowns, 53
UPS, 119
USAA, 88, 93
U.S. Department of Health and Human Services, 188
U.S. Department of Veterans Affairs, 119
user-driven criteria, 180

vacation time, 204–205
value
  created by operational transparency, 108–109
  customer perceptions of, 103–104
  of money vs. time, 194–198
  operational transparency and, 104–105
value chain, 18
  strategy for start-ups, 80–81
values, 97–98
  agile, 102
VanEpps, Eric, 7
Veja, 133–134
Velcro, 24
venture capital, 64–65
videoconferences, 142–143
video rental industry, 17–18, 63, 79
Virgin Trains, 49
Vivractif, 128
volunteering, 204
Vox Capital, 126, 130, 131–132

Wagner, Sebastian, 95
wealth, happiness and, 195–198
Webvan, 80
WeChat, 19–20
WeChat Pay, 19–20
Wegner, Daniel, 11
Whillans, Ashley, 193–212
Whiteriver Indian reservation, 188
Wilson, Anne, 209
Wilson, H. James, 43–59
women, 27–42
    alternative explanations for
      workplace accomplishments
      of, 37–38
    assumptions about family and,
      28–29
    changing the context for, 38–40
    continual learning for, 40–41
    different treatment of, 27–42
    "fixing," 37
    leisure time of, 195
    parity of, failure to achieve, 27–28
    performance appraisals and, 30
    popular myths about, 31–32, 33
    questioning the narrative on, 37
    at Stitch Fix, 65

workforce, aging, 163–177
    ageism and, 166–169
    managing, 170–173
    as opportunity vs. crisis, 173–177
    stereotypes of, 167–169, 177
workweek
    actual vs. perceived time spent
      in, 195
    redefining, aging workforce and,
      170–171
World Bank, 167

Xerox, 171

Yabe, Teruo, 111
Yeomans, Michael, 2–3
Yip, Jeremy, 7
Yoon, Jaewon, 209

Zheng, Yanchong, 116

Invaluable insights
always at your fingertips

With an All-Access subscription to
Harvard Business Review, you'll get
so much more than a magazine.

Exclusive online content and tools
you can put to use today

My Library, your personal workspace for sharing,
saving, and organizing HBR.org articles and tools

Unlimited access to more than 4,000 articles in the
Harvard Business Review archive

Subscribe today at hbr.org/subnow

The most important management ideas all in one place.

We hope you enjoyed this book from *Harvard Business Review*. Now you can get even more with HBR's 10 Must Reads Boxed Set. From books on leadership and strategy to managing yourself and others, this 6-book collection delivers articles on the most essential business topics to help you succeed.

HBR's 10 Must Reads Series

The definitive collection of ideas and best practices on our most sought-after topics from the best minds in business.

- Change Management
- Collaboration
- Communication
- Emotional Intelligence
- Innovation
- Leadership
- Making Smart Decisions

- Managing Across Cultures
- Managing People
- Managing Yourself
- Strategic Marketing
- Strategy
- Teams
- The Essentials

hbr.org/mustreads

Buy for your team, clients, or event.
Visit hbr.org/bulksales for quantity discount rates.